DOING BUSINESS
BOLDLY

DOING BUSINESS
BOLDLY
THE ART OF TAKING
INTELLIGENT RISKS

by

DANIEL KEHRER

TimesBOOKS

*Grateful acknowledgment is made to the following for
permission to reprint previously published material:*

Chief Executive: Excerpts from "What's Wrong with Today's
CEO?" by J.B. Fuqua. Reprinted with permission from *Chief
Executive* Magazine. Copyright © *Chief Executive*, Spring 1987,
Issue 39.

Dow Jones & Company, Inc.: Excerpts from "Profile in Failure:
One Man's Painful Crash" by Patricia Bellew Gray. Reprinted by
permission of *The Wall Street Journal.* Copyright © 1986 by
Dow Jones & Company, Inc. All rights reserved.

Forbes: Excerpts from "A Chat with Michael Milken" by Allan
Sloan. Excerpted by permission of *Forbes* Magazine, July 13,
1987. Copyright © 1987 by Forbes, Inc.

McGraw-Hill, Inc.: Quotes from "The King of Wall Street" by
Anthony Bianco from the December 9, 1985, issue of *Business
Week.* Reprinted by permission of McGraw-Hill Publications.

Reuters: Excerpts from "*USA Today* Posts Its First Profits."
Reprinted by permission of Reuters.

Robert B. Tucker: Excerpts from "Federal Express's Fred
Smith" by Robert B. Tucker from *Inc.* Magazine, October 1986.
Reprinted by permission of the author.

USA Today: Excerpts from "This Kid's Sure Big for Such a
Young Age" from the September 13, 1985, edition of *USA Today.*
Copyright © 1985 by *USA Today.* Excerpted with permission.

Library of Congress Cataloging-in-Publication Data

Kehrer, Daniel M.
  Doing business boldly.
  Includes index.
  1. Success in business. 2. Creative ability in
business. 3. Risk. I. Title.
HF5386.K267 1988   650.1   88-40162

ISBN 0-8129-1312-4

Manufactured in the United States of America
9 8 7 6 5 4 3 2
First Edition

This book is lovingly dedicated
to Kaye, again, for being such an
extraordinary person

And to Paul and Margaret Kehrer,
for 35 years of unbroken
encouragement and support

CONTENTS

BOOK I
THE HEART OF BUSINESS RISK

Risk Dynamic #1: Creative Destruction   3

- Abandoning Yesterday
- Putting Risk Back into Coke
- Why Goizueta Rolled the Dice

Risk Dynamic #2: Risk-Taking Reconnaissance   15

- Avoiding Detail Fog
- Coke's Reconnaissance Effort
- Shorter Product Life Spans
- Coca-Cola's Choice
- Daring to Look Dumb

Risk Dynamic #3: High-Flex   39

- Risking Compromise

Risk Dynamic #4: Championing Change   46

BOOK II
PAYING THE PRICE

Risk Dynamic #5: It's Active, Not Passive   55

- Risk's P.R. Problem
- Fighting "Corpocracy"
- Corporations: Arenas for Risk
- The Wrong Motivations
- Neuharth the Creator

Risk Dynamic #6: Seeing Rewards Over Dangers   78

- Goals and Cutoffs
- Gain Wins Out at Gannett

Risk Dynamic #7: Taking Responsibility   85

Risk Dynamic #8: Risk Is Contrarian   91

- Risk's Key: The Unanticipated
- Investing Means Risking
- The Probability Trip Wire
- Neuharth as Contrarian
- An Investment, Not a Loss

BOOK III
SEEING THROUGH THE RISK MIND

Risk Dynamic #9: Thinking and
Perceiving Differently   115

- Different Motivations
- The Mastery of Risk
- A Future Fortune 500 Risk Taker
- Biotech's Mild-Mannered Risk Taker
- Creating a Risk Culture

Risk Dynamic #10: The Spirit of Wealth Creation   135

- An Entrepreneurial Backlash
- The Casino Fallacy
- Setting Course at Genentech
- A Crucial Choice
- The Patent Minefield
- Capital Injections
- The Pharmaceutical Mother Lode

BOOK IV
GRASPING RISK'S GEOMETRY

Risk Dynamic #11: Perceptions of Control:
An ARTist's Paradox   167

- Control by Illusion
- Venture Capitalists: Agents of Risk
- A Legendary Ad-venturer
- Pro-Active Risking
- Too Much Talk

Risk Dynamic #12: Sharing Risk: OPM and OPB   187

- The Stanley Steamer: Failed for Lack of Risking
- OPB for Adler
- Risk Key: Pattern Recognition
- Why Companies Stumble
- More Risks Today

Risk Dynamic #13: The Flip Side of Flops   203

- Success Littered with Failure
- Presiding Over Failure
- Beware the "Near-Success"
- Derailing America's Bullet Train

BOOK V
RISK-TAKING TACTICS

Risk Dynamic #14: Quick on the OODA Loop   221

- Speeding Up Big Blue
- Setting an Intrapreneurial Tone
- From Stability to Turmoil at GE
- A Cable TV Fighter Pilot
- New Owners

Risk Dynamic #15: Risking from Strength   235

- Shearson's Wall Street Juggernaut
- Coke's Daring Columbia Move

- Another Face-off with Pepsi
- Roberto's Rules of Risk Taking and Deal Making

Risk Dynamic #16: Follow-through   258

- Salomon's Rise and Stumble
- Hot Streak Illusion
- Comfort Can Kill

BOOK VI
REVOLUTIONARY RISK

Risk Dynamic #17: Making Mental Measurements   267

- Measuring Risk's Distance
- The House That Harry Built
- Shaking Things Up

Risk Dynamic #18: Freedom: Concomitant of
Control   274

- Walkaway Management
- Theory Q
- Daring to Think Differently
- Alert to Opportunity
- R&D That Pays Off

Risk Dynamic #19: Seeing the Big Picture   298

- Quad's Risk-Taking Culture
- Toasting a Perfect Zero
- Earning Accolades
- Extended Family

Acknowledgments   311

Notes on Sources   313

Bibliography of Additional References and
Suggested Readings   323

Index   325

BOOK

I

THE HEART OF BUSINESS RISK

"If you can make one heap of all your winnings
And risk it on one turn of pitch-and-toss,
And lose, and start again at your beginnings
And never breathe a word about your loss ...

"Yours is the Earth and everything that's in it,
And—which is more—you'll be a Man, my
son!"

—RUDYARD KIPLING

CREATIVE DESTRUCTION

> *"Even if you're on the right track, you'll get*
> *run over if you just sit there."*
>
> —WILL ROGERS

Capitalism is messy business. It doesn't move in straight lines. Nor is it smooth or predictable. Participants cannot assume order and stability any more than the farmer can count on the weather.

The process of enterprise includes disrupting, even dismantling the old as much as it does building the new. Change is its only constant. But to change is to face uncertainty. *Change requires taking risks.* The essence of making changes is taking risks —not just any risks, but "dynamic" risks. Dynamic risks are forceful risks; they create their own energy and motion. Dynamic risks produce innovation, they launch companies, they improve conditions for workers, they create new products, services and jobs. Dynamic risks constantly revise and improve existing ways of doing things through the ultimate dynamic process we know as trial and error. This risk taking sometimes causes failures and losses, but only *risk* produces progress and profits.

Dynamic risk is sometimes counterintuitive. It doesn't seem

3

logical to rip something apart that's working just fine, to abandon the tried and true in favor of the uncertain. Walter Wriston, former chairman of Citibank, the nation's largest financial institution, offers an adroit description of risk. "If wages come from work, rent from real estate and interest from savings, where do profits come from?" he asks. "The answer is that profits come from risk." Dynamic risks are the picks and shovels of enterprise. These are vigorous risks, willfully undertaken.

Taking dynamic risks is what qualifies companies and individuals to earn profits. It is a process we could call Active Risk Taking, or ART. Its practitioners are ARTists. And like its lowercase cousin, "art," ART is, by definition, "a specific skill in adept performance, conceived as requiring the exercise of *intuitive faculties that cannot be learned solely by study.*" ART is not random or blind, and through a better understanding of risk's dynamics, individuals can become more skilled in its use. Both ART and art involve creativity, innovation, a breaking with tradition, a high chance of failure. Active Risk Taking, however, is not so mysterious as the *process* of art. It is more open and accessible to our probing. It might help if business bisected risk. Active, dynamic risk would be spelled with a capital "R." Lowercase "risk" would define the passive, static variety not aimed at creation or innovation—the risks of smoking, of flood, fire or accident, for example. Lowercase risks are threats without opportunity; they are the ones for which you buy insurance.

Earlier in this century, the economist Joseph Schumpeter described a " . . . process of industrial mutation that incessantly revolutionizes the economic structure *from within,* incessantly creating a new one." He called this process "creative destruction" and said it was "the essential fact about capitalism."

Risk, in turn, is the essential fact of Schumpeter's creative destruction. Risks are the change agents that prevent enterprise from becoming static. All businesses must make inherently risky decisions in crisis situations. But the real risk-taking companies and individuals are those that practice dynamic risk taking—ART—*regularly.* They creatively destroy the status quo in search of something better.

Usually it works. Sometimes it doesn't. The only certainty is that companies that resist change [pronounced RISK] too long will wither and die.

4

Abandoning Yesterday

One thing that will surely squelch the urge to change, take risks and innovate is a company that looks to its *past* for guidance rather than to its future. Innovative risk takers—let's call them *riskers*, or ARTists—have faith in an uncertain future. They know that the realm of new ideas requires a new way of looking at things. That fresh, innovative, risk-taking view becomes impossible if we are locked into "the way things have always been done," believing erroneously that what happens *tomorrow* will approximate what happened *today*.

That makes weather and economics surprisingly similar sciences. As the technology of weather prediction advances, with its supercomputers and satellites, we take it for granted that predictions of tomorrow's weather, or next week's for that matter, will become increasingly accurate. Not so. Weather is much too random, too chaotic. Nor can enterprise, with its increasing sophistication at crunching numbers of infinite variety, hope to predict economic events ever more accurately. Though countless decisions are based on econometric forecasts, the forecasts' track record is poor. As science writer James Gleick points out in *Chaos*, variables such as politics, fashion and consumer optimism are not nearly so measurable as, say, humidity, despite what the economic soothsayers may claim.

The irony is that uncertainty itself has a kind of structure that can at least be dealt with at street level, if not predicted. Science is dealing with it through the emerging discipline called chaos, while enterprise does so at an everyday functional level of risk taking. It's not a choice or accident. It's a necessity.

Risk is the financial world's answer to the science of chaos. It is everywhere in enterprise, as is chaos in nature—in the ebb and flow of interest rates, the tangled web of international currency relationships, the sometimes bizarre pricing mechanisms of the marketplace, the clash of competition, the unpredictability of consumers, and the simultaneous decision making of millions of people who play this game. The dream that enterprise could be reduced to a finite, measurable and controllable process is just that—a dream. In the future, success will stick best to companies that understand and embrace change, risk and unpredictability.

Corporations that take risks find their security not in building a

5

fortress against change, but in knowing they are nimble enough to dodge the bullets of uncertainty. They exercise control by flexibility, reacting quickly to the risks they take to remain in front.

Risk taking looms all the more critical for the 1990s and beyond as flexibility and speed become absolutely vital to corporate survival. The U.S. population as a whole is growing a scant 1 percent each year, and slowing, notes Peter Francese, founder and president of American Demographics, Inc., a unit of Dow Jones & Company. Growth will no longer be an American economic birthright.

In the past, a rising population and economic tide tended to lift all corporate boats. In coming years, however, businesses whose earnings advance only as much as the overall population may not survive. Francese, one of the nation's leading demographic experts, warns that business survival will depend on how well companies adapt themselves to the increasing fragmentation of markets. Companies must learn how to create and sell products and services to ever more diverse groups differing in age, purchasing power, location, lifestyle and values.

Businesses that take risks, that innovate, will be best positioned to benefit from market fragmentation, says Francese, because they are the ones that spend most heavily on research and development. They are the ones constantly changing and offering something new.

But rather than encourage the type of cautious experimentation that defines good management, many American companies have so far spent their greatest resources trying to *avoid* risk. They've forgotten, or never learned, how to "creatively destroy" existing products and methods to make room for the new, the better, the more efficient, even if they now recognize their very survival may depend on making such changes.

Management expert Peter Drucker calls this process "the systematic sloughing off of yesterday." Says Drucker, "Innovating organizations spend neither time nor resources on defending yesterday. The new and especially the as-yet unborn, that is, the future innovation always looks insignificant compared to the large volume, the large revenue. . . . It is all the more important, therefore, for an existing business to commit itself to the systematic abandonment of yesterday if it wants to be able to create tomorrow." This process is a fundamental force of enterprise no less significant than, say, gravity in physics. Progress and profits rise spontaneously from continuous risk taking.

But even businesses that *say* they welcome innovation often resist change and its risks when they find out what's required. Systematically dismantling existing systems that appear to be working well is where company leaders begin having problems with the dynamics of risk in enterprise. There is a potent natural tendency toward caution in the face of uncertainty. This is the dividing point. It is the difference between *accepting* change when it happens to come along, and beating change to the punch by *creating* it, and thus maintaining greater control of it, yourself. Creative destruction requires an investment in unproven technologies, or human resources, in trying to understand new things that the company doesn't yet understand.

Richard Foster, a director of the big international management consulting firm McKinsey & Company, is but one contemporary observer who says U.S. corporations are too complacent, that they approach the future the wrong way. Most corporations spend far too much of their money defending products that are more important for the profits they generated in the past than for what they will generate in the future, argues Foster. That leaves too little to spend on what will be tomorrow's leading technologies. Foster maintains that this defense-oriented attitude has things backwards—that companies must attack, not defend, in order to gain and maintain leadership in their markets.

Some managers today believe that taking risks means taking shortcuts to profit. That's a dangerous misreading of risk. Companies might have to take risks to speed a development along and beat the competition. But risk is not *always* defined by speed. And it is definitely *not* a shortcut. The risk could also lie in holding back a product for more refinement, gambling that the time and money spent in doing so will reap greater rewards later.

The Coca-Cola Company, one of America's oldest and most revered corporate names, was a paradigm of defense-oriented corporate conservatism. The company was built on one product, Coca-Cola, and the corporate mission for almost a century was to defend that product. Coke had been America's leading soft drink for so many years that company leaders believed there wasn't a need to take risks. Coca-Cola was a classic example of a company reacting to conditions rather than taking initiatives.

But Coca-Cola's market lead slowly eroded, and when new blood took control of the company in the early 1980s, it put some boldness back into the Coke brew. Coke's corporate daring, however, illustrates how tricky risk can be. Masterful risk taking doesn't always mean hitting bull's-eyes. Risks sometimes turn out right, but for unexpected reasons, as they did at Coca-Cola. Coke created change, and got more than it bargained for . . .

PUTTING RISK BACK INTO COKE

"I firmly believe we are in business to be risk takers. Our industry size and strength should allow us to take risks without fear of being wiped out financially if we fail."

—ROBERTO C. GOIZUETA,
soon after becoming chairman
and CEO of Coca-Cola in 1981

Roberto C. Goizueta has a cheery, fatherly face etched in a permanent half-smile as if suppressing a laugh. Vanishing black hair only hints of gray. His "call-me-Roberto" sincerity contradicts the hard-boiled stereotype of a corporate titan. Friends and associates describe him as an unfailing gentleman, disarmingly charming and unpretentious. In short, he doesn't seem the type of person who would deliberately rob America of a much-cherished cultural icon.

Yet on Tuesday, April 23, 1985, the chairman and chief executive officer of The Coca-Cola Company stunned everyone from Wall Street to Main Street with a blockbuster announcement: The company was scrapping its ninety-nine-year-old formula for the world's most financially successful soft drink. A new Coke would take its place.

Goizueta's risk put these items on the line:

- The $3.5 billion in yearly sales and $600 million in profits the now obsolete product had been earning for this all-American corporate giant—a $10 billion, Triple-A rated firm that had increased dividends for twenty-three consecutive years and was among the fifty largest concerns in the United States.
- The reputation of the world's most widely known trademark. On any given day, 270 million servings of Coke are consumed worldwide—50 million in the United States.

The beverage Coca-Cola, at least as America had known it, was yanked off the market. Its secret flavoring formula, known as Merchandise 7X, was banished to a vault at the Trust Company of Georgia, under the care of bank president James B. Williams, a member of Coke's board of directors. Coca-Cola officials said the old brew would never tickle thirsty lips again. The new formula was designated Merchandise 7X-100.

Old Coke was out, "New Coke"—or as company officials preferred to call it, "The New Taste of Coke," or worse, "Coke with changed taste components"—was in. With one calculated twitch of his corporate wand, Goizueta (pronounced Goy-SWEAT-a) vaporized a product that had become "America in a Bottle"—a symbol of U.S. capitalism in the 155 countries (plus the South Pole) where Coke is sold. It was, the chairman confesses, one of the most astonishing and visible corporate risks ever taken by a consumer products company.

As far back as 1938, one Kansas newspaper editor described Coke as "the sublimated essence of all that America stands for." That essence had been reinforced a thousand times over by hundreds of millions of dollars in advertising over subsequent decades. Coke was "The Real Thing" (a slogan invented in 1942 and revived in 1969); "The Pause That Refreshes" (from 1929); Coke became "It" in the 1980s. Starting in 1963, America had been told that "Things go better with Coke." Were consumers now being told that, well, they hadn't been drinking the real thing after all? That Coke wasn't really quite "It"?

Executives nationwide marveled at Coke's boldness, or stupidity, depending on their point of view. A marketing expert at Harvard Business School, interviewed about the wisdom of

Goizueta's brash deed, admitted he had shuddered at the risk of tampering with a ninety-nine-year-old "mother brand."

Why Goizueta Rolled the Dice

After nearly a century a little creative destruction at The Coca-Cola Company was overdue. Pepsi was slowly draining off Coke customers. During the 1970s and 80s Pepsi had successfully positioned itself as the drink of choice for growing-up baby boomers.

In the early 1970s, Coke's sales volume had grown at 10 to 15 percent per year. By the end of the decade, it had plunged to an anemic 2 percent annual growth. The number of loyal Coke drinkers *dropped* 39 percent over the decade ending in 1982, while the number of people counting themselves as Pepsi loyalists tripled. Coke still sold more soft drinks, but its once invulnerable armor was pierced. Several years before Goizueta took control at Coke in 1981, the blasphemous idea of a formula change had actually been raised as one way to deal with the Pepsi onslaught. But management would have nothing of it. The offending proposal was summarily buried.

Decades of market leadership had mesmerized Coca-Cola executives into believing that change and risk were foes to be avoided. The company only *reacted* to changing conditions rather than taking initiatives on its own. The thought of changing seemingly successful products and approaches from within was alien. The worst part, perhaps, was that Coca-Cola Company profits continued growing despite its main product's market share slippage. Management couldn't see a reason to fix something that appeared unbroken.

But evidence of the need to change was mounting. Even if Coke did nothing, the marketplace was evolving. In 1980, Coke came perilously close to showing its first drop in net income in many years. Net income that year rose just 0.5 percent. In the five years from 1977 through 1981, the Coca-Cola Company's net sales—after adjusting for inflation—increased a paltry 6.3 percent.

With Goizueta newly in control, Coke's U.S. market share continued its worrisome erosion. In just one year, from 1983 to 1984, Coke's piece of the soft drink pie was sliced 14.3 percent when its market share dropped from 24.8 to 21.7, according to figures reported in *The New York Times*. Analysts blamed the decline squarely on competition from Pepsi.

When Pepsi passed Coke in the crucial battleground of grocery store sales in 1984, Goizueta says, he'd had enough. This was a supreme indignation. His company was outspending Pepsi on advertising by tens of millions of dollars. Coke's marketing programs were considered a big success. Its distribution network reached into every thirsty backwater in the country, and many more worldwide. And still Coke's lead was fading.

An unspeakable indignity loomed: Pepsi could conceivably catch Coke in overall sales by 1986, the year Coke would celebrate its hundredth anniversary. If The Coca-Cola Company was going to take action, take a risk, it had to be well before the centennial celebration. It didn't want egg on its face at its own birthday party.

A few key executives began agitating for action shortly after Goizueta gained full control. They, as well as Goizueta, knew that the soft drink business had been changing for years. The youth market, which drinks most of the sugared colas sold in the United States, was shrinking. Tastes were turning rapidly toward diet and fruit-based drinks. And Pepsi was winning the cola war. Pepsi's slow-motion coup had rattled the executive suite at Coke headquarters.

Something had to be done. Goizueta would have to take his own risk-taking advice. "Not taking action is not a risk-free situation," he says. In his speeches to Coke employees, division heads, chemists and bottlers, the chairman had been preaching a risk-taking philosophy in his Cuban accent, tempered with a southern drawl: "Remember, if you take risks, you may still fail. . . . If you do not take risks, you will surely fail. . . . The greatest risk of all is to do nothing."

In the past, continues Goizueta, "The Coca-Cola Company made an assumption that not to do something is less risky than to do something. So in a way we were taking a risk. It was not an intelligent risk in my opinion, but it surely was a risk." Goizueta's style would be different, more in tune with Wall Street's affectionate nickname for The Coca-Cola Company—"Knockout" (which derives from Coke's stock market trading symbol, KO).

11

* * *

Goizueta has a vein of corporate fearlessness pulsing just beneath a softer, elegantly assembled exterior. Fond of chocolates, he often wears expressions suggestive of a diet of sweets, though his physique says otherwise. The pronounced accent and the sometimes offbeat way he phrases and combines his words make his Cuban roots unmistakable. He was born there November 18, 1931, and attended the same Jesuit prep school as Fidel Castro. He earned a degree in chemical engineering at Yale in 1953 and went to work for Coke's Havana bottling plant. He fled the country in 1960 with his wife and three small children.

In a moment of self-reflection Goizueta describes his willingness to take risks years later as CEO of Coke as having been honed by his decision to leave everything behind and start life afresh in the United States. To Goizueta, that was his greatest personal risk.

Throughout Coke's vast and growing corporate compound on Atlanta's North Avenue, the chairman is known simply as Roberto, at his own insistence. New York executive search maven Gerard Roche, of the firm Heidrick and Struggles, tells of how on first meeting Goizueta he was impressed with the chairman's aristocratic Cuban heritage and commanding presence as leader of a $10 billion corporate colossus. As Roche tells the story: "I was determined to push forward with Roche's rule of getting on a first-name basis with clients as soon as possible. At the first opening, I slid into the dialogue with, 'Well, Bob, the way I see things. . . .' I could see his hands grip the side of his chair, his perfectly tailored figure stiffen, and out came the words: 'Gerry, I don't look like a Bob, and I don't talk like a Bob. And if you and I are going to get along, don't call me Bob. My name is Roberto.'"

According to Goizueta, those who oppose change, who say, "Keep doing what you're doing . . . don't change anything," seem to think that such a course is risk-free. "But that is not the case, because I can tell you just for sure that had we not, for example, launched Diet Coke because it was too risky, the diet segment, which now accounts for over one-fourth of the soft drink market, would not have the Coca-Cola trademark in it, because we did not have a Coca-Cola trademark diet soft drink."

Before Goizueta, the Coke brand name had been sacred. Never had it been bestowed upon another soft drink product. Rarely had it even been considered. Goizueta reversed a century of tradition by introducing a diet soft drink with the Coke name—never mind the company already had a successful diet cola called Tab. It was the first time the Coke trademark was imparted to a beverage other than regular Coke. (The full trademark Coca-Cola was registered at the U.S. Patent Office in 1893, the shortened version Coke in 1944.)

Goizueta believes that this decision, in 1982, to introduce a diet cola with the Coke name ranks as the most perilous of his major corporate risks. "That was the biggest risk," he says, "because had Diet Coke been a failure, we would have extended the trademark to a failed product and would have in the process damaged Tab irreparably."

The Coca-Cola Company and its bottlers fretted over the move. Would extending the Coke trademark help boost the overall soft drink market? Or would it simply dilute Coke's precious image and divert sales from the main brand that took generations to build?

When Goizueta appeared before the National Soft Drink Association convention on December 2, 1982—four months after Diet Coke's launch—he could offer no specific answers to those nagging questions. "The only thing certain about the present environment," he told the audience, "is its uncertainty. " The solution he offered was to "stay hungry and feisty and aggressive in the marketplace."

Goizueta's risk would pay off. Diet Coke became one of the most successful new product launches of the decade. Within two years it was the world's number one selling low-cal soft drink.

Critics had complained that Diet Coke would steal profits from both Coke and Tab. "People said it was risky to extend the Coca-Cola trademark to another product. They did not understand that the diet segment of the market had become not merely a little niche for figure-conscious women, but it was becoming a mainstream part of America. . . . The only product we had there was Tab. We did not have the Coca-Cola trademark in that fast-growing segment of the market. That was the main reason why Diet Coke [known as Coca-Cola Light in some countries] came into being," recalls Goizueta.

The decision to take this risk may have been even more hotly

13

debated within the corporate hierarchy than was the formula change three years later. The Coke trademark had been zealously guarded for nearly a century. The only three other chairmen the company ever had wouldn't consider risking it on something new. But with Goizueta's new aggressive, risk-taking stance, Diet Coke opened the door to creation of what the corporation now calls the "Coke megabrand"—a growing menu of soft drink products that carry the Coke trademark. They include Cherry Coke, Diet Coke, "New" Coke, Coca-Cola Classic, and caffeine-free versions of Coke and Diet Coke.

And in his rush to shake things up at Coke, Goizueta even introduced Diet Coke without market-testing the product—adding one risk atop another. "When people said to me, Why didn't you market-test Diet Coke, I just took a very simple position," he later told *The New York Times*. "Market-testing is to see whether you are going to succeed or fail. But as far as I was concerned, failure was just not an option with Diet Coke."

RISK DYNAMIC #2
RISK-TAKING
RECONNAISSANCE

"Historically, risk takers are people who shatter the illusion of knowledge. They are willing to try something that everyone thinks is outrageous or stupid."

—DANIEL BOORSTIN,
former Librarian of Congress

Shortly after becoming chairman and CEO of Coca-Cola, "America's New High Priest of Fizz"—as Goizueta was dubbed by one newspaper—issued a proclamation calling for "a new corporate culture based on intelligent risk taking." Few outsiders knew at the time just how seriously Goizueta would take his own inaugural decrees about changing to meet the future.

What does Goizueta mean by *intelligent* risk taking? "Well," he grins, "as opposed to dumb risk taking, is the obvious short answer." Now serious, he adds, "What I mean by intelligent risk taking is . . . be sure you have the facts so that you have the cards stacked in your favor. To an outsider it may still appear like a hell of a risky thing you have done. But if you have the cards stacked in your favor—because you have *information* that leads you to believe that you will succeed in what you propose to do—then it is not such a risky thing at all."

He suggests a parallel from the motion picture industry's practice of choosing a best actor and actress each year. Each candidate is playing a different role, says Goizueta, who contends that the only true method of determining which is best would be to compare performances in the *same* role. "If you and I have the same information, and I decide to go ahead with something and you decide not to go ahead, then I may be more of a risk taker than you are. But only if we have the same information. Number one, intelligent risk taking is a question of information, and number two, it's a question of weighing the alternatives." Both require a skill Goizueta has refined to a science, perhaps owing to his roots as a scientist. His attention to detail has become legend throughout the corporation.

But information alone is no guarantee that a risk will succeed. Coca-Cola generated boxcars of research before deciding to risk the formula change. Still, it was unable to predict what would happen. Risk takers can never know for sure whether the information they have is enough . . . whether they are interpreting it correctly . . . or whether it is the *right* information.

An old *Pink Panther* movie, with Peter Sellers, demonstrated why simply obtaining facts isn't good enough. It must be the *right* information, at the same time. In this film, Inspector Clouseau arrives at a small village hotel and encounters a docile-looking dog sleeping in front of the check-in desk.

Clouseau asks the innkeeper, "Does your dog bite?"

"No," the innkeeper replies.

Thus assured, the intrepid Clouseau leans over to pet the dog, which promptly bites his hand.

"You said your dog didn't bite!" an indignant Clouseau barks at the innkeeper.

"Yes," replies the innkeeper, barely looking up. "But that's not my dog."

Our "natural" state of existence, Clouseau learned, is one of ignorance in the face of rapid change, uncertainty and surprise events. The apparently "safe" action of petting the innkeeper's dog was made dangerous by an unforeseen risk: that this might not be the innkeeper's dog after all. Successful corporate risk takers try to anticipate potential losses, but they can't always delay due to lack of information. Since there is *always* information lacking, and there is *never* enough time to seek it out, delay can be a dangerous luxury in enterprise.

In one major study of managerial risk taking, a common response when faced with a risky decision was to delay it, in hopes that it would go away, or some new information would surface. But risks often fail because the risk taker was simply too late getting there. Failing to act is the greater danger in the fields of enterprise, as Goizueta himself points out. Success can depend on the risk taker's own sense of urgency.

Information, however, is a slippery, sometimes deceptive commodity. With risk, information can be aggravating—the more you learn, the less you seem to know. Information overkill. The more scientists learn about dinosaurs, the less they agree on what caused their extinction. Information, some say, is just a nicer term for unpredictability. Economists haven't quite reached that point. Arguments over the causes and effects of inflation, high interest rates, deficits, currency changes and scores of other issues rage on. But the more they learn, the less predictable enterprise seems to become.

Business managers study classical models of how enterprise works, then have difficulty coping when events refuse to conform. Adam Smith's invisible hand assumes that through the wide disbursement of knowledge and information, natural market forces will smooth out the bumps of enterprise. It does work that way over the long term. During the average business career, however, enterprise is not nearly so well ordered. In enterprise, risk begins where classic management theories end. Risk, rather than competition, is the key dynamic that makes enterprise work as well as it does.

In place of stability, enterprise offers us a system dominated by "entropy"—an admittedly obscure term, but wonderfully accurate to help describe capitalism. The word hails from thermodynamics, where it describes the degree of *disorder* and randomness in any system, and also its capacity to undergo *spontaneous change*. Applied to information system dynamics—or for our purposes, risk dynamics—*it measures and evaluates information in terms of its uncertainty*. Entropy is the tendency of enterprise to

17

continuously slip into disorder. As cosmologist Stephen Hawking pointed out in *A Brief History of Time*, it's a kind of highbrow Murphy's law: things always tend to go wrong. Intellectuals also equate it with quantum mechanics—a theory which says things can never be entirely predictable. That view is widely held today despite Albert Einstein's objection that "God does not play with dice."

At The Coca-Cola Company, Goizueta came to believe that action, despite the risk, was his only course. He tells the story of an earlier failure that also taught him the limits of employing "logic" in enterprise. During the late 1950s Goizueta was in Brazil, searching on behalf of Coca-Cola for the right ingredients to produce an orange soda known today as Fanta orange. (Although the Fanta brand is obscure in the United States, it would be one of the world's largest soft drink companies if it were separated from Coke.) His idea was to make the taste as close to real orange juice as possible. "It's only natural," Goizueta says. "Logic tells you that such a product will sell best. Of course, what I forgot is that people who drink orange soda *expect* something different." Goizueta's formula for Fanta—known as Coca-Cola R13—"was a disaster. But you learn from those mistakes. We ended up making it a lot more red, a lot sweeter and less acidic."

In enterprise, decisions *must* be made under circumstances of incomplete knowledge or even pure ignorance. In the face of that uncertainty, learning the *limits of information* is partly the essence of effective risk taking. Overestimating the certainty of information on which companies base a risky decision is a trap to avoid. One lesson of risk dynamics is that risks are most treacherous when decision makers act as if they're *not* taking risks, when they really *are*.

Avoiding Detail Fog

Too much information can also be dangerous, contends J.B. Fuqua, founder, chairman and the largest stockholder of Fuqua Industries, headquartered within sight of Goizueta's office across downtown Atlanta. Fuqua, a self-educated, self-made multimillionaire, walks and talks softly, but carries a big risk-taking stick.

He started building his corporation at age forty-seven and had a Fortune 500 firm by the time he was fifty. Fuqua Industries is now a $4 billion conglomerate with key businesses in photo finishing, financial services and power tools.

Fuqua is decidedly old school. He is known around Atlanta business circles as "J.B.," and his personality is reserved, even dry. But he's proven himself exceptionally spry in anticipating economic changes and profiting from them. And though he never attended college, one of the nation's top graduate business schools now carries his name—Duke University's Fuqua School of Business.

The conglomerate business is largely a matter of buying and selling companies at the right time. Top-flight research and information are mandatory. "You must know enough about the opportunity to assess the risk," notes Fuqua. But while he devours information before taking his risks, Fuqua is careful not to become a prisoner of his own research. There's a danger in seeking too much information. "In fact that's what often happens," he says. "I'm often asked, 'How are you able to make acquisitions when other companies haven't?' And usually it's because they study something to death. And they're not going to make a decision.

"For years my good friends at Coke had a big mergers and acquisitions department. *But they never made an acquisition.* They studied everything to death. The climate's a lot different out there now. But for years and years, Coke never could make a decision." According to Fuqua, "To become successful risk takers, business leaders need to avoid the *fog of detail* that derails crucial leadership skills. CEOs must, first and foremost, be strategists and motivators." His primary example of detail fog derailing leadership is fellow Georgian Jimmy Carter, whom Fuqua describes as an immensely intelligent man whose ability to lead the nation was clouded by his desire to grasp the minutiae of each issue.

According to J.B., three fourths of the information on the average CEO's desk is pure clutter. "The key is to develop a strong ability to see the big picture. That is the best route to spotting upcoming change and assessing the risks necessary to adapt. Good managers can manage any business."

19

COKE'S RECONNAISSANCE EFFORT

By 1980, the marketing research division at The Coca-Cola Company had already documented Coke's dwindling lead over Pepsi. Supersensitive internal reports confined any debate over possible steps to a handful of top corporate executives at the company, and Coca-Cola U.S.A., the division handling Coke sales in the United States. But with corporate profits and dividends still healthy despite a slowdown in earnings growth, the matter received little urgency.

One of the first to pursue the issue was Coke's research chief, who could pinpoint only one logical reason Pepsi was gaining: taste. People had loved Coke for almost a hundred years. Maybe that was long enough. Five years before the change was actually made, Coke's research department was already testing the two critical items: (1) how consumers rated new formulas compared to old Coke and to Pepsi; and (2) how they reacted to the *concept* of a new taste for Coca-Cola. The concept question, however, was extremely difficult to measure. The fact that a Coke division was even *thinking* about testing reaction to a taste change was top secret. Consumers taking part in the tests could not be told outright that such a change was being considered. Tests had to be framed so that the consumers' comments would answer the questions on Coke's hidden agenda.

The first consumer testing showed positive results on both counts. Thousands more taste and attitude tests were done in 1982. New formulas scored significantly better against Pepsi. But there was resistance from consumers to altering the cherished original, even when a new taste was preferred.

In late 1983 Goizueta approved a more formal team project to explore a possible formula change. Changing Coke's chemistry was a relatively simple matter. *Implementing* the change would rattle a multibillion-dollar worldwide network. That's where the effects of the risk would be felt the most.

Consumers, unaware of which company was behind the research, were asked their reaction to changing (improving) the taste of several of the most popular beers and soft drinks, including Budweiser and Pepsi. There was negative sentiment for only one: Coca-Cola. Coke researchers hit on something other Americans long knew: Coke stood for more than just a sugared soft drink. It had become almost generic. Residents of the American Southwest had for years used the term "Coke" in referring to all types of soft drinks, much as we use the terms Kleenex, Xerox and Jell-O.

For Goizueta, that finding made the decision of a formula change *both more risky and more compelling at the same time.* His reconnaissance told him that consumers liked the Coke name more than its taste. "They were *loving* it more than they were *drinking* it," says Coke's CEO. His task, he believed, was to change that by making Coke a *product* they'd choose ahead of Pepsi, instead of just a *name.* Coke, he reasoned, could be whatever The Coca-Cola Company said it was.

Coke chemists were at this time also testing formulas for what would become Diet Coke. It was one of those concoctions, Goizueta claims, that eventually became New Coke. It was essentially Diet Coke with sugar in it—sweeter than original Coke by about three calories per can.

But contrary to stories that appeared after the 1985 formula change announcement, it wasn't the sudden discovery of a "great tasting" new formula that prodded Goizueta into making his risky move. Other formulas had already been tested. The idea for the risk had been fizzing in Goizueta's brain for several years. In fact, Goizueta regrets not having acted earlier. "I wish I would have pushed like hell, even before I was chairman, to have done it sooner," he says.

Thousands more blind tests with this latest "taste discovery" were performed in the fall of 1984 against old Coke and Pepsi. The new formula came up a clear winner, by a three-to-two margin. This, key Coke executives now believed, was a product that could stop Pepsi's advance.

But the big question remained: What could they do with it now that they had it? Give it a new name and put it out beside regular Coke? Introduce it as a *second* Coke? Quietly change the original formula to the new formula? Forget the whole thing?

The information fed to Goizueta and second-in-command Donald Keough, Coke's president, by team members secretly exploring the formula change would be crucial in triggering a decision. The arguments demonstrating Coke's ebbing market share, Pepsi's new superiority in supermarket sales, the apparent consumer preference for Pepsi's sweeter formulation, and the success of the new Coke formula in blind consumer taste tests against Pepsi, all favored a decision to act. That made Goizueta believe there was ample justification for a switch in tastes. Even later, after the formula change flopped and the original Coke formula was brought back as Coca-Cola Classic, Goizueta argued that his critics ("And God knows there were enough of them," he notes) badly misjudged that evidence.

"The product Coca-Cola had been losing market share for over twenty-five years," he says with the conviction of having oft repeated the argument. "It was a product much admired and much revered, like a religious icon, but not *consumed* [his emphasis] very much."

That's overstating the case a bit, given Coke's huge sales figures worldwide. But sales growth for Coke products in the late 1970s had slowed to a trickle, although Wall Street rated the company among the financially strongest in America. Such a high rating normally helps companies borrow money cheaply. But Coke was too conservative to borrow money before Goizueta's tenure, and the rating was primarily window dressing.

Investors bought and held Coke stock for safety and dividends —the company paid the first of a still unbroken string of yearly dividends in 1893. Coke shares were considered safe. But investors never expected huge profits. The company was Old Guard conservative. It was never known for taking the risks associated with major gains.

The company had propped up its portion of the sugared cola market for many years simply by outspending the competition on marketing and advertising by three or four to one. And, says Goizueta, the Coke brand was also being heavily discounted by the bottlers to keep market share alive—a little-known fact that made the market share erosion look even worse inside Coke headquarters. "Sugar colas are the foundation on which The Coca-Cola Company is built," says Goizueta in looking back on the risk he took. "We're not built on the movie business [Coke bought Columbia Pictures in 1982]. We're not built on the orange juice business [Coke owns Minute Maid]. We're not built on the television business. We're built on the sugar cola business, and that foundation was getting weaker and weaker and weaker all the time.

22

"Here's a little parallel," he adds. "Let's say the boxy cars being made by General Motors do not sell. But the stylish Ford models are selling. What does General Motors do? They discount. They move the product based on price, as opposed to on product acceptance. It's nothing new. That's the way we had been moving at Coca-Cola."

Leather squeaks as Goizueta reclines in his desk chair. Fog blocks his usually dazzling twenty-fifth-floor view of Atlanta. "Then," he continues, "because of corporate arrogance—perhaps too strong a term but still valid—we were for many years not willing to confront the fact that maybe the product Coca-Cola is, quote, unquote, inferior as perceived by the consumers. When the Pepsi Challenge advertising campaign came along [a blind taste test pitting Coke against Pepsi], many consumers said, 'My God, the taste . . . I'm drinking the Coke trademark, I'm not drinking the product. The fact is, product Pepsi, without the trademark, tastes better to me than product Coca-Cola.' So when you face a product superiority that is not only discernible, but at the same time is an idea that can be transmitted to the consumer, then you are in a hell of a bind. You might as well face up to the music . . . take the risk."

Goizueta had convinced himself of the need to exercise some "creative destruction"—the systematic dismantling of existing ways of doing things in favor of what is believed to be better. "The question is, do you face up to the music when you are still doing well? Or do you face up to the music later?" he asks, "We could have gone twenty more years, and product Coca-Cola's market share would have kept going steadily down the hill."

Shorter Product Life Spans

By acting soon enough, some companies have been able to avoid facing a crisis later. Consider Fuqua Industries. Several years before Coke's daring moves, Fuqua had begun its own brand of creative destruction. "I've always contended that if you are going to operate a conglomerate, you've got to be just as willing to *sell* as you are to buy," observes the company founder. "Products mature, companies mature . . . the life span of products is getting shorter and shorter."

To demonstrate the point, J.B. took his $2 billion company [at the time] and deliberately chain-sawed it down to a svelte $600 million operation at the outset of the 1980s. He had spotted economic changes on the way and decided some radical structural changes were worth risking. "How many people would take a $2 billion company and cut it down to $600 million?" asks Fuqua rhetorically. "That's what we did because we felt it was a good thing to do, even though the popular belief was that the stock would suffer.

"Ours was a diversified company on the fast track to growth in the 1970s," he says. "When revenues topped $2 billion in 1979, we changed course, trimming operations by over two-thirds to get out of businesses such as petroleum distribution and trucking that we felt wouldn't survive." Fuqua believed rightly that the country was headed for a recession and that oil prices would head down. He sold three television stations for $60 million. A trucking subsidiary was spun off, and Lano Corporation, an oil distribution unit that provided nearly half of Fuqua's revenues at one point, was sold for $180 million in cash in 1981. Fuqua's disappearing act greatly boosted profitability. By the first quarter of 1983, the corporation's per share earnings were the highest of any first quarter in its history.

Fuqua cites his own systematic dismantling as an example of what other companies must face. A good example of a company that *failed* to risk those kinds of changes, he says, is the National Cash Register Corporation, a fast track company in the 1960s and 70s. "NCR was the market leader in mechanical cash registers and other accounting machines, and its grip on this line of business seemed invincible. Then along came the new electronic systems, a field which NCR's managers feared entering. They chose instead to protect their soon-to-be-outdated product lines and were quickly run over. NCR missed the shift to electronic machines and in the span of just four years lost most of the market it had once controlled."

Risk takers must be adaptable, observes Fuqua. "Every CEO pays lip service to change. For most of them, however, change is the one thing they'd most like to avoid if they could. But they can't, and the ability to learn and adapt is vital. The field of electronics over the last thirty years is littered with corporate corpses and tales of 'what might have been' if CEOs had adapted more quickly. Companies that made vacuum tubes were blindsided by the newer transistor technology. Then the transistor makers were scuttled by semiconductors."

This Georgian's solution is executive courage, or risk taking, "to pursue change even when change seems like the last thing that is necessary. That doesn't mean change for the sake of change. The key is *anticipation*—recognizing the inevitability of change and beating it to the punch."

COCA-COLA'S CHOICE

Goizueta also chose to initiate changes when others thought change unnecessary. The result? In his first five years as Coke's chief, the company's soft drink volume increased 25 percent worldwide. The year of his big "blunder," growth in consumption of Coke brand soft drinks was two and a half times higher than the industry average. Half the colas consumed in the United States now have the Coke name, as does one of every three soft drinks.

"When you get so concerned with maintaining what you have as opposed to risking getting more, you're already turning downhill, and chances are you won't keep what you have," he says. But Goizueta, like most others in high-visibility corporate slots, accepts the label "risk taker" with reluctance. "I think that one point being missed by everyone is that risk is very much like beauty. It is in the eyes of the beholder. What to you may seem like a risky thing that we do in The Coca-Cola Company—since I have facts that you don't have—to me is not as much of a risk. Hell, you watch a football game and maybe the quarterback throws a pass and you say, 'That's a hell of a risky pass.' Well, probably the receiver came into the huddle and told him, 'Listen, the defensive back is limping. You can throw to me.' The quarterback has that information that I don't have watching the game. So what to me is a risky pass is not a risky pass to the quarterback.

"Frankly, that's why I feel incapable of judging the degree of risk on an action taken by another person. The best I can say is, 'Based on my own knowledge, and based on what I know, and based on my own personality, I think it's a risky action. But I would have to preface it with all of those things.'"

25

Risk, Goizueta is saying, is relative. The classic tale of two people seeing a business situation in opposite ways is the story of two shoe salesmen visiting a remote Amazon region for the first time. Shortly after arriving, the first salesman wires his home office that sales opportunities are nil since nobody wears shoes. He leaves. The second salesman, however, is ecstatic. "Send all possible stock," he tells his company. "We can dominate the market. Nobody yet wears shoes!"

For risk takers in enterprise, however, *thinking* you have the right information may not be enough. Witness Inspector Clouseau and the innkeeper's dog. When The Coca-Cola Company ran its market tests on a new Coke formula, consumers were not told that the original Coke would be pulled off the market. Researchers were constrained by secrecy from being too specific about a Coke formula switch. As a result, there was a gap in the company's understanding of how consumers would react to the original's disappearance. Even though Coca-Cola had painstakingly tested its new product, and by all appearances company executives took a reasoned approach to such a radical move, the outcome was far different than expected.

The risks of tampering with "success," as Coke did, give product researchers their worst nightmares. Just because consumers like one product over another doesn't mean they will buy it. More elusive psychological factors take hold in the real marketplace— advertising, image, and the key to it all, *perception.* Guessing how a product will be *perceived* in the market is how marketing men and women earn their daily bread. In this case, it was doubly hard. Not only did they have to gauge reaction to a new product, they also had to consider the removal of an old one. The consequences of improperly interpreting the public perception risk blindsided Coca-Cola.

For Goizueta, initial risks signaled other risks. If he *did* introduce a new Coke, how should it be approached? Could it be introduced as a sister product, *along with the original?* To what extent should they call attention to its newness? Should the word "new" even be used? Could the secret be kept long enough to prepare for the change before the competition found out? A leak would sorely damage the corporation's credibility with its network of independently owned bottling companies; rivals would gain valuable time to react. Every course was a risk.

Would consumers compare the new product to Pepsi, as Coke executives hoped? Or would they compare it against old Coke, putting the company in a no-win situation with one of its own products pitted against another?

Should the new product be openly test-marketed in selected regions before any national rollout? That's the usual route for new consumer products. Few corporations want to risk the huge promotional, distribution and other costs associated with introducing a new consumer product coast to coast before it's been tested regionally. There was no end to the questions.

Daring to Look Dumb

Risk takers, by definition, do things contrary to what others do or think. And again, by definition, they may often be wrong. That's why the best of them are not afraid to look dumb, if they've taken what they believe are proper risks. By changing the formula to increase sweetness, Coke would risk looking dumb because of its ad campaign that touted old Coke over Pepsi precisely because it was *less* sweet. Coke would appear two-faced. At the same time Coca-Cola proclaimed its less sweet formula superior on national television, corporate heads were secretly planning to make that formula *more* sweet. That would seem to be a blatant concession to Pepsi's claim that consumers preferred its slightly more sugared recipe. Coke's archrivals would have ample reason to gloat.

Goizueta considered a two-Coke strategy. But there were problems. One key reason for taking the risk in the first place was to make certain Coke did not lose its number one market share position to Pepsi. Splitting consumer sales between two Cokes made that a perilous possibility.

Recalls Coke's chairman: "Why didn't we have two Coca-Colas from the beginning? Well, then we ran the risk that the product which was already losing market share to its main competitor would have been forced to compete against still another, in-house competitor. So not only would poor old Coca-Cola have had to fight against Pepsi-Cola, but it would have had to fight against our own other product as well."

27

No, he decided, if this gamble was going to pay off, he'd have to take the maximum risk of *replacing* old Coke with the new product. And he ruled out the more cautious step-by-step introduction as impractical, cumbersome and incompatible with his other bold choice. Testing in public would tip Coke's hand. The company would seem tentative about its decision, unsure that New Coke was really any better—a weakness Pepsi would surely try to exploit. Region-by-region introduction would still leave two Cokes for consumers to contend with. There'd be confusion. Which Coke would the company be referring to in its national advertising?

Going national, all at once, would cost more. It would bet everything on one roll of the dice. But Goizueta could see no other way. He decided that a bold, positive push behind a reformulated, single-product Coke would force a comparison to Pepsi, rather than to old Coke. He wouldn't meekly slip through a change. He'd tell the world about it. And whether the secret could be kept until he was ready was another risk he simply had to take at the same time, though he'd do everything he could to control it.

Early in 1985 Goizueta made his decision. The formula change was a "go." That night, as he returned to the same house on a quiet Atlanta street where he has lived since joining Coke's Atlanta office in 1964, Coca-Cola's chairman felt confident of the risks he was taking on behalf of his company. His most difficult work was done, he thought. Now it would be in the hands of others to carry forward. And once Roberto makes a decision, he wants things to happen quickly.

In February, with plans for New Coke taking shape, Goizueta made a pilgrimage to the bedside of the ailing Robert Winship Woodruff at Emory University Hospital in Atlanta. Woodruff was patriarch of The Coca-Cola Company. He had taken the reins of the young firm in 1923 as a thirty-three-year-old Emory University dropout, and created the corporate mold that would endure for over half a century. Although fond of the dictum "The world belongs to the discontented," Woodruff had run the company as a role model of arch corporate conservatism. His philosophy was that companies with cash were king, and those that borrowed were beggars. At ninety-five years of age, and still an emeritus

28

director of the corporation, the elderly southern gentleman was nearly as old as the soon-to-be-changed formula itself.

Woodruff had been a domineering presence, known around Coke as "Boss" or simply "The Cigar." For decades he was a legend of American business. A man of supreme marketing skills, he was also legendary in his desire for anonymity. During World War II he had vowed to supply every American in uniform with a bottle of Coke for 5 cents, wherever they were and whatever the cost. Ultimately, the government paid much of the tab for the sixty-four Coke bottling plants that sprouted worldwide to supply the troops and fulfill Woodruff's pledge. It was the birth of Coca-Cola's global soft drink domination.

Among the innovations that Woodruff developed and introduced were the "six-pack" (in the 1920s) and coin-operated, open-from-the-top vending machines. The Coca-Cola Company's official biography of Woodruff describes him as the "mastermind who made Coca-Cola known around the globe" and "the dominant personal force in the world's largest soft drink business until his death." But although he became one of America's richest men and a noted philanthropist, when it came to running Coca-Cola Woodruff was a corporate miser.

It was Goizueta who finally changed all that. Shortly before his tenure began, the company had zero debt. Goizueta made it clear he wasn't afraid to borrow to finance the maneuvers he was planning—moves such as acquiring Columbia Pictures, and buying out bottlers he considered too resistant to change. And if his borrowing meant Coke would lose its triple-A corporate rating or take a beating in the press, so be it.

Goizueta owed Woodruff much. The Boss had, in effect, adopted the Cuban expatriate, treating him like a son, nurturing his career at Coke and grooming him for the chairmanship. Woodruff liked to call Goizueta "partner," and it was Woodruff, even though he was ninety at the time and had officially retired from duty in 1955, who selected Goizueta as victor in the race to replace J. Paul Austin in the top position at Coke. In May 1980, at Woodruff's urgings, Goizueta was named president and chief operating officer. *The New York Times* headlined the story, "LONG SHOT NAMED PRESIDENT OF COKE." Many Wall Streeters had expected Ian Wilson to get the president's slot. Goizueta, being

Cuban and a "technical man," seemed outside the Georgian good-old-boy network that normally produced CEOs in that region. With Woodruff calling the shots, however, the chairmanship and CEO titles followed in March 1981. Don Keough, whom many had expected to become chairman, became president—Goizueta's top confederate.

At the hospital, which Woodruff himself had greatly enriched through his huge donations to Emory University, Goizueta told his frail mentor of the plans to change Coca-Cola's formula. It was a particularly momentous disclosure. Part of Woodruff's legacy was the mystique he had built over half a century surrounding the cola's secret formula, stored in a special vault in the Trust Company of Georgia Bank. When Woodruff took over the company in the 1920s it was deeply in debt, and the formula was being held by a lender as collateral. One of Woodruff's first tasks was to pay off the debt and regain possession of the formula—a task he accomplished in just a few years. That was about the last time the company ever dared assume any debt, until the Goizueta era began.

All this history weighed heavily against Goizueta's new risk-taking style. But just as Woodruff had supported his "partner" Roberto in the past, he did so now as well. He would, however, fail to see the outcome. On March 7, 1985, within days of Goizueta's bedside visit and just six weeks before the formula change announcement, Woodruff, the grand master of Coca-Cola, was dead.

Goizueta's clandestine mission shifted to high gear. Weeks ahead of the launch date, key bottlers—most of them independently owned companies that package Coke on a franchise-type basis—were told (after promising to keep quiet about it) that the company was considering a change in the Coca-Cola formula. Because of the relationship between Coke and its bottlers—which one corporate official describes as "like brothers"—Coke officials say they might have nixed the formula switch had there been major dissension.

Most bottling franchise owners had become fabulously wealthy on the *existing* product. Goizueta himself has fantasized about owning his own bottling company—a position he believes would have made him much richer, much sooner, and without the responsibilities of running a giant corporation. Even his seven-figure chairman's salary doesn't eliminate a yearning to escape the glare of public scrutiny. "You can always find fault with a number of things you have done, but I tend not to worry about the past," he says. If events *had* worked out differently, Goizueta says he might indeed be bottling Coke instead of running the company. "I would be a very rich man," he says. "I don't know a single Coca-Cola bottler who is not rich. I would have been a very rich man owning a minimum of six huge bottling plants, and living in the comfort of the tropics with all the good things in life . . . not traveling half as much and certainly not working half as hard."

The bottlers had one key concern: making money. But they'd been forewarned years ahead of the formula change. Goizueta had cautioned them against becoming simple "caretakers" of a profitable business. "If we were to live by that philosophy, we could kiss volume growth goodbye, watch our sales level off and then decline, and start looking for a new line of business," he said in a speech. "We did not grow from a soda fountain confection to this nation's leading commercial beverage by merely satisfying *yesterday's* markets . . . we are not in business merely to be prudent caretakers. I firmly believe we are also in business to be risk takers. Our industry size and strength should allow us to take risks without fear of being wiped out financially."

Coke executives showed the bottlers evidence to document their product's marketplace slippage, and the obvious implication for long-term profits. If a new formula would stem the loss of market share to Pepsi, then the bottlers couldn't say no. Neither could they be enthusiastic, however, about disturbing their cash cow. They saw the risks as well as anyone, but deferred to corporate brass. If the corporation would push it they'd bottle it.

On April 22, 1985, Coca-Cola bottlers who hadn't yet been told of the impending switch were summoned to a meeting in Atlanta which produced more general support for a corporate decision that had already been made. But like the other bottlers, this group worried. They were aware of Coke's suffering market share, but feared such radical medicine might be worse than the disease. As one bottler lamented after being told of the impending formula change, "We have embarked on a trip, but we don't know what the final destination is."

The crucial day approached. A multicity press conference,

31

based in New York and linked by satellite to Chicago, Los Angeles, Houston, Toronto and Atlanta, was planned for April 23. Invitations were sent to media outlets, promising "the most important marketing announcement in the company's 100 years." Over the weekend, word of the bombshell brewing in Atlanta began leaking out. By the day of the press conference, Coke's "great surprise" was no more.

By now it didn't really matter. An extravagant, upbeat announcement was part of Coca-Cola's plan to blitzkrieg the country with the new product. The sooner New Coke replaced the old, the better, they reasoned. Goizueta figured, correctly, that his announcement would generate free media exposure that would be the equivalent of spending hundreds of millions of dollars on advertising for "the new taste of Coke." Within days, scarcely a cola drinker in the country didn't know about the switch. On the theory that all publicity is good publicity, Coke's risk would be off to a good start on that count alone.

Coca-Cola rented the darkened Vivian Beaumont Theater in New York's Lincoln Center for the slick affair. About two hundred media representatives packed the press conference in New York, ready to grill Goizueta on what was being viewed as his inordinately risky move. Some of them had been fed tough questions by Pepsi officials ahead of time.

At 9:30 a.m., just hours before the scheduled Lincoln Center press conference, Goizueta and his lieutenants met with a battery of Wall Street securities analysts whose job was to follow the company and report on its every sneeze to investors. Coke officials were skittish about how the stock market would receive the news, but confident the long-term results would be positive. Questions were tough, but polite, and for the most part supportive —little preparation for the far more combative and skeptical response Coke would soon receive from TV, magazine, newspaper and radio representatives. Wall Street cares about earnings, not taste and tradition. Analysts were relatively easy to convince that the risk was justified by the product's long market share reversal.

Reporters and the general public were less understanding of Goizueta's risk taking. Coke had to play in capitalism's "creative destruction" arena, and this was a business/financial risk that was part of playing the game. That corporate story—the story of the business risk—was ignored. Coverage of Coke's move took the more immediate, man-in-the-street angle of how strongly people were attached to the original Coke. "Had America's soft drink sultans simply gone mad?'" they asked. Coca-Cola was pummeled as much for having the nerve to consider changing Coke's formula as for the change itself.

Goizueta was partly to blame. The company chose to publicly ignore Pepsi's role in forcing the daring switch. Coke officials wanted consumers to compare their new taste against Pepsi. But their fear of being honest about it placed the focus on old Coke. The tone was set.

At Pepsi-Cola U.S.A. headquarters in Purchase, New York, Pepsi president Roger Enrico pounced on the news like a hungry dog on a meat wagon. The day of Coke's announcement, Pepsi ran a full-page newspaper ad tweaking its archrival and claiming victory in the cola war. Smug Pepsi officials threw a huge block party at Columbus Circle, just six blocks down Broadway from the Coke press conference at Lincoln Center. Pepsi employees were given an extra day off, and the company released a statement that said, in part, "We find it ironic that Coke has spent millions of dollars on an advertising campaign that knocks our taste, while they've been secretly trying to imitate it. . . . When you're in trouble, you make desperate moves. And that's exactly what we think is happening today with Coke."

Rival soft drink companies, smelling blood, reasoned that loyal Coca-Cola drinkers were now up for grabs. Within days, Pepsi had a new ad on the air, targeting consumers dismayed by the Coke switch. James Harralson, executive vice president and chief operating officer of Royal Crown Cola Company, called Goizueta's move "the best opportunity in fifty years for other cola brands to capture a larger share of the soft drink market."

Among the Coke contingent, the day's agenda called for premeditated festiveness. The company, which employs nearly 40,000 people, was known for its lavish media gatherings, and that day brought a bonus—a sense that history was being made. The press, on the other hand, treated Coke's business "risk" like a four-letter word; old Coke's disappearance like a kidnapping of no less news value than the Lindbergh baby snatching; Coke

33

executives like culprits caught red-handed. The tone was decidedly adversarial. As one Coke official describes it, "Coke executives really got jumped on."

And they deserved it. When it came to justifying their risk Coke officials were wimps. They had boldly faced the decision and gone ahead. But as New Coke was introduced, corporate officials clung to the illusion that they could explain their actions with lame statements such as "The best has been made even better" and "Our extensive data convinced us that [the new formula being tested] had achieved a new plateau of taste superiority." Goizueta made the official announcement:

> Coca-Cola, the world's number one consumer product, will begin its 100th year with a new taste, representing the first change in the secret formula since Coca-Cola was created in 1886. . . . Some may choose to call this the boldest single marketing move in the history of the packaged goods business. We simply call it the surest move ever made, because the new taste of Coke was shaped by the taste of the consumer.

At the press conference questions about Pepsi's role were shunted. A top company P.R. executive would later admit, "We were less than candid with the media at the time." It was only later, after the red-hot reaction had cooled, that Goizueta acknowledged rival Pepsi's growing popularity was largely behind his decision to act.

Incessant pounding by the media in the weeks following the press conference wore on Goizueta. He was sensitive to the "hundreds if not thousands of people in this country who have plenty of free advice about how to run The Coca-Cola Company." Later that year he would only half-jokingly tell a group of Associated Press managing editors in San Francisco, "How boring this past summer would have been, for you and The Coca-Cola Company, had we not announced in April a new formula for Coke. What a long, boring summer. There would have been many pages of white space in newspapers and news magazines, and hours of dead air on the television and radio. Just picture those reporters on your staffs with little to do all summer long!"

Pepsi boss Roger Enrico continued to pitch his barbs Atlanta way, calling New Coke "The Edsel of the 80s" and "a colossal marketing blunder." Goizueta's own local newspaper, the *Atlanta Constitution*, said the formula change risk was "a move that will stamp him forever as either a genius or a fool." Public reaction to the formula change went from harsh to ravaging. Television and newspapers were unrelenting with their stories of diehard "old Coke" lovers. A protest group was formed, calling itself Old Coca-Cola Drinkers of America. The company, which had expected some negative reaction, continuously monitored the situation, and initially the damage seemed containable.

Coke officials were frustrated. Their own research had been correct. Consumers *did* prefer the new taste. Post-release surveys, in blind testing, confirmed it. But the *idea* of switching got in the way. The American public was voting on New Coke with its heart, not its taste buds.

Then it got even worse. "Dear Chief Dodo," read one letter among the thousands arriving daily at 310 North Avenue, N.W., Coca-Cola headquarters in Atlanta. "What ignoramus decided to change the flavor of Coke?" Another said, "Changing Coke is like God making the grass purple." The pop-top of public reaction had now burst. Irate phone calls bubbled over at Coke's Atlanta switchboard, where scores of extra lines had to be installed to handle the volume. Letters and telegrams protesting the change engulfed the company. In the seventy-eight days it took the company to bring back the original formula drink as Coca-Cola Classic, the tally was nearly half a million letters and phone calls— the overwhelming majority of them negative.

Goizueta's risk appeared to be going awry. Pre-formula change Coke became an instant rarity. Dealers and individuals hoarded supplies, and the going price quickly hit $50 or more per case. The loss of original Coke became a cause célèbre, getting it back a holy crusade.

Coke-bashing became the rage. The sugar industry grabbed the opportunity to blast Coca-Cola. Jack O'Connell, president of the Sugar Association, a trade group representing the U.S. sugar industry, claimed that it wasn't Coke's first formula change at all. "The truth of the matter has been obscured by the circus atmosphere of the Coke announcement," he said. "Everyone but the consumer knows that the Coca-Cola formula has been quietly adjusted on several occasions in recent years to allow for greater amounts of corn syrup, a sweetener that is considerably cheaper than real sugar. In my opinion, this has been Coke's problem all along. They've cheapened the product by removing the sugar."

Actually, the Coke formula had undergone several minor "corrections" over the decades, including elimination in 1903 of the tiny amount of the drug cocaine it once contained (only about .0025 percent). Other changes involved fluctuating levels of sugar and caffeine. Other ingredients generally believed to exist in the red-and-white can include cola nut, coca leaves, vanilla, nutmeg, lime juice, caramel, cinnamon, lavender, glycerin, guarana (from a Brazilian shrub), phosphoric acid and water.

Madison Avenue's marketing mavens were flabbergasted by the unfolding affair. Not known for their own risk taking, they couldn't quite swallow Goizueta's reasoning. "So what if 61 percent of current Coke drinkers prefer the new stuff?" they groused. "That still leaves 39 percent who might well defect to other brands." Rather than trashing its birthright, Coca-Cola might have fared better by quietly changing the formula without the hoopla, they speculated.

Goizueta had rejected that option. If his information was correct, he reasoned, the payoff would come in promoting the change, not in hoping nobody would notice. It was a close call, based as much on Goizueta's gut feeling or a hunch as on the empirical evidence.

Americans guzzle an average of 806 soft drinks per person each year. That translates to billions of dollars in yearly sales. No right-minded executive is going to jeopardize that kind of revenue without some special sense of where he's going. For Coca-Cola, the unexpectedly vitriolic outpouring was a calamity in the making. Corporate giants had foundered over far less serious blunders. Coke wasn't *just* selling "a simple moment of pleasure," as Goizueta likes to describe the service his business provides. It sold America and the world an image. In changing the formula, he was risking that beloved, multibillion-dollar image.

To Wall Street and the rest of the business community, the negative backlash was serious as well. Analysts pontificated in the press about the "unusual risk of tampering with a highly successful product." Brokerage firms oozed fresh reports assessing the financial impact of Goizueta's move on the company and its stock-holders. The investment banking firm Salomon Brothers, for example, even while embracing Coke's move, said the formula change had injected a "major element of uncertainty" into the company's future. Still, Salomon analysts argued that since 60 percent of Coke's volume and 53 percent of profits came from sales *outside* the United States where consumers rarely have a choice among other colas, the formula change wasn't such a big risk to the immediate corporate bottom line. In a special stock research report issued within forty-eight hours of the New Coke announcement, Salomon Brothers said that taste and brand loyalty weren't nearly so important as image, and that Coke was accurately recognizing the difference by emphasizing the product's "newness" rather than making a quiet reformulation.

With all the negative publicity, however, Coca-Cola's stock retreated only marginally. Three weeks before the formula change, at the close of 1985's first quarter, it stood at $70 per share. Over the next 90 days it dropped as low as $66, but was back near $70 as the second quarter ended. A year later, the stock would reach $125 and split three-for-one.

Taste, it turned out, *was* of secondary importance to consumers of the product. "All the time and money and skill that we poured into consumer research could not reveal the depth of feeling for the original. . . ," Keough would later lament. "Some critics say we made a marketing mistake. Some cynics say we planned the whole thing. The truth is, we are not that dumb and we are not that smart. It's been a humbling experience," said Coke's president.

If Goizueta was humbled by it all, however, it didn't show in his outwardly calm, self-assured demeanor. Tampering with an American icon? Botching a ninety-nine-year tradition? Imperiling $3.5 billion in revenues? Goizueta viewed such second-guessing as background noise in the process of running a corporate Goliath, as he belatedly dragged Coca-Cola's $6 billion hulk (now $10 billion) kicking and screaming into the present. They are "irrelevant things," he maintains. Still, the supercharged nature of the public reflex awed the corporation's chairman. His decisions as leader of the Coke empire had been impugned before. And indeed, he felt at least one of those moves had been *more* risky than changing the formula. But nothing had prepared him for the deluge of damnation he was now seeing.

Despite his pronouncement that the old formula had been permanently and irreversibly banished, a move to resurrect it was under way by mid-May. When June's tally revealed that Coke's sales had gone flat, any lingering doubts about the need to bring back old Coke had disappeared. But reversing engines on the Coca-Cola ocean liner wasn't as easily accomplished as Goizueta would have liked.

RISK DYNAMIC #3
HIGH-FLEX

*"To retire is not to flee. There is no wisdom in
waiting when danger outweighs hope and it
is the part of wise men to preserve themselves
today for tomorrow, and not risk all in one
day."*

—MIGUEL DE CERVANTES,
Don Quixote

"Rubber band risk taking" is a critical risk dynamic for ARTists.
It is the ability to be flexible in risk, to adjust rapidly and snap
back if conditions change or do not meet expectations. Psychologists say that risk takers who can remain most flexible have the
lowest anxiety levels, lots of emotional control, and a strong sense
of reality. They go into risk situations with their eyes wide open,
carefully avoiding the inflexible I'll-make-this-work-if-it-kills-me
mentality.

In team sports, for example, the set play is a staple. In theory, if
each player performs his or her assignment correctly, the result
will be a score. The trouble is, set plays rarely work that way. An
assignment may be missed; the defense may react differently than

expected. On a broken play, team leaders draw on their flexibility —they must *improvise.* Success depends on how quickly they do so.

Risk taking in enterprise works similarly. Much-planned risks like Coca-Cola's may turn into busted plays. Then it's time to throw away the notes. The best public speakers don't talk from notes anyway. Top risk takers don't risk from notes either. They go eyeball to eyeball with their audience, and try to perceive the situation differently. It's not like the risk of investing in the stock market, where you sit back and read the market report each morning. Risk taking can't be one-track. Determination to succeed must be balanced against flexibility.

"I'm all in favor of long-range planning," says Goizueta, "provided that if the future doesn't develop as your plan says it will— and nine and a half times out of ten it won't—you change your plans. Too many people say, 'By God, no. That's what the plan says. I'm going to build those boxy-looking cars because that's what my long-range plan says.' . . .

"There is no such thing as the perfect forecast. The only thing that can compensate for that is to be very flexible. If something doesn't work try something else."

Risking Compromise

A key component of being high-flex is compromise—one of the few points where risk taking and politics agree. J.B. Fuqua makes the point. Before entering business Fuqua was a politician—eight years in the Georgia legislature, and a two-year stint as head of the state's Democratic party. That's where he learned the art of compromise that would later sharpen his risk-taking skills.

"CEOs often view compromise as a weakness, as something best left to diplomats and politicians," he observes. "My own political career taught me otherwise. Compromise is essential to corporate progress and success. Lyndon Johnson, whom I had the pleasure of knowing for many years, had the unusual talent of being tough and able to compromise at the same time. This is a rare quality among today's color-blind CEOs who see business decisions only in black and white. The colored areas, however, are the territory of compromise, and ultimately of progress and profit."

At Coca-Cola, one of Goizueta's own rules of deal making and risk taking is to remain flexible. He compares it to sailing: "You have a start and a finish, but within those two points in a long-distance sailing race you have to adapt your course to the shifting winds so as to put them to work for you. You cannot foretell exactly what the winds will be like *in advance* [his emphasis] of a race, but you sure as hell can take full advantage of them if you are prepared to be opportunistic. You can more easily create your own course during such a race than predict it in advance."

Having taken one of the biggest risks of his career, and of Coca-Cola's hundred-year history, by changing Coke's formula, Goizueta now faced new, even chancier decisions. Should the corporation "tough it out," gambling that consumer outrage would subside once the issue disappeared from the headlines? Coca-Cola's original taste research—still entirely valid—argued that the product would gain acceptance . . . eventually. Or should the company admit a blunder, repent and replace New Coke with the original? Perhaps Goizueta should rethink the two-Coke option. And if so, how could the original be brought back to maximize the positive effect? A reversal might confuse consumers even more. They'd just been told that New Coke was much better. People might simply throw up their hands in disgust at Coca-Cola's flip-flopping and switch to other brands.

Unlike the first risk, which brewed for years, a key issue here was time. There wasn't any. There could be no extensive research studies on the market implications of a decision, no complicated testing of options. If his consumers were voting with their hearts Goizueta decided he'd do the same. Now that Coke's secrets had been hung out for all to see, part of the argument against two Cokes had disappeared. Splitting sales between two Cokes would be better than letting Pepsi win head-to-head against one.

A major downside to the risk: Selling it all to the public could be a nightmare. Suddenly Coke would have to develop a new marketing approach to position each of its new products. There would inevitably be confusion and overlap. Just keeping the names straight would be hard enough. Officially, the old stuff would be known as Coca-Cola Classic, and that's what it says on

41

the can. The new formula was to be called by the shortened name Coke, but with no reference to the word "new" anywhere on the container. At the corporation's annual meeting of shareholders in 1986, a Georgia woman's complaint brought the issue into focus: "I put my money in a machine that says Coke. I expect a 'Coke Is It' Coke. I get the new stuff. That's not what I want."

There simply were no ready answers on the consequences of all these risks to ship upstairs to Goizueta's office. The company would have to improvise its new approaches along the way. Other executives in Atlanta argued that New Coke simply needed more time. If the company waited the furor would subside. But Goizueta, following one of his own cardinal rules of risking, made certain he was *flexible*. He wasn't about to plow blindly onward with the formula change risk if his *new* information—the spontaneous consumer revolt—told him to change course. It was clear to Goizueta that his first risk was in danger of wrecking a good part of two images: the product's, and his own as chairman of the company.

Goizueta knew within four or five weeks that the risk had derailed. Inside, it saddened him immensely, but he says he didn't let it show. When Goizueta quits the office at night he may carry home his work, but not his troubles. "I tend not to worry about decisions. That's a lucky break. My wife [the former Olguita Casteleiro, who met Goizueta at Yale] says I was born with that virtue or fault. When I go to sleep I just unhook the electric cord from the wall and . . . what the hell can you do? You make a decision and the only thing you can do is tomorrow make another decision to correct yesterday's decision if it wasn't right.

"I'm very much an optimist. To me, failure doesn't enter very much into the picture. The fact that [a risk] may fail is something I consider, but, well, you cannot go crazy. There's no way to be in a position like this or any other position of importance if you constantly are worrying or fretting over whether what you did was right or wrong.

"I owe my job to Coke's stockholders," says Goizueta. Indeed, breathing life into shareholder returns had become an obsession from the beginning of the Goizueta era. The price of Coke stock had sagged 25 percent in Austin's last two years at the helm. Defying conventional corporate wisdom around Coca-Cola, Goizueta believed that taking risks was an *obligation* he had to the company's shareholders. From the opening of Goizueta's tenure in the spring of 1981 to the end of 1984, the total return (price gains plus dividends) on Coca-Cola stock was 95 percent, compared with a 42 percent return for the Standard & Poor's 500 stock index. And from 1981 to the end of 1986 the value of an investment in Coca-Cola stock rose nearly 300 percent. An investor who bought $10,000 worth of Coca-Cola stock at the beginning of 1985 —the year of the formula change "disaster"—saw its value reach $13,765 by the end of that year. If they held on for 1986, they added another 45 percent gain on top of that.

The chairman again: "Also bear in mind that this was not a 'bet-your-company'—a term that has been used—decision. There is no such thing as a bet-your-company decision unless your company is a little hot dog stand on the street corner and you cross against the red light." And his thoughts about reversing course: "Risk taking has to go hand in hand with flexibility. If you give me a risk taker that isn't flexible, then you have a dangerous individual on your hands. You know, when people say somebody isn't very intelligent, and on top of that he's lazy, I say thank God he's lazy. A dumb hardworking fellow is the most dangerous person to have around. If you're not going to be very intelligent you might as well be lazy. If you have a so-called risk taker who is inflexible, then you have a problem on your hands."

By July 10, 1985, rumor was spreading that Coca-Cola might bring back the old formula. The price of Coke stock moved up sharply, from $70 to $72⅜. On July 11, eleven weeks after the old formula was retired to the bank vault "never to be seen again," Goizueta brought it back as Coca-Cola Classic. The stock price jumped again. "I tell you one thing," confides Goizueta, "I was just mad as hell that we could not bring Coca-Cola Classic back sooner, but we could not get the lawyers to agree on the name . . . because of contractual obligations we couldn't use certain names like 'original' and that sort of thing. We should have brought Coca-Cola Classic back by June 1. But we were a month and a half late, if you ask my opinion."

The delay originated in Coca-Cola's contract with its independent bottlers, specifying that each bottler will produce and package a set amount of Coke. But just what is the definition of Coke? For many years it had been clear. Suddenly, with the prospect of many drinks carrying the Coke name, it was not clear at all. Goizueta's legal advisors told him the name Original Coke, one of the alternatives discussed, would create legal problems with the bottler contracts. Some suggested calling the new formula Coke 100, a reference to the company's upcoming centennial year. Coca-Cola Classic won out.

The company hastily called another press conference, this time with much less fanfare and a single satellite hookup between Atlanta headquarters and the Hotel Pierre in New York. "The Coca-Cola Company will make available the original formula for Coca-Cola under the name Coca-Cola Classic," the company said in a terse statement.

That night a top Coke executive appeared in a television commercial to inform the public of the decision to bring back old Coke. The official selected to make that appearance, however, was not the ethnic, Spanish-accented chairman Goizueta, but company president Donald Keough, one of the few native Georgians in Coke's top executive ranks. So filled with foreign-born executives were Coke's top ranks that Goizueta would jokingly refer to Keough as the firm's token American. Keough, an affable fellow who seems at ease in public speaking, was considered to have a better on-camera presence than Goizueta's more highly starched style. The two men are close friends, and their offices connect across the executive dining room atop corporate headquarters. One of Goizueta's requests before accepting the chairman's post was that he be allowed to select his successor as president. That was Keough, who had long been considered a marketing whiz around Coca-Cola.

Now Coca-Cola was in a real marketing straitjacket. If the formula change had gone relatively unnoticed, or had been accepted by consumers, marketing efforts would hardly have skipped a beat. For ninety-nine years there had been but one Coke to tout. Now suddenly there were two. One early decision was that the "Coke Is It!" slogan, introduced in February 1982 to replace the "Have a Coke and a Smile" theme, would have to go. "The company's executives are aware that that theme is far too assertive and self-confident for a corporation that just committed the largest public faux pas in the history of marketing," said one Coke official who requested anonymity from *The Wall Street Journal*. Coke's marketing and advertising costs jumped nearly $100 million in 1985 because of the New Coke, Classic Coke and Cherry Coke introductions—a fact revealed two years later in a back page of the company's annual report.

Roger Enrico's "Edsel of the 80s" quip proved premature. As soon became clear at the cash register, when it came to selling soda, two Cokes were definitely better than one. "People joke," says Goizueta. "They say Coke is the Edsel of the 80s. I never knew Edsel was the best-selling car. But Coke is *the* best-selling soft drink in the country." When old Coke returned as Coca-Cola Classic the corporation emerged with two products *and a larger combined market share* than Coke had held *before* the change. In the year of its "big blunder," Coke scored record sales and profits.

The year after the formula change Goizueta was named "Adman of the Year" by *Advertising Age* magazine. Said *Ad Age*, "Mr. Goizueta turned a potentially disastrous decision into a soft-drink marketing coup while staying the course of Coca-Cola Company's other businesses. . . . The company's corporate share is at an all-time high, and the gap between Coca-Cola and Pepsi-Cola Co. is wider than ever." The magazine praised Coke's risk-taking leader who had "cast aside tradition and transformed a stodgy, conservative behemoth into a leaner, swifter operation." By the end of the 1980s Coke had five of the nation's top ten soft drinks, and a bigger market share than ever. Three-fourths of all growth in the sugared cola market belonged to Coca-Cola.

The decision to bring back the original formula as Coca-Cola Classic turned scorn into euphoria. As one newspaper reported, "If [Goizueta] had heard the whine of the small plane circling downtown the other day, he would have glimpsed not an irate customer on a kamikaze run, but an ebullient Coke fan trailing a banner: 'THANK YOU, ROBERTO!' "

CHAMPIONING CHANGE

"Always do what you are afraid to do."

—RALPH WALDO EMERSON

ARTists—active risk takers—must champion change. One critical reason: a rapidly shrinking product life cycle that will be the key corporate battleground of the 1990s. Products that once were expected to produce earnings for three to five years are now becoming outdated in a year or even less. Meanwhile, companies are being forced to create new products at an accelerating pace.

Companies must adapt to those changing currents by taking risks, or be swept aside. As the Greek philosopher Heraclitus put it twenty-five centuries ago: You never swim in the same river twice. Enterprise never looks the same two days running.

U.S. automakers, for example, once took six or seven years to design, build and market a new model. They've narrowed that to five years. But the Japanese do it in three and a half.

In electronics, the product pace is breakneck. *The Economist,* a British magazine, reported that Japan's Sony Corporation would launch over a hundred new audio, television and video products in Britain alone during one six-month period. In the microcom-

46

puter business, notes *Fortune* magazine, new models replace old ones about every nine months. Apple Computer spits out a new product an average of once a week.

Whether the company is a century-old firm such as Kodak, a middle-aged player like Xerox, one of the new high-tech superstars like Sun Microsystems, or America's largest black-owned firm, TLC Group, rapid-fire change is forcing greater risk taking on managements. According to a *Wall Street Journal* study, a new breed of black entrepreneurs "is reshaping the traditional way blacks do business. This new black businessman is colorblind, takes direction from Wall Street, [and] acquires companies that cater to mainstream America. . . ." Black-owned businesses don't focus purely on ethnic markets any longer. In fact, changes being wrought by a new breed of risk takers make it a bit silly to use the qualifier "black" next to the words "financier," "entrepreneur" or "businessman."

The new breed is increasingly willing to take big risks to open up new markets. The most influential member of this group so far has been Reginald Lewis, whose New York–based TLC Group bought Beatrice International in 1987 for just under $1 billion, in partnership with Drexel Burnham Lambert. TLC scored big with its leveraged buyout of the McCall Pattern Company in 1984, and controls businesses with around $2 billion in annual revenues. In the Beatrice deal, Lewis and his group beat out other bidders, which included William Simon's Wesray group, Citicorp, Nestlé and Shearson Lehman Hutton.

Xerox fought its way back to competitiveness in the later 1980s in part by slashing its average product development time from five years to less than two. Kodak once took its own good time to develop a product, making certain every detail was ironed out before introducing it to the public. If that took ten years, so be it. The time Kodak spent was a corporate bragging point. Taking risks to speed things along was considered a breach of proper corporate conduct. Now things have changed at the company's Rochester, New York, base camp. Management realized Kodak could not survive under its old way of doing things.

Thus, when the firm introduced its new Create-a-Print product in 1988, the development cycle had taken only twenty-two months. Kodak achieved that level of corporate swiftness because middle managers were free to make decisions *and take risks* that

47

would previously have been kicked upstairs. Without Kodak's newfound risk-taking zeal, Create-a-Print—a system permitting consumers to make their own custom prints in the store—would have taken more than twice as long to develop and bring to market. Kodak's new color copying machine would have taken five or six years to develop, but took less than three when risk taking was encouraged.

"Indeed," observed *The New York Times,* "Kodak is in the throes of a cultural upheaval that could serve as a case study for what happens when an old company faces new ground rules. It has changed its internal power structure, its manufacturing methods, its dealings with suppliers and competitors, almost every aspect of how it does business. And perhaps most striking at a company that used to view risk as anathema, it is encouraging its people to take chances for the sake of speed. . . . Compared with its old lumbering self, Kodak is a whirling dervish."

Taking risks to slice development time can yield huge rewards. Quick development means the product can use more state-of-the-art technology, and can be more readily adjusted to fit changing markets. A product that's first on the market can also command a premium price. Italy's Benetton, whose colorful clothing shops now clog the American urban landscape, gained an edge by making uncolored clothing, then dying it at the last moment to fit current fashion.

Product acceleration, however, means more than simply making decisions more rapidly. In the past, most businesses used "sequential" product development. First the design people carried the ball. Then engineers got involved. Later it became a financing, then a marketing issue—like an assembly line. Companies now must risk abandoning that approach, replacing it with an often more chaotic system where everything happens at once. Japanese firms that have long favored this system have a name for it: *wai-gaya,* the best English translation of which is hubbub.

At Coca-Cola, Roberto Goizueta emerged from his formula change risk as victor, but not without scars. His risk—"the boldest single marketing move in the history of the packaged goods business"—had contained many classic traits. It demonstrated, perhaps more clearly than any high-profile corporate risk of the eighties, that risk and change can provoke unforeseen reactions that require still more change in a chain reaction–type sequence. And Goizueta himself became a symbol of the corporate ARTist willing to delve in a little "creative destruction," recognizing that to do nothing would be slow death. Says Goizueta, "If I had a blunder like this every year I'd be home free. . . . We took the product [old] Coca-Cola from the heart of the people—they were *loving* it more than they were *drinking* it—and moved it to their hands and onto their lips." Only after old Coke was taken away did cola drinkers realize their love affair, and when it was brought back they started drinking it more than ever. "Just like you may not treat your wife very well until she says, 'Well now, you know something, I have a boyfriend,' and all of a sudden your wife starts looking better and better every day.

"On top of that," continues Coke's CEO, "we now had a two-share product which we could never have had before. So we have the best of both worlds."

As the "lesser" half of the new duo, however, New Coke started life slowly. Within a year of old Coke's return, Classic was out-selling New Coke four to one, and giant fountain users such as McDonald's and Kentucky Fried Chicken had returned to Coca-Cola Classic. Some bottlers no longer wanted to handle New Coke, and the product just plain bombed in many regions, including Atlanta.

"I would like to tell you that we planned the whole thing, but we didn't. On the other hand, we knew on April 23 that the option of bringing back Coca-Cola as Coca-Cola Classic was in our back pocket when we made that decision," recalls Goizueta. Nevertheless, outsiders marveled at Coke's recovery from the ticklish affair. "At any other company, the New Coke fiasco would have spelled a rotten year financially, and a death knell for the product and the executives responsible for it," observed *The New York Times*. But this wasn't "any other company." This was the new change-minded Coke, and profits for the soft drink maker that year soared.

Wall Street analysts also expected blood to flow from the Coke executive suite, but none was seen. Goizueta stood behind his crew, refusing to assign blame by firing people who were party to the risk. Coke's chairman had not taken a blindfolded plunge into the pit of corporate risk taking. Nor did he emerge from it wiser and wealthier by pure luck. He remained convinced that it was not a "bad" risk that he and Coca-Cola had taken. It was a "necessary" risk, he argued, supported by years of declining market share and the need to adapt to changing market conditions. And the risk was partly the product of Roberto Goizueta's personal philosophy toward running a business aggressively—refusing to simply be a "caretaker" of profitability.

"Back in the 1970s we had gotten a little bit fat and happy. But the more successful and larger a company gets, the more bureaucratized it becomes . . . decisions take longer, and not being wrong becomes the important thing as opposed to being right. You have gained so much and you start worrying about losing some of what you have gained. But the moment you start worrying about losing what you have gained you begin going downhill. We surely have examples today. Whether IBM is such an example . . . is a question to be raised. Whether General Motors is such an example . . . is a valid question. Whether Procter & Gamble is such an example is a valid question to be raised." According to the chairman, Coke was precisely such a company in the 1970s: "We were more concerned about not losing market share than about gaining it.

"Interestingly, in the overseas market—where we *are* the soft drink industry—market share has no meaning. It's per capita consumption that is important. But when you have 70 percent of the market you become complacent; you then try not to rock the boat. I think one company that was like that and was brought back is General Electric, under Jack Welch. Another company that was brought back is Dow Chemical [under Paul Oreffice, Dow's CEO and a member of Coke's board].

". . . All the changes in history take place in spurts. If you go back and check that spurt, that's when a prince became a new king, and all kinds of changes took place. But then when he's king he wants to preserve that kingdom exactly the same way he created it. And I think that is the danger. Heaven knows I'm going to try not to, but the temptations are to say, 'You've been so successful for the first five years, don't screw it up, just keep things the same.'" How does Goizueta the risk taker intend to fight that temptation? "Well, you have to do it consciously. You keep reminding yourself every day and you change people. . . . The company has to keep renovating itself all the time, and I have to be frank with you, I'm fifty-five and I'll be watching over my own

50

shoulder that I don't spend the next ten years preserving what I have built in the last five."

Goizueta knew his formula change risk might explode when he lit the fuse. No matter how closely the odds and alternatives are calculated, a dynamic risk still carries an element of danger, and with it the possibility of loss. The risk didn't work out the way Coca-Cola's executives planned it, but they couldn't complain in the end. If there were ultimately rewards Goizueta could legitimately lay claim. Coke had earned the rewards with its risks.

BOOK

II

PAYING THE PRICE

*"A business always saws off the limb on which
it sits; it makes existing risks riskier or
creates new ones . . . Risk is of the essence,
and risk making and risk taking constitute
the basic function of enterprise . . . This risk
is something quite different from risk in the
statistician's probability; it is risk of the
unique event, the irreversible qualitative
breaking of the pattern. . . . "*

—PETER DRUCKER

*"Only those who dare to fail greatly can ever
achieve greatly."*

—ROBERT KENNEDY

RISK DYNAMIC #5

IT'S ACTIVE, NOT PASSIVE

*"If the risk/reward ratio is right, you can make
a heap of money buying trouble."*

—UNKNOWN

Many businesses have tricked themselves into believing they can avoid or eliminate risk and still innovate, still make progress. Slowly, through the last several decades, business has assumed the lofty aura of a science, dominated by management theories, formulas and dictums. The new laboratory technicians of commerce, drawn from the nation's swollen pool of MBAs, often believe they can eliminate the uncertainties of enterprise . . . some of its risks. The explosive growth of America's new information-based society has contributed mightily to the illusion that risk can be eradicated. The technologies of corporate decision making, of processing these data and crunching endless rows of numbers, are used as weapons against risk.

Today every business decision comes wrapped in statistics. We look to statistics to form opinions, divine trends, and make choices about risks. With access to these deep and fertile data mines, managers become kids in a candy store. When problems arise they throw data at them, only occasionally inquiring whether the information actually nets any tangible progress. Management consultant Peter Drucker's counsel is ignored. Risk, Drucker has said, is *not* about statistical probabilities or avoidance. It is about *breaking patterns*—daring to do something that hasn't been done before. When businesses have statistics and other information to "measure" their risks and advise them on decisions, they expect the final results to fit their information. When it doesn't they wonder why.

Statistics have become a new type of corporate currency for purchasing peace of mind in decision making. If there's a number, our obsession with statistics says it must have an economic use. A number by itself seems coldly objective. But statistics are easily manipulated or misinterpreted. Statistics do lie.

Successful risk-taking companies discover that what *actually* happens and what they *expect* to happen by examining the "evidence" may be radically different things. General Foods found that out when its regional test marketing of a new drink mix product appeared to score a huge success. Sales figures for all flavors of Great Shakes were high, so company executives gave it a national release. When it flopped, they were puzzled. The *numbers* had predicted success. General Foods discovered too late that during the test, consumers eager to find a flavor they liked had continued buying them one after another. But they hated them all and stopped buying. This doesn't mean all research or statistics are evil, only that they can be misused by those who disregard chance, change and unpredictability.

Business has many economic means of measuring the costs and benefits of risks *once those risks have been taken,* and once they have proven to be either a success or a failure. The great difficulty in studying risk taking in enterprise is that while risks occur only *before* events, they can only be reliably measured *afterwards*.

Neither do sophisticated financial theories provide convenient ways to measure the costs of *not* taking a risk, although that's where a company's most devastating loss can lie. Risk is a constant of nature. And constants, of course, can't be ignored too long, or erased. Consequently, if enterprise suppresses risk in one place it pops up in another. That leaves only one available course—active risk taking, or ART. By practicing ART, a business sets its own agenda; it taps into risk's exclusive and abundant abilities to produce real profits. Risk taking becomes the lumberyard in which enterprise builds its own economic future.

Applying scientific analogies to business lures us into thinking about risk the wrong way. Science is *perceived* by our society as something precise, highly technical, based on predictable patterns, even though most science is really not like that at all. By ascribing the same perceived qualities of predictability and precision to *enterprise,* we start thinking of risk as a scientific problem that can be solved—as a corporate cancer that can one day be cured. Ignoring risk's role as a powerful tool for progress accents *passive* varieties of risk that produce nothing, instead of the *dynamic, active* varieties that spawn innovation. It also fosters 1980s-style "paper enterprise"—the corporate raider's game of asset musical chairs that seems active enough on the surface, but does little to encourage creativity and commitment to long-term growth.

For decades, business and academia alike have tried to measure passive risk taking with little success. The standard approach asks questions such as, What risks must a company *accept?* What risks can be avoided? The goal in trying to measure risk is always the same: to understand risk better so that it can be *minimized.* Never is risk presented as something to be sought out. The questions *should* be: What methods can help enterprise more effectively *take* constructive, dynamic risks? How can managers become *better* risk takers? What should companies do to *increase* their risk taking?

Many businesses have come to believe that risks, in pursuit of enterprise, *can* be eliminated. The best we can hope to do, however, is shift risk from one hand to the other, not eliminate it. Risk by definition involves uncertainty. It always courts the unknown. Markets are not static. Yet businesses normally approach the problem in reverse, asking themselves how best to interpret *predictable* changes. Predictable change, however, isn't what's important. *Un*predictable change is the chief economic variable risk takers must face. Thinking that enterprise can completely control risks assumes it can control the unknown. It cannot. The alternative to accepting risk is accepting further economic decline, productivity stagnation, and a declining standard of living.

Risk's P.R. Problem

Risk remains a wholly disagreeable idea for most people. It is commonly considered a *negative* quality. Corporations exhaust huge resources attempting to avoid risk, despite the massive economic upheavals of the past decade, which are forcing a broad reassessment of what American enterprise must do to survive and prosper in the 1990s and beyond. The reassessors find that inviting change and taking risks are two critical ingredients to that survival. All others either believe risk is something *the other guy* should take or harbor secret hopes that, somehow, profit, progress, innovation, and all that is good in business can be achieved by taking the *minimum* number of risks. Sadly, that's not possible.

Post–World War II American business took survival for granted. We were a nation of sellers existing in a seller's market. Our economic thinking was geared toward functioning under relatively stable conditions, on a belief that tomorrow would be essentially the same as today. It was a philosophy that ignored risk in favor of growing big and fat like Coca-Cola. Top executives relaxed and handed the reins to caretakers with instructions not to do anything too risky. American enterprise partied on risk avoidance during those years, leaving later generations to pay the bill.

The economic upheavals of the 1970s and 80s shattered old illusions of stability. Key economic benchmarks—inflation, the value of the U.S. dollar, the prices of oil and other commodities, interest rates, the stock market—demonstrated remarkable volatility and uncertainty. Combined with explosive technological advancement, rapid government deregulation of business, and—perhaps for the first time in the nation's modern history—stiff (and growing stiffer) foreign competition on many economic fronts, those upheavals have triggered greater appreciation of risk taking's importance in enterprise.

The new economic order is a *buyer's* market where each enterprise must be unusually nimble, not a seller's market where survival was assured to even the poorly run enterprise. It beckons entrepreneurs and executives at all levels of enterprise to adopt new beliefs, new standards based on change and risk. It compels businesses to face up to uncertainty and paradox, and learn new risk-taking skills that can help transform them to meet tomorrow's market demands.

Flexibility, as we've already seen in one case, will become an increasingly critical part of this risk-taking shift. A high-flex quality in enterprise makes a company and its managers able to take greater risks. Business can no longer depend on long, stable product or service life cycles. This is one reason the Japanese have been so successful. They build flexibility into their economic systems—an ability to turn on a dime, or at least a manhole cover.

Fighting "Corpocracy"

In the postwar American economy, risk aversion was epitomized by a bloated government bureaucracy that offered little incentive for taking risks of innovation. Business often found government bloat a tempting target for sarcasm. Yet at the same time, large segments of *corporate* America evolved into a corporate equivalent of bureaucracy, dubbed "corpocracy." This corporate paunch has manifested itself as an unwillingness to take risks, thus denying the most important quality that brought America its high standard of living in the first place. Meanwhile, America groped to discover why its economic growth rates were so poor, why it was having trouble competing against the rest of the world. This caused much wringing of hands as the "America in decline" theme became popular.

On a November day in 1986, a top Reagan administration official, Richard G. Darman, then deputy secretary of the Treasury, put his finger on it. Darman said that this "bloated, risk-averse, ineffective and inefficient" corpocracy had become "a problem of rising and popular interest and concern." The former Harvard professor's assault on corporate complacency drew flak as well as support from far corners of American business. Newspaper accounts reported "consternation in the highest levels of the White House" over the speech. Some corporate leaders sought to avoid Darman's mud: "In the office equipment industry, I think Mr. Darman would find a long history of investment in research and development, a more recent history of downsizing companies to effectively compete, and a history of risk taking," responded William Glavin, chairman of Xerox. And Gerald Greenwald, vice chairman of Chrysler, claimed that "Chrysler and the American auto industry do not fit Mr. Darman's description." Some found the remarks outlandish. "I can't help but be shocked at that kind of angry outburst by so high a government official," said Andrew Digler, chairman of Champion International Corporation and head of the Business Roundtable. "I don't know the bloated, risk-averse, inefficient and unimaginative executives that he described. I don't believe he does either."

Darman, who later became a managing director at Shearson Lehman Hutton, followed up by wondering aloud if all of American business hadn't become afraid of risk. He contended that risk takers such as Steven Jobs and H. Ross Perot are "exceptions who prove the rule: Most corporate leadership is a rather conventional gray." Said Darman, "We pride ourselves on being entrepreneurial risk takers; but many climb to the top of the corporate ladder on the strength of their demeanor and a failure to make observable mistakes." Darman's point was that business executives making huge salaries should be held to a higher standard of creative performance than has generally been expected or demonstrated. That means more than simple corporate stewardship. It means taking risks, practicing ART, once again.

Of course not everyone can be a risk taker for an economy to survive, Darman admitted. "But the question still presses itself upon us: Are we becoming a bit too gray, losing our youthful energy and missionary vision as we age? Is our pioneering spirit flagging?" His answer was yes. As proof he pointed to America's lagging economic performance: From 1950 to 1965, U.S. business productivity grew 3 percent annually. From 1965 to 1973, it grew at 2 percent annually, and at a mere 1 percent per year since that time.

Worse, he said, is that U.S. manufacturing productivity has consistently grown much more slowly than that of Japan, Germany, France, Canada, and even much-maligned Great Britain. In fact, America's productivity growth ranks near the *bottom* among the industrialized countries it trades with. Two smoking guns have severely wounded American economic growth: *poor productivity* and *an aversion to risk.*

Corporations: Arenas for Risk

Business can change that. Corporations are the shells within which innovative riskers can ply their craft, if management encourages it to be that way. As one management expert puts it, the corporate structure provides an arena for the exercise of productive power and risk taking. The individuals involved may be personally at risk or they may be gambling company resources: time, money, jobs, reputation. There are rarely cases, however, where it is purely the corporation's assets and reputation that are at stake. The decision makers also put their own prestige, career advancement possibilities, reputations and money on the line in guiding companies.

One step toward eliminating entrenched risk aversion is the widespread movement toward corporate restructurings. These remodelings are updating the look of many of the largest companies in the United States for the better, and are beginning to scrape away caked-on layers of risk avoidance.

But the aging process that can gradually weaken corporations is not easily halted or reversed. Restructuring and risk must be continuous, not a once-in-two-decades event. Restructuring will not yield long-term results for the corporate body unless there are shifts in the *thinking* of executive leadership as well. Foremost among the changes needed to foster growth and innovation is an improved willingness to take risks.

American companies, with all their sophisticated organizational structures to help them navigate the economic seas, will find themselves off course if they swerve to avoid risk too often. In recent years, the new corporate discipline of "risk management" —an outgrowth of the insurance function—has spread rapidly. Instead of creating more "risk management" positions to help them avoid, contain and control passive risk, innovation-seeking companies could try something completely new: an executive position responsible for *promoting* ART throughout the corporation.

Call that person a "risk relations officer." Perhaps "vice president for risk activation" has a better ring. What about "director of corporate risking"? Whatever. Title doesn't matter. But having a corporate watchdog to make certain the company doesn't short-change dynamic risk could pay valuable returns long-term. Actually it shouldn't be necessary at all under a successful corporate culture of risk taking. Better yet, just make ART part of every-body's job description and be done with it.

The Wrong Motivations

The object—some say the duty—of enterprise is to *make* risk, not simply to respond to it. Companies that claim to seek innovation while maintaining an environment hostile to risk taking without fear, and hostile to failure, will only be frustrated in their endeavors. Developing a corporate risk culture that makes its own change and innovation requires both talk *and* action. Companies of all sizes have tended to stumble when trying to instill such risk-taking cultures because their basic approach to motivating people is skewed *against* risk. The norm in corporate motivation has long been *fear*—fear of missing out on a raise, of being reprimanded for mistakes, and ultimately fear of losing the job entirely. But workers with innovative minds are seldom motivated by fear; and a fearful person is not inclined to take risks. Those who do fear failure do not make good risk takers. As Tom Peters notes in *Thriving on Chaos,* "You can't ask a fearful person to break all the conventional rules and regularly take what feel like risky initiatives."

When top management demonstrates its own willingness to take risks, *and* a tolerance for others who take risks, even if they fail, achieving innovation becomes easier. As small entrepreneurial companies grow into large ones, their risk resolve will be severely tested. Making the transition from being a solitary risk taker to being a corporate risk "encourager" is difficult for some entrepreneurs who now find themselves heading those larger companies. They must change from risk takers to risk *leaders.* They must develop a high tolerance for risks taken by *others* besides themselves.

Existing, successful public companies also fear making *short-term sacrifices in anticipation of longer-term gains*—a key building block of ART. Private companies face fewer such drawbacks. Public companies face greater scrutiny. The very real power of stockholders gives many corporate executives the perception, at least, that their operations must be geared to short-term profits. This rampant affliction sets companies nationwide to seeking the quick fix on quarterly and annual report bottom lines. They spend less and less on research and development because the payoff is too distant. Risk is considered "unaffordable," especially in an age when managements of public corporations can easily find themselves the targets of shareholder lawsuits.

This creates a rather bizarre juxtaposition in the world of American enterprise. Corporations willingly go on a rampage of mergers and acquisitions, spending hundreds of millions, even billions, to buy into other industries. It's far easier, and considered less risky, to buy an existing widget maker than to start your own. The attitude sticks. And corporations that will pay top dollar—and sometimes well beyond—for an acquisition won't part with the price of paper clips if it's something they might have to gamble on creating themselves. "In the United States, we still have many companies with a downright cynical attitude toward innovation," noted Chester A. Sadlow, executive vice president for advanced production technology at Westinghouse Electric Corporation. "They have a curious R&D philosophy . . . to be the first company to be second. Wait until someone else has broken his pick pioneering, then jump in with vast resources to capitalize on the demonstrated opportunity . . . why take the risk of being first when the second bite of the apple tastes as good, if not better, and you know it is safe to eat? Why be innovative when you can develop a much better product through reverse engineering?" Sadlow answers his own question. It's because risk aversion spreads like a disease, eventually killing off the life support systems of an industry—its inventors and innovators.

In their book *The Bigness Complex: Industry, Labor, and Government in the American Economy*, Walter Adams and James Brock make a related point. Big companies, they argue, account for a disproportionately small amount of technical innovation in America because they have no appetite for risky research projects. Smaller, risk-taking companies produce almost twenty-five times as many innovations dollar-for-dollar as do the sluggish, risk-averse corporate giants.

John Diebold, head of the Diebold Group, Inc., a top international management consulting firm, sees a narrowing of opportunities for corporate risk taking under a system that stresses short-term results, but resists the greater risks of long-term investment. "I think that there are only two classes of company in the United States today that can take a really long-term [and more risky] view," says Diebold, who is credited with coining the word "automation" in his book of the same name published in the 1950s. "And that is, a privately owned company where they can take a long-term view, and embark on an investment that has negative results for a long term; or a public company that has a stable enough profit-earning business that it can sweep losses under the carpet for a long time as the risk is developed.

"If you aren't one or the other it is very difficult to take a long-term view if it has a negative short-term consequence," Diebold points out. "In other words, if it's a question of going into something that has sizable operating losses in order to get a market position or a product position, it's very difficult to do that in America today if you're not one of those two types of companies. It's very tough for the CEO of an American public company to take a beating on earnings for any sustained period because it's the right thing to do for the long term. And that, in the aggregate, is a societal problem . . . a very big national problem."

In such an immediate results-oriented climate, it takes brave corporate executives to risk substantial amounts of short-term profits on the chance of future development and innovation. Malcolm S. Forbes, the feisty chairman of *Forbes* magazine, says that a corporate aversion to risk, based on the fear of harming short-term earnings, is "the bottom in management savvy." According to Forbes, "The main motivation seems to be 'caution,' which is better spelled 'cowardice,' by managements who are reluctant to risk investing in a future whose benefits they may personally not be around to reap."

This is precisely what sets Gannett Company apart. Its CEO *was* willing to take a $500 million earnings thrashing over five years on his belief in building something new and valuable for the long term. . . .

NEUHARTH THE CREATOR

*"No-risk managements run both no-win and no-fun
businesses."*

—ALLEN H. NEUHARTH,
chairman, Gannett Company

*"There is no security on this earth, only
opportunity."*

—DOUGLAS MACARTHUR

In 1952 a brash twenty-eight-year-old would-be newspaperman
risked $50,000 of borrowed money to start a weekly sports news-
sheet in South Dakota called *SoDak Sports*. He had a fresh journalism degree on the G.I. Bill from the University of South
Dakota, and a bronze star earned as a combat infantryman in Europe and the Pacific during the war. The paper flopped. But without that short-lived sports tabloid America might never have seen
USA Today, the nation's first and only truly national, general-
interest daily newspaper.

USA Today, a new concept in newspaper publishing, was a
heart-stopping risk of money and prestige for the risk taker and
the company behind it. Before it ever earned a dollar of profit, the
venture cost its founding company nearly half a billion dollars in
before-tax start-up losses. Even more amazing, it was bankrolled
by a firm long noted for its conservatism and steady, if uninspiring
growth. In a nation grown accustomed to decades of newspaper
closings, it contradicted the trend and critics alike who gave it
little chance for success. Yet, by its fourth year, *USA Today* had
become the second most widely read newspaper in America, and
a prototype of risk-taking innovation at work in modern enterprise. And by the end of its fifth year, the paper was able to
celebrate its first monthly profit.

The twenty-eight-year-old whose sports tabloid failed was
Allen H. Neuharth, who'd later become chairman of the $3.5 bil-
lion Gannett Company Inc.—the nation's largest newspaper company by far, and one of the world's most powerful diversified

media conglomerates. Neuharth considers the launching of *SoDak Sports* the first major business risk of his professional career. "We begged, borrowed and stole all the money we could," he recalls. "That was true entrepreneurship. Two years later we had lost it all, our venture went belly-up, and we were bloodied and bowed.

"I ran away from home, went to Miami, found a job as a reporter for $95 a week," says Neuharth, whose formerly jet-black hair has turned to silver. "There, when I wasn't working or having fun in the sun, I thought a lot about what went wrong with my plan to become rich and famous in South Dakota. Gradually I got it. I didn't really have a plan. I only had an idea. I hadn't really considered the *risk/reward* [his emphasis] ratio. I hadn't figured out how to pay the rent. My first venture went broke because of a lack of a practical plan and because of mismanagement. I had mismanaged it."

The foundation of this ARTist's future risk-taking course in business was formed right here. Once burned, he drifted toward conservatism. "It was touch and go whether I would become the most conservative conformist on earth or take the lessons that I could learn from my own mismanagement," he says. But Allen Neuharth could be neither conservative nor conformist.

Thirty years after the abortive birth of *SoDak Sports* he gambled a bit more—this time an estimated $400 to $500 million in losses over five years—to launch another paper. It was *USA Today,* Allen Neuharth's bid to firmly establish for himself and Gannett a bold legacy in American journalism and business history. To reach that plateau, Neuharth would first have to risk losses that averaged nearly a quarter of a million dollars *each day* for half a decade. He'd have to launch *USA Today* over the vehement objections of his own chief financial executives. He'd have to be willing to sacrifice an unbroken two-decade string of earnings gains by the corporation he headed. He'd have to create a newspaper unlike any other from scratch, and develop a coast-to-coast printing and distribution network to go with it—the likes of which had never been seen before. He'd have to watch his company struggle month after month with massive losses from a product many "experts" said hadn't a prayer to survive. And he'd have to do it all knowing that failure could mean the end of his career.

It is Neuharth who credits his earlier "devastating loss and

66

injury" with providing the lessons, strength and willingness to take on the kind of risks it took to build something new. "If I had not been bloodied at an early age as I was with that risk, and then had time to regroup and have at it again, I doubt that I would have taken the kinds of risks that I have taken in the last twenty-five years," says Gannett's chairman. "The experience of a failure, large or small, is a very cheap price to pay in terms of your willingness to take risks later on. Learning that you can take risks and fail without the world ending is invaluable . . . you learn as much from failures as you do from successes."

If it's true that the media control America, then, arguably, Allen Neuharth is one of the nation's most powerful men. Yet other media moguls such as Ted Turner, the cable television impresario and onetime CBS suitor; Rupert Murdoch, the cagey Australian turned U.S. citizen and owner of a vast international newspaper and broadcast empire; and Mort Zuckerman, the Boston real estate developer-cum-publisher who owns *U.S. News & World Report* and *The Atlantic*, are more often household names to the American public. Why? Because they all run large national media outlets, either print or electronic.

Gannett's newspapers, on the other hand, have traditionally been found only in smaller cities across America—cities like Battle Creek, Michigan; Rockford, Illinois; Palm Springs, California; Rochester, New York. Jack Germond, the political columnist and former chief of Gannett's Washington news bureau, once described the chain as "a bunch of shit-kicking little newspapers."

Gannett, which owned a dozen newspapers when Neuharth joined the company as a reporter, now shepherds nearly a hundred dailies with over 6 million in circulation, plus another 35 nondaily papers. Still, his brethren in the publishing trade sometimes snubbed Neuharth because his empire lacked a presence in major cities. During the early years of Neuharth's reign at Gannett, the company was considered just plain dull. It focused on medium-sized papers in cities where it had a monopoly, or nearly so, and could squeeze out ever-higher profits. It was bland and safe, but Gannett's owners chuckled all the way to the bank. His media conglomerate achieved huge financial success in what Neuharth admits were the "minor leagues" of publishing. According to *The Wall Street Journal*, he once attributed the company's absence of any big media deals to simply having "no guts." Snipers on Wall Street—which generally loved Gannett's profit-generating brand of fiscal conservatism—and at rival media giants took to calling him "No-Guts Neuharth."

Neuharth joined the small Gannett chain of newspapers headquartered in Rochester, New York, in 1963. The company, like so many others in the field, had been founded in 1923 as a family-owned business. But no Gannett family members remained, and to Neuharth that meant greater possibilities for risk taking and advancement. In 1966 he got a shot at what he considers his second big career risk. Neuharth convinced Gannett's chairman and CEO at the time, Paul Miller, to let him start a new paper near Cape Canaveral—the place from which President John Kennedy had said the nation would go to the moon and back. At about the same time, Gannett's managers were considering "going public" —offering shares to the public for the first time—and Neuharth had a hard time selling a cash-eating start-up project that could damage the company's financial profile at such a critical juncture.

Neuharth's plan to launch *Today*, "Florida's space age newspaper," called for a $3 to $5 million commitment in three to five years "to see if we could produce a profitable new newspaper." This time Neuharth was determined to do it right. He established a group of experts who secretly studied the market and laid the plans for the new launch—moves he would emulate a decade and a half later on a far bigger risk. Neuharth considers the Florida start-up as a small-scale model version of his later risks launching *USA Today*.

Twenty-eight months and $5 million later, the Florida project moved from red ink to black on its ledger sheet. "I don't want to oversimplify it," says Neuharth, "but with *USA Today* we just multiplied many times over what we had done with starting the new publication in Florida in 1966. . . . Many of our people who were involved with that had a mini-scale experience that was translated into *USA Today*."

When Neuharth took on the Florida project Gannett insiders speculated it was a make-or-break assignment. If it was a success he'd emerge as the leading candidate to run the company. It *was* a success, and Neuharth soon began acquiring new titles at Gannett Company—president and chief operating officer in 1970, chief executive officer in 1973. He completed the sweep with the chairman's title in 1979.

One of Neuharth's first moves that year was an aggressive program to hire and promote more minorities and women. A decade later Gannett had more than twice as many black journalists working for it than the average media outlet, and was considered the most progressive major media firm in the country when it came to hiring women and minorities and promoting them up through the corporate ranks.

During the 1970s the Gannett organization continued to gobble newspaper properties and spit back an astoundingly endless stream of earnings increases. By 1988 Gannett Company had tallied twenty consecutive years of record earnings, without a single down quarter. That feat greatly endeared Wall Street to the Allen Neuharth school of newspapering and made Gannett America's sixty-sixth most profitable industrial corporation and number one in profits in the printing and publishing industry.

During the 1970s, as Gannett grew from thirty-three papers to eighty, the once regional company began to form a national base of print and broadcast properties. A major acquisition in 1977 of the Speidel Newspapers added thirteen new properties in eight states and signaled the emergence of Gannett into the newspaper big time. But it was still the big time in a small way. Even as Gannett's flock of small-city dailies grew, that flock remained essentially a diffuse group of small, independently run papers whose primary link was in the ledger sheets of their common corporate parent. Gannett seemed forever doomed to the shadows of the nation's mighty papers such as *The New York Times, Washington Post, Chicago Tribune, Miami Herald* and *Los Angeles Times.*

It was during the 1970s that, according to Neuharth, "Many of us at Gannett spent lots of time speculating and dreaming of things that we could do with the resources that were now ours around the country." Each time Gannett's base broadened a little more it set Neuharth's mental gears grinding. "Several things were clear to us. We had huge resources—by the late 1970s, we had the biggest news-gathering organization in the country—but less than 20 percent of what we were gathering each day reached a consumer," he points out.

Gannett had the beginnings of a nationwide distribution system in its family of papers. Most of those were p.m. newspapers, and Gannett had a huge investment in production equipment—printing presses that were being used only five hours or less out of every twenty-four. Late-night hours, when a.m. papers go to press, found many Gannett-owned presses idle. That investment in fallow equipment spelled a major untapped resource and opportunity for the publishing giant, if it could figure out a way to exploit it.

Neuharth doesn't recall just when the idea for USA Today emerged. "It wasn't a bolt of lightning that hit me at ten o'clock one night while I was sitting in the living room," he says. But emerge it did. In the beginning, thoughts of launching a national general-interest daily paper were confined to what Neuharth describes as "mostly bull sessions" in the company's back rooms and Rochester saloons. When Allen Neuharth completed his consolidation of power at Gannett in 1979, the gears shifted. That year Gannett completed its biggest acquisition yet—Combined Communications Corporation, which included newspaper, television and billboard advertising properties. Gannett bought the company for $372 million from its founder, Karl Eller. That was also the year an organized approach to developing a national general-interest newspaper was put in motion. "That's when I finally said, 'Well, let's get serious about this,' " Neuharth recalls. The ex-army infantryman formed a task force "specifically charged with seeing whether we could utilize our resources to produce, distribute and sell a national general-interest daily newspaper."

Or, at least Neuharth knew it would be a newspaper. When he told his top four Gannett executives he was committing $1.2 million to research something new, he didn't tell them specifically what he had in mind. A company statement in early 1980 about formation of the special task force was vague, saying only that it would explore new venture possibilities across the entire communications field—electronic as well as print. He pointed them in the right direction, and wanted to see if they would arrive at the same general conclusion he already had—that America was ready for a new type of general-interest daily newspaper.

That internal Gannett task force was code-named Project NN, although Neuharth begs ignorance on just what the two Ns stood for. "Damned if I know," he pleads. "I thought it stood for 'New

Newspaper.' Some other people said it stood for 'National News-paper.' And a few of the jesters or critics in the company said it stood for 'Neuharth's Nonsense.' But anyway, it was NN and you can take your pick."

For people to study the angles and report back on the possibil-ities, Neuharth turned to fresh talent. All five members of the group were young, and three were only in their twenties. It was a collection of specialists. Says Neuharth: "One was a specialist in technology and how you harness the satellite for this purpose." Using satellites to transmit complete page makeups from the com-posing room to a series of printing plants around the country would be critical to the demanding deadlines of writing, printing and delivering an entirely new product every weekday morning to cities and towns across the country. Whether the technology existed to do what Neuharth wanted to do, and whether Gannett could tap it, were two crucial questions that had to be answered.

Other publications, notably *The Wall Street Journal* and the Paris-based *International Herald Tribune* (the last remaining ves-tige of the once-proud *New York Herald Tribune*), had already demonstrated that satellites could indeed be used to transmit a *black-and-white* page image to printing plants around the world. But nobody had demonstrated that it could be used to produce high-quality *color*, heavy on photos.

And lots of splashy color is what Gannett's visionary leader had in mind. From the genesis of the idea for *USA Today*, Neuharth believed his competition would *not* just be other daily news-papers, but television as well. The electronic news disseminators, however, weren't necessarily viewed as enemies. Neuharth per-ceived that the advance of electronic information technology—computers and television—against the seemingly archaic technol-ogy of printed newspapers was cumulative, not displacive—that availability of information made consumers hungry for *more*, and that a repackaged newspaper with a fresh mix of information had just as much chance of making it as any other information product, electronic or otherwise. After all, television had not killed radio or movies, even though that was widely expected when the tech-nology evolved. Nor did the onslaught of VCRs doom Hollywood, as some of the big studios had so direly predicted in the early 1980s. Instead, VCRs whetted consumer appetites for more.

USA Today, said the ex-G.I., would become a flashy print version of the boob tube. Neuharth even demanded that his circulation department design a newspaper vending machine that looked something like a TV set.

Neuharth believed that color would be a major requirement to attract big national advertisers to the pages of a new national publication. But color is expensive. And *high-quality* color is exorbitant—if you can even get it. Higher cost would mean higher risk. New presses would be needed. Quality control would be crucial. Unlike most national magazines, which are printed at one location and then mailed, a national daily newspaper would have to be printed at many different plants around the country. *USA Today*, in fact, is now printed at 36 different sites. Quality would have to match. A paper produced for a reader in Washington, D.C., would have to look the same as one produced for a reader in Portland—just as McDonald's wants its Big Mac to be identical in every location. That would require tremendous technical modifications to many Gannett presses accustomed to printing only meatball color.

Before he could consider taking the next step toward his risk, Neuharth had to find out if the current state of the art in satellite transmission would allow him to beam high-quality color images from a central location where the paper is produced, out into space and back to earth at various printing sites around the country. To find that out, Neuharth hired away a bright young technician from *The International Herald Tribune* to study the problem. Gannett's chief would eventually learn that the technology did exist, and today *USA Today* zaps page images globally in time periods ranging from three and a half minutes for a black-and-white page to fifteen minutes for a full-page color advertisement.

Another of Neuharth's hand-picked whiz kids for Project NN had expertise in Gannett's circulation capabilities; a third was involved in marketing through Gannett's national advertising and sales organization in New York. The fourth member represented the editorial side, and the fifth was a generalist to coordinate it all. "We assigned these bright young minds to work in a secluded cottage [which Neuharth owned] in Florida to study newspapers across the USA and elsewhere in the world—how the new technology could be applied; how circulation and distribution for a national daily would work," says Neuharth. "We knew that in the USA nearly 70 percent of the people cannot remember life before television. That's about 150 million people. For all these potential readers who grew up as viewers, we knew that we would have to provide a newspaper that would be quick instead of slow, interesting instead of dull, and visual instead of verbal. In many ways, *USA Today* transfers the tube to the printed page." Each major risk would have to be overcome. Could a national quality-color newspaper be printed, every day, on time? Would readers buy it? Would advertisers buy it? Could one organization distribute such a paper to the entire country?

The project NN team worked under top-secret conditions trying to answer those questions. Neuharth didn't want word of the project leaking out. Gannett was not alone in its quest. Visions of a national general-interest daily newspaper had titillated American journalists and publishers for decades—perhaps as far back as the mid-nineteenth century, when a weekly version of Horace Greeley's *New York Tribune* distributed across the most heavily populated portions of America became tremendously influential.

In more recent years, Dow Jones had published a highly regarded, feature-oriented national weekly paper, launched by Dow's chief executive Bernard Kilgore in 1962, called *The National Observer*. As legend has it, Kilgore's dying words in 1967 were, "Will my baby make it?" Over the next ten years, the company suffered $16 million in losses on the *Observer*. Kilgore's baby was doomed. All the same, the black-and-white paper was required reading in many journalism schools until Dow Jones, unable to make it profitable, finally pulled the plug in 1977.

With *The Wall Street Journal*, however, Dow Jones had proven that a timely, topflight *daily* could be produced and distributed for national consumption, at a tidy profit. As 1980 approached, ever-fattening *Journal* revenues, technological advancements in high-speed printing, computerized page composition, news gathering, and satellite transmission of ready-to-print pages brought the idea of a national *general-interest* daily out of journalistic fantasy and into the realm of possibility.

Neuharth was well aware of the newspaper industry's fascination with the thought of a national daily, with the *Journal*'s success, and with rumblings his counterparts at other major media companies had been making about "going national." Among at least four other corporations testing the waters for a national daily were two large media conglomerates, The Washington Post Com-

73

pany, which owns *Newsweek* and other properties, and The New York Times Company, owner of a string of papers and broadcast properties.

Both publishers, which had the two most prestigious newspapers in the country, already had a small national following and products that certainly deserved to be more widely read outside New York and Washington. Why not take a slimmer version of the paper, toss out the local stories, dump in more national advertising, and distribute it nationwide?

Sounds simple, but printing and distribution problems would be immense if the paper were to compete for timeliness against other dailies across the country. And whether national advertisers would go for the idea was an unknown. Despite its failure with the *Observer*, Dow Jones was also exploring the idea of a national daily, as was Australian mega-publisher Rupert Murdoch.

The New York Times did launch a national edition in 1980, although its distribution was (and is) small and rather low-key. It was also strictly black and white, in keeping with the paper's stodgy, even elitist image. "It's targeted at a different audience than *USA Today*," Neuharth explains, "and it is published on a considerably smaller scale. But they took an existing prestigious newspaper and went after a little slice of the national audience."

Five and a half years after Gannett blazed the trail, *The New York Times* announced plans to expand its national edition with a new cultural, lifestyles and trends section—an apparent response to *USA Today*'s success.

According to Neuharth, *The Washington Post* also considered that route, but opted for something quite different, bringing out a tabloid called *The Washington Post National Weekly Edition*. Says he, "I think that Donald Graham [who heads the Post Company] would tell you that he didn't want to risk the reputation and success of *The Washington Post* by diluting it with a national record—and understandably. But he had a vehicle that anyone would consider using." Neuharth was being kind. He doesn't get on well with Graham, and the feeling is mutual. Of *The Washington Post*'s venture, Neuharth has also been quoted as saying, "We didn't think they would have the balls to risk weakening their Washington monopoly by trying anything major nationwide."

According to Neuharth, newspaper owners have seldom been big risk takers. "It is my feeling that newspaper owners and publishers have traditionally been rather conservative in their business and journalistic judgments. Some call us dull and drab. I've kidded a lot of my friends in the business—but not entirely in jest —that I felt that a hell of a lot of them have gone through life determined that, by God, they're not going to try anything for the first time. To the degree that you can generalize about newspaper owners or publishers or editors—which is always dangerous— they are not the boldest risk takers in the country."

Allen Neuharth and his powerful ego could not go along with the long traditions of resisting change. A host of important shifts have taken place in recent years that affect publishers, says Neuharth, "but not everybody has properly managed those changes. It's clear that we're living in an information society and that public attitudes and expectations in terms of the media are far different. I believe that the public wants to know more, see more, hear more, read more than ever. Despite our own hesitancy in understanding that, all of these things have been feeding on themselves. The public has been consuming more and therefore they are hungrier, and they have a greater appetite than we have satisfied."

He suggests examples of attempts to feed the hunger: Ted Turner's success with Cable News Network, and the explosion of specialty magazines in the 1980s. "You also see it in *USA Today,*" he notes. "My instincts tell me, and I think recent history supports this, that the more it happens, the greater the hunger will be by more people. And maybe instead of targeting the top 7 percent of the audience out there [the paper's aim], that slice will increase to 10 or 12 percent. The challenge is to capitalize on this tremendous hunger for news and information that's feeding on itself. Those of us in the information business, if we are smart, will use the greater resource that we have as we expand our own operations. We'll figure out more ways to produce and sell news and information to more people at a higher profit. That may be an oversimplification, but I think that's what it is.

"Everything is a risk and I encourage people at every level of management not to run scared, not to be afraid to take the risk. I encourage them to weigh the pros and cons of those types of decisions. But to my knowledge, and where I have been involved, nobody at this company has ever had their wrist slapped for taking a risk—even if they were risks that turned out to be failures. . . . "

75

Neuharth has the reputation of looking out for his people, of remembering favors rendered.

"I'm looking for people with vision," he says. "If you have vision you're going to take risks. If you don't have any vision you're dull, and you work to maintain the status quo. There's something inherent in people's personalities that leans them in the direction of, or away from, risk taking." Neuharth presses the point by describing a former Gannett chairman: "I have said many times, about him and to him, that he never made a serious mistake in the thirty years he worked here. He never took a real risk and never had a brilliant idea either. But he never made a serious mistake. You need some of that, but for me the key decision makers must have vision, and vision must involve risk taking."

Gannett was forced to consider risky new alternatives if it wanted to own a national general-interest daily. Even though it owned more than eighty newspapers, there wasn't one big enough, or with a broad enough appeal, to interest readers in many parts of the country at the same time. Neuharth considered buying, from Time Inc., the other newspaper in Washington, *The Washington Star*—once rated the best p.m. daily in the country. "We looked at that twice, but each time we did we felt that if it were to survive it would have to do so as the second newspaper in Washington's local market," recalls Neuharth. "We concluded both times we had an opportunity to acquire it that we weren't smart enough to make it profitable. And it didn't give us what we wanted for the bigger picture, the national picture."

USA Today would have to be created the hard way, the expensive way, the risky way—from scratch. But as Neuharth says, "Any personal venture I've ever been involved with has been risky. That's life. Sure, *USA Today* was a risky venture. But again, all ventures are risky. Outsiders considered *USA Today* even riskier than it really was because they weren't privy to the facts. Our approach to *USA Today* was the same as that of many other business ventures. This was a considerably bigger scale, but the approach was the same—to assess the risks and the rewards, and then judge what the risk/reward ratio was. We do that whether we buy a little newspaper, a big newspaper, a TV station, or start a newspaper."

The "facts" his team reported back, however, included heavy downside risks. Gannett's presses weren't in good enough condition to print the paper Neuharth envisioned, and there weren't enough of them. They'd need a huge new investment in people and computers to keep track of circulation on a national scale. The satellite transmission technology was available, but expensive. Getting a million papers into readers' hands each day would create distribution nightmares. They'd need tens of thousands of news racks. And advertisers would be fearfully slow in coming. They'd probably wait at least a year on the sidelines checking out this new animal before spending a dime to ride along. Up-front costs would quickly reach tens of millions; total costs hundreds of millions. Gannett Company's unbroken string of quarterly earnings gains would be in dire jeopardy.

On the positive side, however, Gannett had identified an audience for the product: America's increasingly mobile society, attuned to the abbreviated format of television news, and color, quality and consistency. That, Neuharth and his team knew, they could deliver. If it worked, Gannett would have generated immeasurable new prestige for itself and its media empire. And the new enterprise could conceivably be worth $1 billion or more. That was Neuharth's reward in the risk/reward ratio he studied.

SEEING REWARDS OVER DANGERS

*"You don't concentrate on risks. You concentrate
on results. No risk is too great to prevent
the necessary job from getting done."*

—CHUCK YEAGER,
former test pilot

There is no standard measure of a willingness to take risks. But psychologists who have studied the risk-taking mind conclude that effective risk takers are best able to clearly establish in their own minds the link between risk and opportunity, between risk and achievement. They recognize both the potential gains and the potential losses, but are more willing to overlook the downside. They are, if you will, optimists who see the glass as half full. Such ARTists who focus on rewards over dangers make *their* choices and take *their* actions based on where *they* see that opportunity. Somebody else who doesn't see the same opportunity couldn't take the same action—you can't take a risk if you can't see it.

Risk takers in enterprise tend to remain focused on the possibility of opportunity and gain as they evaluate and pursue their risks. A more risk-averse personality, on the other hand, is always more concerned with *avoiding losses*. Risk takers are drawn to endeavors where they perceive the odds to be challenging but not overwhelming, where their wits and business skills can help them win that opportunity for themselves and their companies.

Sigmund Freud taught us that things may not be exactly as they seem. Your spouse might say one thing and mean something else entirely. The hidden meaning injects uncertainty and risk into our lives. When the topic is enterprise rather than sex, however, man suddenly prefers to believe that all is rational, straightforward and therefore *predictable*. Yet the pursuit of economic enterprise is filled with just such say-one-thing, mean-another effects. It is what makes risk in enterprise so unavoidable and so essential.

Still, we are all taught from childhood that "danger" is a signal to retreat. Society's taming process doesn't always recognize and encourage the risk-taking, creativity-producing personality types who focus first on opportunity, second on danger. More often, it instructs its children that risk is something to be avoided. No one can argue its wisdom in the physical realm—thin ice, railroad crossings and traffic lights can't be ignored. But we are easily overconditioned to avoid all risk. Danger in the economic realm of enterprise can be a *positive* sign indicating "Opportunity Ahead," and meant to spur action rather than squelch it. By forgoing risk, we forgo the opportunity as well.

As psychologists have pointed out, motivations to take risks and overcome that taming process are complex, and risk takers often show a strong ability to deal with complex situations. *They consistently excel in tests of abstract reasoning.* Uncertain situations force ARTists to proceed without all the facts—without having the lines of realism fully drawn. Riskers must continuously employ a brand of abstract reasoning to span the inevitable gaps between what is known and what is sought out. And they must make those abstract leaps of faith themselves, filling in their own "facts," their own reality in the absence of complete information.

Goals and Cutoffs

Still other psychological research finds that risk takers have a high level of what psychologists call "need satisfaction." They *want* many things. They have high aspirations and expectations that they are willing to take risks to satisfy. They clarify their own expectations and use them as fuel rods for taking risks in a two-stage process—*deciding on their risk-taking goal, and setting a "cutoff" point beyond which they will not risk any more.* These ARTists would derive more satisfaction out of a smaller payoff obtained through risk taking than they would from a larger gain if it was obtained conservatively.

The risk-taking mind is full of paradoxes. For example, when choosing between two ways to make a profit most people will pick the safer route, even though the profit is smaller. But when given the choice of two ways *to avoid a loss*, those same individuals will travel the more risky avenue.

What's going on? According to a report in *Psychology Today*, "What tilts the balance toward safety or risk is not the content of the choice, *but the way it is framed.*" Perception—a kind of propaganda effect—wins out, and perception is crucial to the risk-taking mind-set. Here's how it works:

You and I will flip a coin. If it's heads you get $1,000. Tails, you get nothing. Now suppose you also have the option of skipping the toss in return for a fixed amount of money. What is the least amount you will settle for? You have a fifty-fifty chance in the coin toss. Do you give it up for $500? Studies on this question show that the average person will take about $350 in sure money.

But turn the situation around a little. Suppose you are given $1,000 to begin with. Now you have the $1,000 and must flip a coin to determine if you keep it all or must give it all back. How much of your $1,000 will you now give up to avoid tossing the coin? Here again there is a fifty-fifty chance of keeping or losing the $1,000, so do you give up $500 to be assured of keeping $500? Since most people were willing to take $350 in the first case, they should be willing to give up $650 in this one. But research doesn't show this result. Most people will give back no more than $350.

In reality, both situations are the same—you have a fifty-fifty chance of gaining $1,000. Because of the way the first choice is *presented*, however, it appears to be a choice between two gains. And, according to the psychologists, *when only a gain is involved in two risk decisions, people tend to be more conservative.*

The second case was constructed to make the choice appear to be one between two losses. And, *when faced with a choice between two losses, most people will take a greater risk*—in this case, by refusing to give up more of their money in return for keeping a sure amount. (In the example, most people wanted to keep $650 of what they had, but would take $350 in the first case.)

The same tendencies translate into other decisions we make in business and investing, as well as in other areas of our lives. Faced with two investment opportunities that both look attractive we tend to go with the more certain winner, even if the potential gain is smaller. When we face a choice in business between two potential losses we're prone to take more risk to avoid the larger loss. The vast majority of people choose a route that is framed positively over one framed negatively, even if the choice is exactly the same.

We tend to avoid taking risks in pursuit of gains, but we choose risk more often to avoid sure losses. In other words, most of us are not really averse to risks at all. Rather, we are averse to *losses*. The task business managers face is to encourage people to *take greater risks in pursuit of gain, rather than risking only to avoid losses.*

For most Americans, a possible financial loss counts much more heavily than a potential gain. One behavioral scientist who recently identified this risk-taking paradox is Amos Tversky, a Stanford University psychology professor and winner of a MacArthur Foundation fellowship—the so-called genius award. Working with Tversky in this field in Daniel Kahneman, a professor of psychology at the University of British Columbia in Vancouver. When *Discover* explored the new research in 1985, the science magazine detected an increasing interest in applying it to fields of economics and enterprise. Perhaps, the article suggested, executives might come to believe that business decision making depends much *less* on "cold hard statistical facts" and much *more* on perceptions of risk and reward. This research has helped shift attention toward an economic middle ground between the purely logical and the purely random—the realm of *calculated* risk taking. This realm of enterprise borrows a little from both poles, recognizing that progress and innovation take place always with incomplete information, in a world of change and surprise.

GAIN WINS OUT AT GANNETT

At Gannett, Al Neuharth was personally locked in on the potential rewards of the risk he was considering, not the potential damage. His answers to obstacles were to break them down. Not enough presses? Get more. Lease them from somebody else if need be. Old ones need repair? Then fix them. Some board members nervous? He'd fix that, too.

As it became increasingly clear that Neuharth was dead serious about what many at Gannett considered a wacky idea, dissension developed. It came primarily from the financial side of the corporation. Those with an editorial background were willing to give just about anything a shot. The number crunchers, however, were plenty worried. Some thought the chairman was leading proud Gannett down the proverbial primrose path.

They had a point. The venture under consideration would cost a mind-blowing sum to launch and maintain for the years it would take to reach profitability—*if* it ever got there at all. Neuharth agreed, but *he* was willing to take those risks for the payoff he perceived would be theirs in the end. To keep his own mind on track, Neuharth stopped inviting his top financial officer, who opposed the project, to planning sessions. By mid-1980—two years before *USA Today* was launched, and a year before a final decision would be made—Neuharth had already decided he'd take the risk unless evidence against it became overwhelming. Gannett might be wounded if the paper failed, he thought, but not mortally.

Gannett's board of directors was informed of the project in the fall of 1980. Like all individuals involved, they first had to sign statements agreeing not to divulge the information. Neuharth made sure they were aware of the risks, but he was also clear in letting them know which way he was leaning. He targeted mid-1981 for a final decision—a decision he later described as the toughest the company had ever faced.

Neuharth had enough encouraging information to risk a little more. In early 1981, still short of making a commitment to publish, Gannett produced a prototype of its proposed national daily to send out for "field-testing." By now, rumors had spread about a secret Gannett plan to start some type of new daily publication. Some accounts got it wrong, however, suggesting that Gannett was developing a sports and business paper to compete with *The Wall Street Journal*. Much of the reaction was disbelief that fiscally conservative Gannett would consider *any* high-risk venture.

For months, Gannett editors and writers grappled with the prototype, trying to discover the right formula to fit Neuharth's concept of a colorful, "quick-read" paper that could compete with television for consumer attention—and presumably advertiser dollars as well. They needed a publishing "first"—the kind of newspaper never seen before. Graphic designers worked up slick new ways of presenting information—colorful layouts that would later set a new standard for other daily papers. They made liberal use of high-quality color photos, and articles ranging in length from short to microscopic. There was such an abundance of short items that staffers once held a contest to guess the total number of "stories," which turned out to be over six hundred in one forty-page prototype issue. The tone was upbeat, and use of color approached that of comic books. (Ironically, one of Neuharth's personal eccentricities at the time was that he dressed only in black, white and shades of gray—having added the dimension of gray only when his own hair color demanded it.)

A small number of potential readers and advertisers were now given a look at Neuharth's prototype creation. The two crucial groups were advertisers and readers. Advertisers were confused by the paper. There wasn't anything else like it. Was it a newspaper, a magazine, or what? They didn't know where it fit. Readers gave it thumbs-up. The splashy look, quick read, outstanding sports and innovations like the weather maps were a hit. Media pundits who grabbed a look, however, concluded that Gannett would be crazy to risk going ahead.

"At that point it was still an R&D project," recalls Neuharth. "If the field-testing had been totally discouraging we could have pulled the plug." But it wasn't. As development continued, "the answers kept coming up green," he says.

Skeptics doubted that a company with experience only in community dailies, reporting mainly local news, could become an overnight force in national news coverage. But *USA Today* didn't intend to compete head-on with other prints news gatherers. It planned to invent a new mix of news, features and entertainment that would treat America's weary eyes, without taxing its brain.

On the pages of America's leading business publications, the critics called Neuharth's venture "foolhardy," an "ego trip" and "superfluous" in the face of expanding news coverage by cable (Ted Turner's Cable News Network) and broadcast television. Doubters also pointed out that Neuharth was foolishly risking his company's consistent record of earnings growth by launching a paper that was sure to lose hundreds of millions of dollars before it ever made a dime. The same reservations, of course, had been constantly raised from within Gannett. Neuharth heard, and filed, those objections. He had his own way of looking at the information, his own reasons, and to him they spelled innovation and opportunity, *ahead of* risk. Did those outside critics think a powerful and potentially profitable new voice in the American media could be created from scratch without some heady risk? Neuharth certainly didn't. He agreed with Walter Wriston. The reward, the eventual profit, could come only from the risk.

Besides, Neuharth had many pluses on his side:

• A nationwide organization, generating huge amounts of cash, that he knew could sustain the expected losses from a start-up. And every dollar of those losses would be tax-deductible.

• Printing and distribution facilities scattered across the country at existing Gannett newspapers.

• Experience of knowing what his resources were and how to use them.

• Strong backing from many allies on his board of directors.

• A "now-or-never" itch in his newspapering britches that told him the situation was ripe for the risk.

RISK DYNAMIC #7
TAKING RESPONSIBILITY

"What we obtain too cheap, we esteem too lightly; 'tis dearness only that gives everything its value."

—THOMAS PAINE

Taking risks always implies taking responsibilities. But risk goes beyond simply "accepting" responsibility. ART generates *new* responsibilities from *new* risks.

Responsibility is a general partner in the joint venture between risk and opportunity, and ARTists must show themselves more than willing to accept the consequences of their behavior. When a risk falters, risk takers move to fix it, not place the blame. When something fails they immediately analyze why and start scouting the next step. They believed in what they did and are not out to second-guess themselves.

Risk *avoiders* tend to prefer freedom *from* choice and responsibility. Evidence of that comes from the realm of investment risk taking. Meir Statman, a Santa Clara University finance professor and a researcher in investment psychology, suggests reasons most individuals avoid risky investments: "When presented with freedom of choice, investors often behave in ways that reveal that what they really want is freedom *from* choice." Most investors display an aversion to *responsibility* . . . which is to say, an aversion to risk.

The aversion to investment risk taking is plain from the way people behave, observes Statman. They pay huge sums for the advice of stockbrokers, investment advisors, pension fund managers and others, even though evidence shows that such advice does not help investors beat the market. "Why do investors engage in a search for data even when they have no ability to interpret it?" asks Statman. Making any investment involves risk and, therefore, responsibility. And that implies regret when the choice turns out badly. Statman claims that the main service the brokers and advisors provide is to be scapegoats for investors who make the wrong choices and want to pass off their regret to somebody else.

Investment risk taking is particularly unruly because of the vast and growing amounts of information on investment markets. These data skyscrapers—available at the touch of a button on your home computer—give the illusion that all is *not* chaos after all; that perhaps uncertainty's veil *can* be temporarily lifted by simply grabbing onto a few more facts or historical performance charts.

The fact is, you can look at market averages over three-, five-, and ten-year periods and see they've gone up nicely. But this does not reflect the specific fates of the thousands of investors who bought and sold on ups and downs along the way . . . some making money, many losing. Thus, investment *averages* are indisputably misleading to most people who read them. The man with one hand in the fire and the other in an ice bucket is, *on average*, at a comfortable temperature, too.

The key to understanding this problem is the idea of "discontinuity," argues James Gleick in *Chaos*. "When a quantity changes, it can change almost arbitrarily fast. Economists traditionally imagined that prices change smoothly—rapidly or slowly, as the case may be, but smoothly in the sense that they pass through all the intervening levels on their way from one point to another. That image of motion was borrowed from physics, like much of the mathematics applied to economics. But it was wrong. Prices change in instantaneous jumps, as swiftly as a piece of news can flash across a teletype wire and a thousand brokers can change their minds. A stock market strategy was doomed to fail, argued Benoit Mandelbrot [IBM's genius mathematician, who introduced fractals to the world], if it assumed that a stock would have to sell for $50 at some point on its way down from $60 to $10." Mandelbrot's point about stock prices was made abundantly clear in the market crash of October 19, 1987.

In investments, as in other realms of risk taking, the risk is largely in the eye of the risk taker. This can have both positive and negative ramifications. Witness one of Wall Street's best-known crooks, Ivan Boesky. Before the crash of his multibillion-dollar risk arbitrage empire in 1986, Boesky had been called by *The New York Times* "one of Wall Street's best known risk takers"; *Time* magazine labeled him "the biggest and boldest of the 'arbs.'" With a touch of unintended irony, Boesky himself professed to not be much of a risk taker. Rather, as he once said at a press briefing introducing a book he wrote, "It is the average investor who buys a stock on the basis of an analyst's recommendation, and then prays it will go up, who is taking the bigger risk."

Boesky contended that because he had developed a strict discipline about risk arbitrage, it involved less risk. "There are no simple formulas," he said. "Good judgment plays a greater role than technical competence, and subjective analysis outweighs risk calculation." He may have had the theory right, but either didn't believe it or chose to ignore it by using illegal means to leapfrog the system and its inherent risks.

For Neuharth, at Gannett, responsibility for the risk was something he would gladly take. There was nothing cavalier about it. He was deeply and personally a part of it. The project was *his*, even if others chose to call it "Neuharth's Nonsense." But if it succeeded he'd want the credit. He privately told reluctant Gannett board members that he was staking his personal career on it; that if it failed he'd step down.

Most of Gannett's directors were impressed by Neuharth's documentation behind the risk, even though he admitted much of it was guesswork. After all, this had never been done before. There were no models to follow, other than the much smaller Florida project. He made certain the board was not given a whitewashed version of the potential downside. At the same time, he assured them it was not a bet-the-company risk either; that Gannett could

87

recover if it failed. While it may have been Gannett's money at stake, it was Allen Neuharth's personal prestige on the line—a make-or-break move by the chairman.

"It wasn't as though we were betting the company on this venture. If *USA Today* meets its financial targets, it might be 15 percent of the Gannett Company," he says. "We were *investing* some of the company's resources in another enterprise. I had been credited, rightly or wrongly, with a reasonable record of success with Gannett at that time, and I recognized that it would probably be damaged if this went belly-up. I thought it might also be enhanced if it succeeded. I think in any new venture—any risky venture—there is a point person, and if the venture fails that point person is more likely than others to be embarrassed and suffer the consequences. Conversely, I think that in any new venture that succeeds, there are always at least a hundred architects. But that's a fact of life. So what the hell."

When the formal surveys of consumer reaction to the prototype were complete, the results gave Neuharth a boost. Publishing professionals might be skeptical, but readers weren't. Neuharth figured that if Gannett's pockets were deep enough, if it could overcome the huge production and distribution problems, at least the paper could be assured of an audience.

As the crucial go/no-go board meeting approached at the end of 1981, Neuharth consolidated his position. He argued forcefully, perhaps autocratically, that money Gannett would spend was an *investment*—never a *loss*—a vintage risk taker's distinction. What was Gannett's chairman thinking at that crucial time? "I focused on the risk a lot," he confides, "but I never went home at night saying, 'My God, what am I doing?' I went home at night saying, 'Jesus, I'd better get started early in the morning so that I can be involved in this exciting new venture.' By that point, the risks had been carefully weighed, and the decision was to go. Once that decision was made I didn't spend time worrying about it."

Neuharth had too much positive evidence. To back out now would confirm Gannett's bush-league, no-risk image. It was the force of Neuharth's will, and his unique perception of the potential gain, that made *USA Today* a reality; that resulted in his taking the risk. He took it despite the fact that three of his four top executives had told him they'd say no if the decision were solely theirs to make. But even those executives, who were also board members, decided to back the boss, and vote to proceed, when the time came.

At the final directors' meeting of 1981, Neuharth announced to the board, "Now today we're going to say yes or no on the go-ahead for *USA Today*." The board already knew well what Neuharth's recommendation would be. And the chairman knew that by taking the risk he was setting himself up for anyone who cared to take a potshot. Many would cheer if he failed.

Neuharth told the board that in his final analysis he believed the potential for gain outweighed the downside risks. The chairman went around the table polling the board members. Yes votes piled up. When he came to Andrew Brimmer, an economist and the first black to serve as a governor at the Federal Reserve, Brimmer paid Neuharth a high compliment: "The way in which Gannett has approached the problem of whether to undertake this high-risk venture is a classic Harvard Business School case study, as far as I'm concerned." He ticked off the highlights of Neuharth's three-year effort to explore the proposed venture and its risks up to that point—Project NN's detailed research, the surveys, the careful crafting of a prototype, the attention to seemingly small details such as the design of vending racks. Brimmer pronounced himself "totally enthusiastic and supportive."

More yes votes. Neuharth's tactics had succeeded in rallying support even from the skeptics. The vote was unanimous to adopt a five-year business plan to launch *USA Today*, beginning in the fall of 1982.

"The conviction was a strong conviction that we ought to do this," recalls Neuharth. "The commitment was a strong commitment. And not just mine. There were varying degrees of enthusiasm during year one, year two and year three. In the beginning there were some skeptics, but never any cynics. Our board has been through enough things with us so that they are appropriately skeptical and critical, but not cynical. All they need is to be shown that what we're doing has some logic to it and that the reward looks okay and that we can handle it properly."

With other media giants eyeing the same potential, how is it that Gannett, under Allen Neuharth, was the one that took the risk? "I think it's the company and the individuals," he says, slipping lower in his chair. "I think the company was positioned better than anyone else who was looking into the possibility. And I think the individuals, the decision makers in the company were more prone to aggressive endeavors, whether they were acquisitions or new ventures.

"Every time you do something and it works, you gain some confidence, and some people say we had a pretty large ego and were kind of cocky. Well, maybe that's appropriate, I don't know. But I certainly would plead guilty to the fact that the top management folks at Gannett at that point had a high degree of confidence. We had to, or we wouldn't have done it. Whether that translates into big egos or cockiness I'll leave to others to decide.

"But there had to be a high degree of confidence. Our confidence had grown because of what we had done up until that point. . . . There is no mentality in Gannett anywhere at the top that is interested in just preserving an empire. That's dull. That's not our bag. That's not what we're here for."

RISK DYNAMIC #8

RISK IS CONTRARIAN

*"Every good and excellent thing stands
moment by moment on the razor's edge of
danger and must be fought for."*

Sign outside H. Ross Perot's
office in Dallas, from Thornton Wilder

Chief executive officers in American companies today face more uncertainty, more unpredictability and *less* job security than ever before. Enterprise *demands* ever greater efficiency, growth and profits, despite ever more competition and increasingly volatile business conditions. In such an environment, it's hard for a CEO to buck the trends, to deal with the uncertainty, to be a *contrarian*. Success under these conditions requires a kind of faith in uncertainty, a willingness to abandon the past—though it may be eminently defensible—to create change and innovate.

At first glance, innovations often appear not worth the bother. The *current* way of doing something has been lovingly fine-tuned. Innovations and risk may seem clumsy at first—a cure that's worse than the disease. For an enterprise to attempt something innovative, the chance of loss simply *cannot* be predicted.

If it could, the enterprise would not be innovating at all, but duplicating an existing success—or failure. Innovation is *unique*. Nobody else has done it *quite this way*. That doesn't mean it has to be a major innovation—a subtle innovation is nonetheless an innovation. You can bunt for a base hit just as easily as swinging away.

Ironically, some of the best innovations are not immediate successes for the simple reason they haven't existed before. And since they haven't existed before, the consuming public doesn't yet know how badly it "needs" the product. Allen Neuharth said all along that *USA Today* would not replace other newspapers, but that it would become an *additional* read. We survived nicely without VCRs, but it's amazing how badly we've come to "need" this innovation. There was a time when we obtained cash only during banking hours. Now millions of people simply "must" have access to a twenty-four-hour teller machine. And baking cookies at home, or buying them packaged in the store, once sufficed. Now cookie lovers line up to get them freshly baked at the local cookie emporium.

Risk's Key: The Unanticipated

Contrarian-style risk takers *count* on surprises, count on the fact that, by definition, these surprises cannot be anticipated, and that a company's best shot at success lies not in doing away with risk, but in accepting it, understanding it, and turning it to an advantage. Confident, contrarian risk takers are often accused of arrogance. They can be disputatious people. In less noble terms, they tend to argue a lot. But management science itself is guilty of arrogance when it seeks to make enterprise into something ordered and predictable, which it cannot be. Enterprise is irregular, disordered and turbulent.

Risk, then, becomes a useful tool in pursuing contrarian economic goals, rather than a problem or imperfection to be sliced from the economic equation. Risk taking is a means of profiting from uncertainty and accommodating the unknown. Executives who are successful ARTists recognize that knowledge is, and always will be, incomplete, that risk and opportunity are closely linked, and that trying to avoid risk by gaining ever more information produces stagnation and lost opportunities.

Yet America's economic system remains ill-equipped to account for risk; and, by implication, for failure as well. We calculate the national debt, the inflation rate, producer prices, the value of the dollar, the amount of money in our banks, the direction of interest rates, the gross national product, and all kinds of other numbers. These we call leading indicators of our nation's economic health. Yet this system ignores risk, because there's no number attached to it.

Our economic system possesses an innate aversion to risk. It's an aversion that obscures our ability even to recognize the risks that others have taken before us. There are no corporate graveyards to visit, no roadside markers to bankruptcy to remind us of capitalism's rich heritage of risk and failure. We tend to think of business as a type of military institution that lives on, no matter how many soldiers pass through its barracks. In the military, acting "contrary" is strictly against the rules.

But enterprise is nothing like the military. Enterprise is extremely *fragile*. Barely perceptible shifts in market forces can destroy mighty economic structures before management has time to change. Even corporate giants such as General Motors, Time Inc., IBM, General Electric, CBS or Coca-Cola have been burned by unforeseen change.

Consider VCRs. American companies thought that market would be too insignificant to risk much on trying to be first to develop the technology. Now most of the billions of dollars VCR sales have generated belong to the Japanese. Not a single American company makes this machine. Tens of millions of VCRs sporting Yankee labels such as GE, RCA, Zenith and Montgomery Ward populate American living rooms, but they were all made by a handful of Japanese firms. What makes that particularly damning for American enterprise is that it was an American company that invented the technology in 1956. Ampex Corporation, of Redwood City, California, was also first to make and market a machine referred to at the time as a VTR, for videotape recorder. Over the next twenty-five years, however, entrenched American business interests, hell-bent on protecting existing products and profits, fumbled away this new technology to the Japanese. U.S. interests

93

worried about protecting the old, and were unwilling to take risks on something new.

Although Ampex was first, the company had little idea of the importance its invention would have. In the early 1960s, Ampex formed an alliance with Sony, a young, aggressive Japanese electronics firm that had made its name and money in transistor radios. It was Sony that first saw the potential of the VTR, and later the VCR, as a *consumer* product. Other American companies besides Ampex dabbling in the technology, including RCA (which owned NBC) and CBS, saw video technology as something exclusively for professional use—especially by the TV networks.

Sony threw its weight into getting a VCR on the market, and was first with such a machine in 1971, a forerunner to its introduction of the Betamax some five years later. In the early 1970s, RCA was dabbling with its SelectaVision technology, and in 1974 test-marketed a machine that was never heard from again. RCA executives decided to focus on video disk technology, which offered better picture quality, but with one glaring drawback that would doom it: It did not offer consumers the ability to *record* on their own, as did tape technology.

RCA had been one of America's best hopes. This was the company that had been a contrarian risk taker years earlier, developing color television ahead of everyone else. Under its chief executive, David Sarnoff, RCA dumped huge R&D sums into a technological direction Sarnoff considered promising, even though everyone else at the time thought it was foolhardy. That was the 1940s. Year after year RCA doggedly pushed its technicians on the color technology. Sarnoff was gambling there'd be a huge consumer market for color sets. He was right, of course, and RCA was the early leader. The Japanese used the same approach later on to grab the VCR market.

In the early seventies, one of the best hopes for eventual U.S. dominance in VCRs emerged from a start-up company called Cartridge Television, Inc., out of Palo Alto, California. With a fresh public stock offering, and additional financial backing from heavyweights like Sears and Columbia Pictures, Cartridge jumped out to a quick lead. But as with any new technology introduced in a rush, there were bugs—with the hardware, with distribution, with financing, with advertising and marketing. Within a year Cartridge needed a capital infusion of probably less than $50 million to keep things going. But it could find no backing from the major U.S. electronics firms plodding away on their own video technologies, and which preferred to do things their own way, even if they were trailing behind. By 1973, a company that might one day have dominated the market was dead for lack of risk capital.

In 1976, Sony successfully introduced Betamax in the American market. Powerful U.S. business interests greeted Sony with the classic anti-risk response: *Litigate, rather than innovate.* Universal Pictures, with its parent company MCA, along with the Motion Picture Association of America, sued. They claimed that this new technology, allowing consumers to tape programs off television sets, violated corporate copyrights on the TV shows they produced. The legal action dragged on for years, with a lower court decision going against Sony in 1981. The case was finally decided by the Supreme Court in a 1984 decision in favor of Sony.

By then, U.S. manufacturers were long gone. The battle for supremacy of the American VCR market was being waged completely in Japan between Sony and the gigantic electronics firm Matsushita. Sony's Betamax technology was pitted against Matsushita's VHS competitor. The only role U.S. companies were now playing was choosing which of the Japanese combatants to buy their machines from.

James Lardner, who chronicles the history of the VCR in his incisive book *Fast Forward,* sums up: "Only one important feature of the home video world as we know it could never have been imagined from the forecasts of 15 and 20 years ago: That the ambitious plans of more than a dozen American companies—the likes of CBS, RCA, Avco, Magnavox, Motorola, Kodak, Bell & Howell, Fairchild, Zenith, MCA and Polaroid—would go up in smoke, and that when the smoke cleared, the Japanese would control the field."

American business apparently didn't learn much from this episode. Unless domestic firms take some risks they may also find themselves locked out of a booming market in high-definition (HD) television in the 1990s.

Avoiding risks, says Lester Thurow, dean of MIT's Sloan School of Management, "is the route to economic failure. . . . Some American firms will fail with a more aggressive stance vis-à-vis new products and new technologies, but the entire economy will fail in the long run under a general strategy of risk avoidance. With foreign competition now armed with equal if not superior technologies, markets have objectively become much riskier and tougher for Americans. If it is to succeed, American industry is going to have to get used to employing strategies that would have been regarded as too risky 20 years ago."

During that period the military spirit of the corporation prevailed, demanding uniformity, crushing change, discouraging individual choice and individual risk, always acting as a rigid unit. Enterprise, to achieve its best, must function just the opposite, with each individual pursuing his or her own vision. Actually, enterprise at its best lurches forward in barely controlled chaos. No military could tolerate it.

A risk-averse system cannot adequately deal with the two common words that ultimately control our economic destiny: uncertainty and change. When the human species is faced with change and uncertainty, it is forced to take risks. Risk *is* change, and since we fear change, we fear risk—until we realize that change and risk together mean opportunity.

The Chinese have long recognized this. As James Lipton, a novelist, once observed, "The ancient Chinese, seeking an ideograph to represent the turning point we call crisis in English, performed a miracle of linguistic compression by combining two existing characters—the symbol for danger and the symbol for opportunity—to create the character *wei-ji*, which stands as an eternal assertion that, since opportunity and danger are inseparable, it is impossible to make a significant forward move without encountering danger, and, obversely, the scent of danger should alert us to the fact that we may be headed in the *right* direction."

William C. Clark, director of the International Institute for Applied Systems Analysis, in Vienna, even equates efforts to *eliminate* risk to witch-hunting. For several centuries spanning the Renaissance and Reformation, society's idea of risk assessment meant witch-hunting, he says. And while modern risk assessors don't incinerate their fellow citizens, Clark claims the attempts to squelch risk "are logically indistinguishable from those used by the Inquisition.

"The 'risk problem' is not uncertainty of outcome. Instead it is the challenge of coping confidently, effectively, and creatively with the surprising world around us. The fundamental question is not how to calculate, control or even reduce risk. It is how to increase our risk-taking abilities."

Investing Means Risking

In all sectors of American enterprise, there can be no "taking" without "risking," although we would dearly love to have it otherwise. Nowhere is this tendency more clear than in the investment field. Everyone wants the big gains, but no one wants the risk. Risk takers like Allen Neuharth who dare to think otherwise see the risk of loss not as a loss at all, but merely as an *investment*. The process is similar whether $500 or $500 million is involved. All risk taking is a form of investment.

"Safe investment" is only a relative term, and a bit of a misnomer. Making any investment is predicated on some degree of uncertainty, which is to say on risk. If you invest money in the stock market you take the risk that overall investment perceptions will change unfavorably, and the market as a whole will go down. The stocks that you own may or may not follow that trend. Even if the market goes up the company you invested in might run into trouble or go bankrupt. If you put your money in CDs you're taking less risk with it, but what about opportunity loss—what your capital "could have" earned if you had invested it elsewhere? When you put money into long-term CDs during a period of low interest rates, for example, you take a considerable risk of opportunity loss. While your money is locked up earning a small return, opportunities in hundreds of different investments may be passing you by.

Risk taking with investments includes reacting quickly, and quite often going against the crowd with a *contrary* position. Contrarians are the salmon of the investment stream—always swimming against the flow. When everybody is buying they're selling, and vice versa. They believe that individuals, when left alone, are tolerably sensible and reasonable when it comes to making financial decisions, taking risks. As a member of a *crowd*, however, an individual at once becomes a blockhead. It may be okay to take a risk based on the "bigger fool" theory of investing for a while. Even if you buy at a foolishly high price there will be a bigger fool that you can sell to at an even higher price. But it won't work for very long. Your risk is that you will be the last fool. Contrary to belief, the supply is not inexhaustible.

The Probability Trip Wire

Comprehending probabilities is one major impediment to contrarian risk taking. How many of us believe, for example, that if the ball in a roulette wheel has just landed on black four times in a row, the odds have now improved that the next spin will turn up red? It's a common but an infamous scientific fallacy: The odds are the same as they were at the first spin, fifty-fifty.

"An essential part of worrying is knowing what the chances are that something will happen," wrote William F. Allman in a now defunct science magazine in 1985. "But just a little knowledge of probability theory can be a dangerous thing. Everyone knows that when the odds of something occurring are, for example, 50-50, then half the time, on average, the event will happen. But fewer realize that the average usually nears 50 percent only after a large number of events. With a small number, wide variations can occur. . . . Some of us conclude, incorrectly, that chance is self-correcting—that is, a deviation in one direction promotes a deviation in the other to compensate for it."

That is the essence of the fallacy, and the reason an awful lot of people lose big at gambling. It's crucial not to make this mistake in risk taking: *Just because you have been wrong before doesn't mean the odds are now better that you will be right.*

NEUHARTH AS CONTRARIAN

USA Today was a true contrarian move at birth. In the 1970s and 80s, newspapers were falling dead at an alarming rate. Nobody ever *started* a major newspaper. That was inconceivable. The very year *USA Today* was born, some two dozen papers expired. Critics wondered if the *USA Today* launch wasn't a foolhardy exercise in swimming upstream.

It certainly didn't seem that way to Neuharth, the contrarian thinker. "By the summer of '82," he says, "it seemed pretty clear to me that anyone in possession of all the information we then had would have to conclude that this was a venture the company should undertake." But, he adds, "*How* to do it was still not very clear at all. There were all kinds of options that affect the degree of the risk and the costs of the venture—the degree of commitment that you make up front; how long a period and what kind of business plan you develop; whether to phase it in market by market or whether to drop it on everybody simultaneously." He hadn't really decided how far he'd be willing to go if things turned sour.

Gannett adopted a five-year plan that envisioned profitability for *USA Today* by the end of 1987, when the plan said circulation would reach 2.4 million and the newspaper's market value would be "$1 billion or more."

September 15, 1982, was launch day for Allen Neuharth's great new experiment in American print journalism. He chose the Washington/Baltimore metropolitan area as the birthing ward. At 1:30 a.m. on the fifteenth, Neuharth and other Gannett executives were at the Journal Publishing Company in nearby Springfield, Virginia, watching the first of 150,000 full-color copies of the premier issue come off the presses. He was checking quality, as he would at other print sites as more cities were added. It was just second nature to Neuharth, who in 1966 had personally checked to see that copies of the Florida newspaper *Today* were being properly delivered to individual doorsteps.

In the gathering light of this late-summer morning in Washington, the first issue of *USA Today,* bearing a 25-cent price tag and lots of colorful pizzazz, was delivered to newsstands. Later that morning the President of the United States and the leaders of the House and Senate (Senator Howard Baker would later become a Gannett director) joined eight hundred other invited guests at a launch party Gannett threw on Washington's mall.

"People ask what would have made me quit," says Neuharth. "Well, if on September 15, 1982, when we launched in Washington and Baltimore, we hadn't sold any, we would have stopped publishing." But copies did sell, and five days later the paper appeared in Atlanta. It was clearly Neuharth's baby. Throughout the incubation period of the biggest risk of his life, he remained an almost fanatical taskmaster, pushing each of his employees to do more, to do better. In the early going he was there feeding and diapering his newborn, stalking the newsroom, often rewriting headlines himself.

Even the choice of which story to lead with that first day was risky. It would set the tone for the newspaper's future coverage. While all the other major papers chose the assassination of Lebanon's president as the lead, Neuharth went with Grace Kelly's death as the top story. His gut told him that more Americans were interested in the untimely death of Princess Grace than in one more Middle East killing.

Media critics called the paper a print version of *Good Morning America*. They complained that America's first national daily paper looked like a "mediocre piece of journalism." It was dubbed McPaper, junk food journalism, and the near beer of newspapers. Nevertheless, the push to add cities was relentless. Minneapolis met the paper on September 27; Pittsburgh on October 4; Portland and Seattle on November 8; and the last city added in 1982 was San Francisco, on November 15. Then twelve more major cities were added over the next ten months, and by the end of 1983, *USA Today* could truly be called a national paper.

It could also be called a money pit. Gannett Company's operating expenses that year—the first full year of *USA Today* operations—jumped 17 percent. But that was expected. In 1984 they jumped another 16 percent. That *wasn't* expected. In both years the biggest chunk of the increases could be traced to the drain from *USA Today* operations. Later reports estimated the combined 1982–83 loss at about $165 million.

Before the launch, says Neuharth, "we knew about what kind of earnings we could generate, and, if you will, to what degree we could subsidize *USA Today* for a certain period of time, without the company going down the tubes. That doesn't change the degree of risk very much. But I think it is easier for a company with that earnings capacity, or deep pockets if you will, to take that risk than one which didn't have the deep pockets."

Later, he would learn that Gannett's pockets would have to be even deeper. The financial team had badly underestimated the size of the initial losses. And when *USA Today* became an early hit with readers, the paper's introductory program was accelerated, boosting costs still more. Although Gannett released no fig-

100

ures about the paper's losses, the company admitted that during
USA Today's first two full years of operation, expenses "significantly exceeded original company expectations." In the three
years before USA Today was launched, Gannett's income averaged 12.6 percent of total sales. In 1982 that dropped to 11.9
percent, and in 1983 to 11.3 percent, on the effects of the USA
Today money drain. According to one report, Neuharth described
the higher-than-expected losses two years into the risk as "a fuck-
ing disaster." He pressed harder for controls.

Early going for the newspaper was anything but smooth. Distribution problems plagued the system as Gannett learned the hard
way that putting the same paper in readers' hands across a 3,000-
mile stretch of countryside wasn't easy. Much of the Washington-
based USA Today staff had been borrowed from other Gannett
papers around the country. Those papers began to complain that
they were footing a large part of the bill for Neuharth's risk. Gannett placed tens of thousands of its TV-look-alike USA Today
vending racks on city streets—literally overnight at times. Some
communities objected to the invasion of coin boxes. In court, Gannett won the issue on freedom of the press grounds. Advertisers
remained on the sidelines to watch. To lure them in, Neuharth's
paper would need an independently audited circulation count.
But USA Today's system to track circulation on a national scale
was a calamity. This was one critical area where Neuharth had
failed to anticipate trouble.

Since Gannett refused to disclose how much the new venture
was really costing, Wall Street had a field day playing the "Guess
How Much Al Neuharth Is Losing on USA Today Game." Gannett
had never divulged earnings or losses from individual properties,
so it wasn't unexpected. The chairman's reasoning: "We think
that the shareholders and Wall Street should judge the Gannett
Company on its total performance, and we reveal everything that
the law says we must reveal, and more. But we think it might be
counterproductive to subject ourselves to second-guessing on
every piece of the action. There are times in a company of this
size when certain operations do extremely well and others do
rather poorly. Our job as managers is to ensure that the total performance of the company is satisfactory or better."

When the paper was launched, Value Line, the nation's largest
stock market advisory service, estimated that Gannett would lose

"well over $10 million" in its first full year of operation—a woefully low estimate. Other analysts pegged the losses much higher, and by 1984 and 1985 investment firm research departments were putting the yearly drain at $80 million—still below what Neuharth was most likely spending. *Value Line's* comments in its September 17, 1982, issue were relatively kind to Neuharth as well: "The national newspaper is Gannett's most ambitious but riskiest venture to date. Though it won't compete with *The Wall Street Journal*, *USA Today* will be going against numerous local newspapers having much the same format. . . . Win or lose in the national market, the start-up period will be long and costly." And shortly after the newspaper was introduced, *Value Line* wrote again, "This media venture reflects a lot of daring and imagination. The survival rate for the fledgling dailies of other publishers has been virtually nil during the past 15 years. So Gannett has no good examples to help guide the success of *USA Today*."

By the end of 1983, *USA Today* had become the third largest newspaper in the country, behind *The Wall Street Journal* and New York's *Daily News*. On its third birthday, the paper published an interview with its founder. It read, in part:

Question: Is *USA Today* still a good investment for Gannett?

Neuharth: We think the risk-reward ratio looks even better now than it looked at the beginning. If *USA Today* continues toward a successful, profitable venture, the investment in it will have been much, much less than it would take to acquire an existing publication like it, if there were one.

Question: Does it bother you that because *USA Today* has a different format, it probably will be difficult for it to win Pulitzer Prizes in many categories?

Neuharth: No, it doesn't bother me at all. Don't forget that Pulitzers were set up many years ago for traditional, old style newspapers. *USA Today* is not a traditional newspaper . . . I don't expect that the Pulitzer judges will dramatically change their overall approach to prizes in the near term. [Neuharth emphasized the same point in a later speech: "*USA Today* is a newspaper that is designed, written and edited for readers and for the advertisers. Not for editors or publishers, not for reporters, not for journalism critics, but for readers and advertisers."]

Question: Has Gannett's growth awakened fears of too much media concentration?

Neuharth: Not in my mind. But I fully understand that bigness in the media makes some people a little nervous. The potential dangers are there, if there is overconcentration of the media. But I don't believe they are real dangers because readers, viewers and listeners are pretty sophisticated. They can pick and choose. Large media companies that deliver inferior news products to readers are just not going to get away with it for long.

When *USA Today* was launched it was offered on newsstands for 25 cents. In tune with Gannett's philosophy of hiking prices to whatever the market will bear, that bargain rate gave way on August 27, 1984, to a new 35-cent price.

But the price still wasn't enough to suit Neuharth, a marketing whiz in the newspaper business. He was fishing for the highest price people would pay for the new product, without cutting too deeply into circulation. It was a crucial choice. The paper needed every dime in revenues it could squeeze out. But if the price was too high, circulation growth would stall or drop, and that would mean less revenue from advertising, which is based on total circulation. The first price hike hurt circulation, but not severely. *USA Today* publisher Cathleen Black reported that circulation dipped less than 10 percent, then rebounded.

Neuharth was encouraged. Another move to 40 cents would add $13 million annually to the bottom line. But a jump to 50 cents could bring in even more. It was during one of his periodic "note-comparing" sessions with another media chief that Neuharth uncovered just the tip he needed to make the riskier move to 50 cents. Warren Phillips, chairman of Dow Jones & Company, confided to Neuharth that one of his mistakes had been raising *The Wall Street Journal*'s price from 35 cents—which takes two coins —to 40 cents, which required readers to fumble for three coins to buy the paper. Dow Jones had discovered—the hard way—that its readers were more upset by the inconvenience of having to dig for three coins than they were at paying the extra nickel.

(Phillips had been one of the few colleagues who publicly cheered Neuharth's venture. Calling *USA Today* "... a skillful execution of a well-thought-out concept," Phillips suggested that

103

with circulation falling at most other newspapers, publishers should keep their mouths shut unless they, too, were willing to take a risk like Neuharth's.)

Gannett's chief reasoned that his readers would just as easily part with two quarters as with a quarter and a dime. "We learned from the *Journal's* experience," says Neuharth, who decided not to repeat his colleague's blunder, and went directly to 50 cents—a two-coin price—precisely a year after the boost to 35 cents for *USA Today.* The price increase took effect on the same day "The Nation's Newspaper" published the fattest edition in its three-year history—a plump sixty pages with twenty-six pages of ads. In 1986, *USA Today* would zoom past the *Daily News* to become the second largest newspaper in the country in paid circulation, still trailing *The Wall Street Journal* by a wide margin. In "total readership"—accounting for multiple readers per copy—*USA Today* even claimed the number one position.

An Investment, Not a Loss

While Neuharth had made it clear that he was staking his personal reputation on *USA Today*, the corporation had much to gain or lose from the risk as well. Almost from the time Gannett went public in 1967, Wall Street analysts had been calling it one of the best-run, most consistently profitable newspaper companies in the country. Neuharth doubted that his risk would completely destroy Gannett's good graces on Wall Street, but he worried that analysts and investors might initially "misjudge" the bold venture.

"And they did," says Neuharth, who remained highly sensitive to Wall Street's reading of his risk. Gannett stock dropped four points the day after *USA Today* was announced, and lost several hundred million dollars in total market capitalization over the next three months. "We expected that might happen," admits Neuharth, "and we tried to put the venture in perspective. But understandably, some analysts, who liked the way the company was performing, were asking themselves, 'Here's a company with an outstanding earnings record. Why take the risk?' "

Neuharth, who had run Gannett on a "No Surprises" platform for years, has the answer to that question, and it fits America's best risk-taking traditions. Why risk? Because it was the only way to *build something new and valuable,* he says. Gannett was doing fine; it was making money; there was no urgent need to find a way of making more. But Neuharth took a risk anyway. It wasn't a risk in any negative sense to Neuharth, it was an *investment.*

Throughout the years of mounting losses, Allen Neuharth steadfastly maintained that only two things could jeopardize the ultimate profitability of *USA Today:* "Either very very poor management on our part, or a major national depression." No hedging here. And with statements like that, Neuharth kept the heat on his staff, and himself, to have a profitable enterprise after five years. The *Los Angeles Times* reported a Gannett executive saying, "*USA Today* is the fulcrum on which the whole reputation of Gannett and particularly Neuharth lives and dies. If it breaks even on schedule, Neuharth will retain his clout. If it is not profitable, however, there could be a board revolution. . . . If the board votes to close *USA Today,* I think Al would resign," an informal offer Neuharth had made before the paper was ever launched. *The Wall Street Journal* added its assessment: "So much of Gannett's reputation and resources ride on *USA Today* that if it fails, Mr. Neuharth's other grand plans could falter."

Neuharth, however, didn't see the point of being too rigid about schedules. "If you are confident that your risk will be ultimately successful enough to give you the risk reward, then I think it would be unwise to look at the calendar and say, well, gee, it's December 31, did we have a profitable period? And if not then let's lock the door. We won't approach it that way.

"We attempted to get them [Wall Street analysts and stockholders] to understand that this was an *investment* [his emphasis], and they had seen us make many investments involving many dollars over the years and had often questioned whether we were paying too big a price for those investments. But they had always been satisfied ultimately that the investment was okay. *USA Today* was simply a bigger investment than the individual ones we had made up until that time. But we believed that the risk/reward ratio was better than for a smaller investment because we were going to get a bigger return. Just saying that wasn't enough, and many people still thought it was a little experiment that would go belly-up in a year or two," says Neuharth.

Even with *USA Today*'s losses cutting into corporate earnings,

105

however, Gannett managed to post gains each quarter throughout even the newspaper's worst period, "although I think we came a little close there in the first quarter of 1983," admits Neuharth. Some analysts were unimpressed. However they looked at it, "Neuharth's Nonsense" was stealing 40 to 60 cents in per-share earnings from company stockholders, and even though gains elsewhere more than made up the difference, Gannett shares by the end of *USA Today*'s first year were said by some investment firms to have no particular appeal.

Neuharth, his board of directors and his Gannett team stuck with it. By the time *USA Today* entered its fifth year, revenues were up and losses were declining. The paper's 1986 revenues reached an estimated $220 million, up $50 million from the year before. That year, *USA Today* accounted for 10 percent of revenue gains from Gannett's newspaper business, and the company announced that *USA Today*'s losses had dropped significantly.

Through it all, Gannett's stock continued an upward trek. The per-share price of Gannett stock jumped more than 300 percent (not counting the regular dividends that were also paid) between 1981 and 1987—the most critical money-losing years in *USA Today*'s young life. Although *USA Today* exacted a heavy toll on Gannett's ledgers, dividends paid to shareholders were increased each year, nevertheless, by an average of 9 percent annually. There could be no carping about "Neuharth's Nonsense" from the company's stockholders.

Allen "No-Guts" Neuharth began winning plaudits for his risk taking from Wall Street and American business luminaries, academia and even the journalism profession. "Gannett is dependable," declared one stock advisory service. "It has displayed an enviable stamina even as its increasing size and market diversity have exposed it more to the rigors of economic uncertainty. The credit goes to management whose fine-tuned sense of business has enabled Gannett to deploy its capital effectively." An analyst with the investment banking firm Kidder, Peabody & Company was more succinct, describing Al Neuharth as "a genius leader."

In 1984, 1985 and 1986, *Fortune* magazine's annual survey of the most admired corporations ranked Gannett second among all U.S. corporations as most admired for its innovativeness. That magazine also rated Gannett the most profitable of nineteen publishing companies in the Fortune 500. For several years running,

Financial World magazine named Neuharth "Outstanding Chief Executive of the Year" in the publishing industry, and the *Wall Street Transcript* plied similar honors. *Saturday Review* magazine dubbed *USA Today* one of America's most underrated products—"the perfect reflection of the way we live now; the future of newspapers and the most influential force in American journalism today." The Wharton School of Business honored Neuharth as one of America's outstanding entrepreneurs, and the *Washington Journalism Review* called him "an extraordinary press lord, still at the top of his form." Even the *Harvard Lampoon* found *USA Today* tempting, flooding newsstands with a parody version of the paper on its fourth anniversary in 1986. That, too, pleased the chairman, who later boasted that his publication was the youngest ever chosen as the subject of a *Harvard Lampoon* parody.

As it matured into a more steady product, the breezy *USA Today* was also honored by the journalism community, though perhaps indirectly. In 1986 its editor, John Quinn, was named editor of the year by the National Press Foundation, "because of the unique contribution that he and *USA Today* have made to print journalism."

Fred Smith, the entrepreneurial, risk-taking founder of Federal Express (as legend has it, Smith once met a Federal Express payroll in its early days with winnings from a Las Vegas blackjack table), also cites Gannett as a key example of innovative risk taking in American enterprise today. In one of his rarely granted interviews, Smith told *INC.* magazine, "Pogo, the cartoon character, pointed out one time that the way to be a great leader is to see a parade and run like hell to get in front of it. I don't know many innovations where somebody sort of just dreamed up an idea out of the clear blue and went off. I mean, there are usually some fairly discernible trends available for a long time indicating a demand for a product or a service. And the time to act on that—to get to the front of the parade—is when that demand and the technology needed to meet it begin to converge.

"Take the example of Gannett and *USA Today*," says Smith. "We've been a national society in America for about 25 years now, largely as a result of television, but it is only recently that you could describe anything like a market for a national newspaper.

107

And that's because there was only recently the technology available to send the copy via satellite to print sites all around the country quickly and inexpensively. So there was the convergence of a societal change or expectation and a technology that allowed someone to fulfill it. Al Neuharth was one of the first to see it.

"He's been sitting there taking it on the chin year after year, with hundreds of millions in dollars worth of losses. But I think he's going to prevail. . . . Remember, Neuharth didn't have to start *USA Today* to pay the dividends and turn on the lights. But I think he was aware of a threat to his existing business—Gannett's local newspapers. There is, to one degree or another, a death cycle underway with the local papers. The TV gets you the news faster now, and has more or less co-opted the trendy, glitzy part of the news. And for more in-depth discussion of the issues, there are many other vehicles that do it better. So what the local newspaper is left with is the births and deaths and marriages and the latest stabbings and the stupid machinations of local politicians. Long term, you've got to say that, other than as a direct-mail advertising medium, the papers have lost much of their rationale." Neuharth recognized the same cycle, but interpreted it a little differently. Instead of acquiescing to television's growing influence, he decided to remake the American newspaper in a new image designed to appeal to changing consumer taste.

"It's at that point," notes Smith, "that the innovator says to himself, 'Now's the time that I ought to take a risk. I see the threat on the supply side. I see the opportunity on the demand side. And, oh, by the way, I'd like to do something new and useful and important.' And when that happens, that's when organizations tend to innovate."

Malcolm Forbes, Sr., chief mechanic of the Forbes publishing empire, part-time business pundit and longtime proponent of constructive business risk taking, first suggested Neuharth's gamble was folly. "When they announced their plans for *USA Today*," stated Forbes in 1982, "I would not have bet a nickel on it. In fact, I would have sold my [Gannett] stock." But three years later Malcolm marveled at Neuharth's pluck. "In daily newspapers, deaths far outnumber births," wrote Forbes in the pages of his magazine. "Not many today have pockets deep enough, enough blood in their fiscal veins to hemorrhage every day until a new newspaper can get a healthy hold. Gannett's Al Neuharth is that rare one—strong of heart, with exciting vision and fiscal muscle. The result? *USA Today* is apt to become one of the most extraordinary concepts and successes in U.S. press history. It's colorfully alive, chockablock with arresting features and ample McNuggetted news . . . I bet, and we can all ardently hope, *USA Today* is here to stay." Neuharth was amused by Forbes's flip-flop. "A very thick skin is one of the ingredients necessary to entrepreneurship," he says. And if imitation is indeed the sincerest form of flattery, British press lord Robert Maxwell flattered Neuharth with his plan to launch a European daily modeled on *USA Today.*

Nobody was calling him "No-Guts Neuharth" anymore. By·the latter 1980s, in addition to its newspapers, Gannett also owned and operated ten television stations, including the number one rated station in Washington, D.C., and stations in Boston, Phoenix, Atlanta, Minneapolis and Denver. Neuharth alone controls 10 percent of the nation's TV market—a share he intends to push higher. There were also sixteen Gannett-owned radio stations around the country by that time. And, of course, there was *USA Today,* which in its sixth year had grown to about 1.7 million circulation, and a claimed total readership of some 5 million people. Gannett also owns *USA Weekend,* a Sunday supplement magazine it bought from CBS in 1985 for $43 million.

If those aren't enough ways for Gannett media properties to influence consumer minds, the company also owns the largest outdoor advertising business in North America. If they don't reach you via the morning paper you read, the radio station you listen to, or the television station you watch, they'll get you with billboards while you're driving down the road. To find out what you're thinking, Gannett uses the poll-taking organization it owns, Louis Harris & Associates—acquired for about $4 million cash in 1975. Neuharth also has his own book publishing division.

Gannett is now venturing into producing TV programs as well. A Gannett venture produced the *America Today* news program for a hundred and fifty PBS stations, and joined with Robert MacNeil and James Lehrer to produce *The MacNeil/Lehrer NewsHour.*

The best fit for Neuharth's risk-taking style, however, was Gannett's partnership with GTG Entertainment, created by former NBC programming wizard Grant Tinker. With $40 million of backing from Neuharth, GTG introduced a televised version of *USA Today* with the same name. Like its print sibling, the TV version was to be a breezy, entertaining information show (not quite "news"), taking its lead from stories headed into the next day's paper. GTG had 156 stations signed up for the program when it debuted in September 1988 to very poor reviews.

The irony of a newspaper patterned on television now producing its own television program wasn't lost on the journalism establishment. "I've always thought of *USA Today* [the paper] as a television program that you can wrap fish in," former CBS news guru Fred Friendly told *The Wall Street Journal*. "This completes the circle."

Neuharth loves to keep track of it all. On the wall behind his enormous white stone desk is a map of the nation, with tiny lights indicating the locations of Gannett properties. Company operatives constantly travel the country searching for more properties so the boss can keep adding lights to his map.

The executive suite in Gannett's Arlington, Virginia, headquarters, at the edge of Washington, D.C., hardly bespeaks Neuharth's humble South Dakota roots. Nor is humble a word often used to describe the Neuharth personality. The size of his ego fits the size of his risks. This is a temperamental man who'll call somebody an S.O.B. at a staff meeting, who has commissioned the minting of special company coins with his likeness, and who has erected a huge bust of himself in the lobby of corporate headquarters.

On a crisp October day there's a morning fire crackling in one region of his personal office, which has a view from here to eternity. Just outside the boundary of a city that allows no buildings taller than twelve or fourteen stories—so as not to block the view of the U.S. Capitol and other cherished monuments—Allen Neuharth is perched on the thirty-first floor of a silver bullet structure a stone's throw from the Potomac River, Kennedy Center, Watergate and the Lincoln Memorial, and out of reach of the bureaucrats who control such matters as building heights. The Gannett operation run from this location spans thirty-nine states, the District of Columbia, the Virgin Islands, Canada, Great Britain, Guam, Hong Kong, Singapore and Switzerland. The company employs over 36,000 people (about 2,000 on *USA Today*) and has about 11,000 public shareholders.

110

Gannett would be even larger if Neuharth always got what he wanted. In 1985 he tried to buy *U.S. News & World Report*. Boston real estate tycoon Mort Zuckerman beat him to it. Neuharth even proposed a friendly merger of Gannett and CBS the year of Ted Turner's futile bid to capture the broadcasting giant; and also talked merger with Time Inc. Both deals fizzled.

The last quarter of Neuharth's critical five-year game plan would be *USA Today*'s first profitable one. Ad revenues that year soared 40 percent to over $100 million. The big celebration came June 16, 1987, when *USA Today* posted its first monthly profit ever. Reuters news service filed this story, datelined Arlington, Virginia:

> *USA Today*, the Gannett Company's flagship national newspaper, posted its first monthly profit ever in May, six months ahead of schedule, Gannett's president, John Curley, said. *USA Today*, the colorful newspaper that had been losing money since it was founded in September 1982, had a $1.1 million operating profit in May, compared with a loss of nearly $900,000 the previous month, Mr. Curley said. The breakthrough in profitability "confirms that *USA Today* is here to stay," he said at a news conference.

Even though soaring newsprint costs and an industrywide slowdown in advertising growth torpedoed profits for the paper's sixth year and kept that goal an elusive one, *USA Today* had indeed cleared its highest risk hurdles.

BOOK
III
SEEING THROUGH
THE RISK MIND

"Security is mostly a superstition. It does not exist in nature, nor do the children of men as a whole experience it. Avoiding danger is no safer in the long run than outright exposure. Life is either a daring adventure or nothing."

—HELEN KELLER

RISK DYNAMIC #9

THINKING AND PERCEIVING DIFFERENTLY

"When the risk is taken out, there isn't much left."

—SIGMUND FREUD

"Everything worthwhile carries the risk of failure. I have to take risks every day. I'd rather not, but the world doesn't give [us] that option. . . . You're never going to get what you want out of life without taking some risks. . . . "

—LEE IACOCCA

What is it that makes one person more willing to take risks than another person? Many psychologists who have studied the risk-taking mind claim that risk takers *think* differently than risk avoiders. Risk takers see relationships between events and trends in enterprise, and their nuances, that other people haven't yet seen, or will never see. Risk takers *perceive* risk differently than risk avoiders. Where most people perceive safety, risk takers may perceive peril. And what the risk avoider considers dangerous the risk taker may view primarily as *opportunity*.

Consider Michael Milken's tenure as high-yield bond chief at the investment banking firm Drexel Burnham Lambert. By inventing new forms of financing based on so-called junk bonds, Milken radically changed the way much of American industry finances itself. Nobody had thought about junk bonds the way Michael Milken did. Other financiers considered them, well, *junk*. Milken saw in them a great, untapped opportunity, and his unique perception of bond risk radically shook the business of finance. He preached that companies *had* to change and take risks to keep up—to tap opportunities before change in a more negative sense was *forced* upon them.

In one of his rare interviews, Milken described a classic case of opposing risk perceptions: U.S. Treasury securities. Investors from widows in Des Moines to giant pension funds own them because, common wisdom holds, they are the safest investment around. Since Uncle Sam prints the money, he can never default. But, Milken told *Forbes*, Treasuries "have tremendous interest rate risk. In my 20 years in business you could have gone bankrupt several times investing in Treasuries." That's because even though the Treasury security itself is fully guaranteed, *the market in which it trades is not*. If interest rates rise the market assigns your Treasury security a lower value than what you paid for it. If you sold then, you'd take a loss.

Working at Drexel in the mid-1970s, Milken took a contrary view of traditional bond financing techniques. He surmised that bloated corporate giants which were awarded the highest bond ratings, and which had long earnings histories, wouldn't necessarily be the survivors in a world of accelerating economic change. He cited General Motors in the early 1980s as an example. GM was cash-rich—the earnings champ of the auto industry—so it did nothing to change. Poor old Ford, meanwhile, started experimenting, taking more risks. By 1986, Ford had galloped past GM, and for the first time in decades topped its larger rival's earnings.

The leaders, the risk takers, observed Milken, are always probing, always looking to change course if conditions change, or if previous decisions simply appear to have been wrong. Milken argued that *future* earnings were more important to a company

116

and its investors than past earnings on which ratings are largely based. And those future earnings would come from the best-managed smaller companies—companies already taking risks and producing change, but that were often unable to raise needed capital because their low-rated debt (bonds) was considered "junk" on Wall Street.

All this revolutionary change wrought by Milken might have remained positive had he and other Drexel executives not chosen to use high-yield bonds another way—to pay for hostile corporate takeovers. In 1988 the Securities and Exchange Commission (SEC) accused Drexel, and Milken, of a laundry list of securities law violations stemming from the firm's dealings with such takeover stocks. The civil charges (the SEC lacks authority to file criminal charges) included insider trading, stock manipulation and fraud.

As *The Wall Street Journal* observed September 8, 1988, "That Mr. Milken should have such an exalted place in these controversies is at least in part a reflection of the enormous changes he has helped bring about in the financial world. Thanks largely to his efforts, a generation of entrepreneurs has been able to raise sums of money they could once only dream about. . . . Whatever one thinks of Mr. Milken, he clearly is a man who, more than most, isn't interested in traveling with the crowd."

Milken changed Wall Street's thinking, and brought high-yield bonds into the economic mainstream. His brush with the law highlights the fine line that often exists between positive risk taking and more extreme actions that go beyond legal boundaries. Still, it was largely through Milken's architecture and insight that billions of dollars in static capital were routed to more dynamic, risk-oriented uses, even if some people disagree with the wisdom of that shift. Among the early beneficiaries were Triangle Industries, MCI and Stephen Wynn's Golden Nugget Inc.

One of the changes Milken said American corporations must risk in order to stay competitive is to pay workers, in part, with equity interests in the company. One man who built a company around that concept is Robert A. Swanson, founder and CEO of Genentech, and an individual who embodies many risk-taking dynamics. In the 1970s, before the term "genetic engineering" entered the American lexicon, it was Swanson who believed that

117

the *theories* scientists had just identified could lead to commercially valuable *products* much sooner than anyone else realized. He went on to construct the world's pace-setting genetic engineering company.

Because they think differently, ARTists like Swanson find it easier to take risks and be creative or innovative. Dr. Frank Farley, a psychologist at the University of Wisconsin (UW) who has been studying the risk-taking personality for over twenty years, believes risk takers use "transmutative" or "transformational" thinking. It's this form of thinking that permits riskers in enterprise to more easily translate one way of seeing a problem or issue into a different way of viewing it. Swanson took the *idea* of producing valuable pharmaceutical substances in microscopic genetic factories, and built around it a real, workable structure to begin the enterprising process of moving from point A (idea) to point B (the commercial product). Likewise, Milken latched onto what had been an obscure financial instrument, saw how differently it could be used, and changed the way companies and investors alike thought about junk bonds.

Risk takers using this form of transmutative thinking can take an idea, swivel it under the light like a prism, and see that seemingly bland, yellowish light anew, broken down into all its glorious colors. They see enterprise for what it is—full of paradox, without borders, often disturbing to conventional beliefs. In this plot line, intuition plays a key role in recognizing opportunities and figuring out new ways to exploit them.

"In their minds, *risk takers can see analogies and similarities better than many other people*," says Farley, whose studies of physical riskers have made him one of the nation's leading authorities on the psychology of risk. They approach risks from many angles, and it gives them more confidence, better odds and greater creativity. They "transform" or "transmute" one way of thinking into another, thus supporting their own risk urges.

By contrast, risk avoiders tend to think and see things in one light only. Problems have one solution—often "the way it's always been done." Lack of risk taking blocks their ability to devise creative solutions. For Swanson, on the other hand, the words "It can't be done" are unknown. Colleagues say his mind is highly focused on his goals and that he will forever prod employees to find a way to accomplish those things that "can't be done."

Different Motivations

The ARTist's basic motivation in enterprise also differs from what motivates the risk averter. The main motivation and highest ranking goals of the financial risk taker, according to the UW psychologist, are success and competence. The main goal of a financial risk *avoider* is achieving happiness. "And here's the interesting thing," says Farley. "We find that the financial risk takers, for whom success and competence are major goals, are already typically quite happy people. They are happy in the *process* of their risk taking. It goes with the territory. While their opposites, the financial risk avoiders, see happiness as a goal."

Risk takers have a strong desire to feel competent at what they are doing in business—*to feel they are having an impact.* They crave a self-perception of competence, skill and influence that is achieved by taking risks. "How do you get that sense of competence?" asks Farley. "You get it through acting on the world. That's how you come to know yourself. If you never act on the world, take chances and do something, then it's going to be harder for you to come to know yourself and know your competence."

Farley's "Type T" (as he calls them) risk-taking personalities— the "T" comes from thrill-seeking—are motivated by uncertainty, the unknown, novelty and risk. "If you're not willing to expose yourself to uncertainty or the unknown then you don't have much of a chance of being very creative in this life," he says. "And I believe that entrepreneurs are creative; they are creating new enterprises, just as an artist is a risk taker and creates new conceptions of the world around us, or like a great scientist who creates a new conception of physical reality that is a form of risk taking." It's risky because they are entering the unknown, the realm of uncertainty, according to Farley. "The greatest scientists, for example, live their lives out there on the edge of uncertainty, breaking the bounds of knowledge, going way beyond what we now know. And in a sense, an entrepreneur is also going beyond what we have now and creating a new thing—and that's risky."

Only a distinct minority of the population belongs to Farley's "Big T" personality category. "As a group they tend to be more creative and more extroverted, take more risks, have more experimental artistic preferences and prefer more variety in their sex lives. . . . Their tendency to seek the novel, the unknown and the

119

uncertain, combined with their risk-taking characteristic, further enhances their likelihood of being creative. . . . I believe these are the people who are likely to have enormous impact on our society's character—for good and ill," he says.

How do Farley's Big Ts do in enterprise? "They are likely to be unhappy and ineffective in a highly structured work environment, particularly one that emphasizes routinized performance and rigid top-down management. Providing them with the right work environment—one low in structure and authoritarianism but high in arousal value—may be the ticket to greater creative production."

Yet another distinguishing factor of the risk-taking mind is its jealous regard for independence of judgment. Farley's Type Ts like to make their own decisions; they like to have elbow room, freedom of choice. For them, a key ingredient of having ideas and taking risks is the independence and freedom to go ahead and take them.

Does gender influence the willingness to take risks? Opinions on that issue have clashed. Male executives have often used the women-aren't-risk-takers argument to avoid hiring women for higher-risk, higher-paying corporate positions. Yet, what psychological research exists on the subject tends to show no significant difference between the risk-taking desires of men and women. Just one example: A study of investment preferences of men and women published in *The Journal of Psychology* found that there is no difference between the sexes in the emphasis they place on a desire for investment security. Many factors affect the decision to take risks with capital, this study concluded, but sex is not one of them.

Farley maintains that while men tend to take more physical risks, woman are equally active risk takers in other realms: "Risk can occur in many arenas, and I think that female risk taking may be more channeled in the direction of the psychological side of risk taking. We find in our research that women express a strong interest in entrepreneurship, in financial risk taking. They indicate the drive and desire in those areas." What often blocks their risk efforts, Farley argues, is a shortage of backing and opportunity—start-up loans for a new business, for example.

Today women are routinely taking up ART—arguably, at a

growth rate considerably higher than for male riskers. If you consider that change involves risk and uncertainty, then the movement of more and more women into business, including starting their own companies, puts them square in the ranks of active, creative risk takers. According to U.S. Department of Education figures, the number of women earning MBA degrees skyrocketed over 300 percent from the mid-1970s to the mid-80s. At the same time, MBAs awarded to men increased only 25 percent. And the federal government's Bureau of Labor Statistics reports that the ranks of self-employed women have also swelled. Over the ten years to 1987, the number of self-employed women leaped some 50 percent. The number of self-employed men grew only about 10 percent over the same period.

Some women have been unable to find adequate outlets for their risk-taking desires within the corporate structure. They are finding—in record numbers—that going into business for themselves is a better answer, and one that fulfills a chief goal of today's entrepreneurial risk taker (male or female)—*greater control.* "The time comes when you say either you're going to stay and remain on the treadmill, or you're going to move out and make things happen for yourself," says one of the many women who left the corporate sphere to become an entrepreneur. "The pats on the back do not really substitute for true growth."

Michaela Walsh, president of Women's World Banking, which helps women worldwide obtain venture financing, says: "I think that women's attitudes about risk taking and the types of risks they take are different than the attitudes of men and the types of risks men take. I think women tend to function in smaller arenas, and tend to be more pragmatic. Risk taking by women is much more related to their own family environment. Men, I think, tend to think more on the grand scale, to take risks for conquering the world. Women will take risks incrementally—more risks, smaller scale risks. They tend to deal in more complex relationships than men."

A related opinion comes from Paula Mannillo, director of finance for the Women's Economic Development Corporation, in St. Paul, Minnesota: "Women do concern themselves considerably with how they are going to run their lives, and with balancing their lives between work and family and all the other obligations that women frequently have. So there is a great deal of concern about how they structure and take risks. I think that women take risks in a different way. They judge risks not only in terms of money and reputation and so forth, but more in terms of how it might affect the rest of their life, in ways that sometimes men may not."

What makes one woman more willing to take risks than another? The same things, it would appear, that drive men. Mannillo contends, "There is an indefinable quality that I find in people who do decide to go ahead, and it has something to do with persistence and drive. The people who go ahead and really get their businesses up and going have this quality of doggedness, of not giving up, of figuring out another way if the first way doesn't work."

The Mastery of Risk

Dr. Suzy Boehm, a White Plains, New York, psychologist, says that risk taking and the concept of "mastery"—the idea that you *can* succeed at something—are closely related for women, as they are for men. Here again, there appears to be little difference in how the two sexes approach risk taking. "You take a risk with the idea that you can master something," says Boehm. Women who feel that they are at a disadvantage when competing against male-dominated businesses may be less inclined to take the risks necessary to proceed. But the women who have gained enough confidence in their abilities as riskers to see beyond gender are more apt to be bigger risk takers. Those whose risk taking has been reinforced, either by success or by *positive* failures, find risk taking easier. Comments by women riskers support Boehm's contentions. As one woman entrepreneur in Massachusetts said, "You learn a lot about your capabilities by putting yourself on the line. Running a successful business isn't only a financial risk. It's an emotional risk as well. I get a lot of satisfaction from having dared it—done it—and been successful."

The process begins early in life. "I think that's what you are talking about with girls when they are young and keep being told, 'Be careful!' Girls are told that more often than boys, and that reinforces a risk aversion," observes Boehm. "As a result, women don't grow up with the sense that they can try something that may be scary and succeed, where males may have had that kind of experience growing up." According to this psychologist, "The women who are at a point in business where they are taking risks have already overcome so much that they are not necessarily a representative sampling of women. They are women who have been brought up one way and are acting in another way. In some cases they may be overcompensating. They may be taking more risks because they have to prove that they are not averse to taking risks. In the business world, I think that overcompensation has been an issue with women."

Walsh points out that risk taking by women in enterprise differs in other parts of the world. She says the willingness to take risks is often linked to the cultural role that women play. "In some cultures, women are just incredibly powerful in business; in others, their role is not as entrepreneurs. If you look at West Africa, most women are traders, marketing types who work in a cash economy, and they are very effective and very powerful risk takers. If you look at some of the dynasties in Asia, they're really owned and controlled by women; and they do it quietly, and they are incredible wheelers and dealers and risk takers," she says.

Walsh goes along with the idea that although women are inherently no more risk-averse than anyone else, American society cast them in that role and made it a self-fulfilling prophecy in the past. "Women in the United States have not been conditioned to look at risk in a positive way," says Walsh. "I think most women have regarded risk, particularly as far as money is concerned, as a frightening or a more negative result. In other words, they are conditioned that if you take a risk you are going to lose; while the fact is, if you take a risk, generally you will win. But they have not been conditioned that way. It's a socialization process that begins in childhood."

People who feel they control their own lives are more willing to be bold. Anyone—male or female—who lacks the feeling of control may also lack a strong inclination to take business risks.

A FUTURE FORTUNE 500 RISK TAKER

Colombe Nicholas says the single most critical element behind *her* risk taking is precisely the type of control the risk psychologists talk about. Nicholas is president of Christian Dior America, among the largest concerns in the United States headed by a woman. She describes herself as a "clear-cut risk taker"—perhaps a necessity in the fickle business of fashion. Growing up in Piqua, Ohio, in the early 1950s, and later as a young teen living in Montreux, Switzerland, Nicholas has led a driven life. Always hearing "You can do it" from her parents reinforced her own natural tendencies to be a risk taker, she says. "Try it. What's the worst that can happen? You can fail; then you try something else," they would say.

Today, as head of Christian Dior America, the U.S. arm of a French parent company, Nicholas directs licensing and product development in the United States. Dior has annual revenues of some $380 million. In the volatile, desultory business of fashion, only the strongest, most innovative risk takers survive for very long. "I was never made to fear failure," says Nicholas, explaining why she does not fear taking business risks. "And as a result, I just naturally tried harder. If I did something that didn't work out, my parents would say, 'Gee, that's too bad. I know you're going to do a heck of a lot better the next time. How are you going to do it the next time so that doesn't happen again?' Failure was always put behind me, and the next sentence was, 'How are we going to move forward and do better?' " The same approach works for her as a corporate chief executive.

In 1980, Dior's new French corporate parent wanted to move more aggressively in the United States. That's when Nicholas became the newly Americanized corporation's first, and so far only, president, with a mandate to, as Nicholas puts it, "grow the business." Despite periodic financial woes at the parent company, Nicholas grasped that mandate and held on. As head of a separately incorporated U.S. subsidiary of a foreign parent, she found herself with autonomy over the U.S. market, including her most crucial tasks of product development and design, and strategies for marketing and advertising.

Nicholas knew immediately that a new image strategy had to be devised. But the risks were formidable. Christian Dior himself had died in 1957. The image that he had created—one of classic designer elegance backed by high-quality product—was deeply ingrained in the fashion marketplace. Nicholas needed to make big changes to "grow the business" without prostituting Dior's tradition of elegance. "When your designer is dead the only thing you have to keep is the name," she says. "You have to maintain the integrity of the designer's name."

She also knew she needed to gain the attention of the department store buyers who determine what merchandise reaches the selling floor and ultimately the hands of the consumer. "We had to show them that Christian Dior was not a stodgy old company, that we were progressive and that we intended to keep pace," she explains. "But how do you do that? So I told myself we really needed to come up with an advertising campaign that would be rather controversial, and shocking and unusual and daring."

Within months of that decision Dior had just such a campaign, which became known as the Three Diors (a concept borrowed from the exploits of three people in the Noël Coward play *Private Lives*). The ads featuring the trio—two men and a woman—carried a strong hint of a scandalous *ménage à trois*. Over the objections of some Dior licensees, who pay the bulk of the advertising expense, and predictions of doom by some fashion business naysayers, Nicholas launched the controversial campaign in 1982. "It's amazing the effect that the campaign had on buyers of department stores," she reports. "Department stores hated it, loved it, whatever you might want to say. But they noticed it. Buyers would come up and say, 'Boy, that Christian Dior line looks terrific.' It was the same product as six months before, but they had not looked at it in a contemporary light.

"It could have backfired. The buyers could have said, 'Dior should stay in its place. They're just classic, they're elegant,'" says Dior America's president. "And I might have lost more than just the consumers if they had said, 'That's not *my* Dior. The Dior I know isn't involved in these wicked things.' So I think it was a chance that I took, but it paid off. It totally revolutionized my marketing strategy and Dior's position in the U.S. market."

"It's not a science. That's the trouble," Nicholas continues, trying to explain the business of fashion. "Whether skirts should be long or short, or green doesn't sell." For her, making those decisions, taking those kinds of risks is based on "a gut feeling. I'll look at it and say, 'You can't give that away.' Why do I know you can't give that away? I couldn't begin to tell you. It's just that over the years I've developed a sense of taste."

125

If the decision is more black and white, Nicholas is a "cut to the bone" manager. "I always try to reduce things to the most simple common denominator," she says. "What is the problem? You get the person to focus on cutting through everything that's out there. There are so many extemporaneous things going on around us that don't really apply—yet people *think* they apply— that it's hard to get them to focus only on what we're trying to achieve" with the decision or risk at hand.

Nicholas is a compulsive list maker, too—a big joke around the Christian Dior America headquarters on Broadway in New York's fashion district. She views herself as a "fixer"—identifying problems, fixing them, and moving on to other things. "But I don't know why," she reflects. "Maybe it's confidence in myself, confidence in my ability." And she does credit her law degree with helping her think more analytically—a quality that both contributes to her willingness to take risks and to the chances those risks will be successful.

Failure isn't part of her vocabulary. "I never think of failure," she says. "I refuse to accept that. And I beat the people up around me; we never discuss that. It might have to do with my personality. I am a rather positive person. And if you yourself don't believe in something 100 percent, how the hell do you expect anybody else to? Somewhere, when I decide to go for it, I will just block out that it might not succeed. I think that you have a gut feeling that it's going to work. And you know I've never been able to describe why I've been able to know that this was the thing to do. I don't think it's something I learned in school. I think it's street sense. I can't define it, but I know it's there and I know I've got it."

Others seem to agree. Within seven years of taking over, Colombe Nicholas's aggressive leadership had boosted Dior America's revenues nearly threefold, while the number of product licenses, which she negotiates individually, jumped 50 percent. *The Wall Street Journal* named her one of the five women most likely to be running a Fortune 500 company in the 1990s. For Nicholas, the motivation for taking risks in business is perfectly clear: "Hitting the home run," she states without hesitation. "And it's self-satisfaction. I find it absolutely the most boring thing to be safe. And if I do have a weakness, it is that I do take risks to the point of being controversial.

"You have to decide what motivates you in life. And I think what motivates you changes during different times in your life. At some point you're very motivated by money," Nicholas says. "But there comes a time when you're earning enough money that it matches up with what you perceive to be a comfortable lifestyle. The money becomes secondary, and then you start to look at the power that is involved in your job—how many people do I control, am I a decision maker, am I the master of my own destiny?"

BIOTECH'S MILD-MANNERED RISK TAKER

"It is almost impossible to exaggerate the importance to the general welfare of the willingness of individuals to take a personal risk. The worst thing that can happen to a society, as to an individual, is to become terrified of uncertainty."

—WALTER WRISTON,
former chairman, Citibank

There's a bit of Indiana Jones in Robert A. Swanson, founder and CEO of Genentech, Inc., the world's leading biotechnology company. He's a mild-mannered businessman on the surface. But Swanson is in the risk trenches daily, battling for the Holy Grail of biotechnology. He aims to build the nation's first new, fully integrated pharmaceuticals company to be created in decades. He may already have succeeded, but won't admit it. This destined-to-be-great corporation, launched one beery night in 1976 on Swanson's belief in a radical new technology called genetic engineering, arose because its founder conceived a new enterprise ten years before others thought it possible. Then he was willing to bet on it, and—most importantly, perhaps—entice scores of other talented people to do the same.

Although he didn't frame his first dollar from the sale of a biotechnology product until 1985, Swanson aspired to sell over $1 billion in genetically engineered goods by the early 1990s. The

127

soft-spoken, cherry-cheeked and balding superstar of the biotechnology business tenants a cramped corner of Genentech's swelling ten-building compound in South San Francisco on a thumb of earth jutting into the bay. On a table there's a copy of *Fortune* magazine, which once described Swanson as "an unimpressive-looking fellow." His persona combines a touch of understated 1970s California-style mellow with a hint of East Coast liberalism turned middle-aged.

A conversation with Swanson is filled with little gulps of silence, as he ponders each sentence. His comments often trail off to incompleteness as his mind works on a new idea. Beneath the bespectacled facade of Genentech's chief, however, there's a biobusinessman of steel. He rolled the dice to start a new company based on a barely discovered technology. And he bet that his tiny firm would be first to commercialize the products of genetic engineering, years ahead of when the experts predicted it would be possible. Now the new industry this ARTist helped create could be the most promising enterprise of the 1990s. That's when the biggest fruits of risks taken by Swanson and others will be harvested.

For Bob Swanson, whose early risk taking made him godfather of biotechnology while he was still in his early thirties, the decision to take the biggest business risks in his life first required that he undertake some mental time travel. In the battle to launch Genentech in the mid-1970s, Swanson grappled inside himself with the many risks. At home in his San Francisco apartment, the MIT grad thought about the consequences of failure—for his friends and associates, for the investors who had agreed to back him, and for himself. He thought about the black eye his own young career would suffer, too. "Putting all of that into perspective was very important to me," Swanson said years later in an interview at the bustling Genentech headquarters, where construction is a constant.

As he struggled with those early risk choices, Swanson projected himself far into the future. "I tried to imagine myself as an old man, looking back over my past life, at a time when it was too late to change anything," he explains in his painfully reserved fashion, a personal trademark. "And I was saying to myself, 'What would you have wanted to do? What kinds of decisions would you have wanted to make? Would you have wanted to stay in venture capital? Would you have wanted to start your own company and given it a shot, even if it failed? Or would you have wanted to move into management within a larger organization at a time of change?' " he says. "It was a way of determining what things were really important to me."

Those mental gymnastics helped Swanson dissolve lingering doubts he had about making a commitment to risk launching Genentech. "For me the answer came as I looked back," he recalls. "The answer was, 'Go for it. You're not going to like yourself as well when you're that old man if you don't decide to take the risk and start your own company now.' " Swanson set his plan and charged ahead.

Over a decade later Swanson was still charging. His goal, from the start, had been clear: build a new pharmaceuticals company from the ground up, based on technologies yet to be invented, and reach over $1 billion in revenues by the early 1990s. The fact that medical science had scarcely whiffed the technological potential of genetic engineering was no impediment to Swanson, the young San Francisco venture capitalist. Others agreed that one day, in the distant future, the results of genetic engineering just might be commercialized. But to form a company *then*, a decade or more in advance, seemed foolhardy. Except to Robert Swanson, and a handful of others.

At MIT, Swanson had been fascinated with how raw ideas become finished products consumers hold in their hands. Here was the rawest of ideas—stitching genes obtained from DNA into host cells to produce useful human substances such as growth hormone, insulin, the anti–blood clotting agent TPA, vaccines for AIDS and herpes, dietary supplements and fertility aids, among dozens of others. Swanson leapt at the idea of bringing it into commercial reality. This recombinant DNA (rDNA) technology—later dubbed gene-splicing—had been described in scientific papers of the early 1970s, but it was still unproven. When Swanson considered forming a company, nobody had yet altered a living microorganism's genetic instructions and taught it to produce a substance it would not naturally produce.

Most scientists believed it could work—in theory. But few thought it could be accomplished soon. And fewer still believed it could produce *commercial* products—and corporate profits—

129

before this wide-eyed twenty-eight-old reached middle age. Other technological advances of this magnitude throughout history had taken that long or longer to evolve from pure science to business enterprise. Gene-splicing was at the very earliest point. It was pure, basic scientific research. And for drugs, which must survive rigid, bureaucratic testing requirements stretching years, the time period from idea to cash register could best be measured glacially. Those were the products Swanson wanted his company to make.

ARTist (active risk taker) Bob Swanson welcomes the positive, thoughtful type of risk that spawned his corporate slogan: "Make It Happen." "Maybe that slogan is related somehow to this positive form of risk taking," he says. "If you want to get something accomplished you have to figure out how to get it done. Your sense of risk has to be in the right area." And things *do* get done at Genentech. The company's unbroken string of biotechnology industry firsts stretches across more than a decade: first to clone, first to manufacture, first to win FDA approvals, first to sell, first to profit.

Creating a Risk Culture

Genentech became a microcosm of the business risk cycle, compressed into a single decade. From the germ of a spanking new technology, a major new corporation was formed. It became an instant leader, but needed continuous capital infusions, and creative, ARTful *leadership* to put it all together and hold it together during years when it survived primarily on hope and force of will —Swanson's will. It had to overcome intense technical, legal and financial obstacles.

Later its rapid growth and success posed new problems: how to maintain in a much larger organization the momentum and the risk-taking culture that had been easier to instill in a small entrepreneurial group?

As the 1980s were ending, Genentech's 2,000-member work force bulged with high-tech professionals with fat portfolios of Genentech stock accumulated over years of equity participation. In the beginning, however, the ultimate value of the stock was questionable. Swanson had lured many of his top-notch scientists

130

and managers with offers of shares in the company. Many doubted the stock would ever be worth anything, including top Genentech scientist David Goeddel, who sold five hundred of his shares early on. By 1988, he ruefully told *Barron's*, those five hundred would have grown to 120,000 shares, worth $5.5 million. Another early Genentech employee sold just enough of his initial cache of Genentech stock to purchase a Volkswagen. His comrades now figure it cost him about $1 million.

But Genentech's belief in sharing the wealth is best demonstrated by the likes of bubbly young Kathryn Bowman, a receptionist working from cramped quarters in one of Genentech's flock of squat blue and white buildings that seem to multiply like cells in a petri dish. "Whatever the stock price is the day you start to work for Genentech," she enthusiastically explains to a visitor, "is *your* price. You can continue to buy the stock at that price even if it goes up later." Employees receive a 15 percent discount from "their" price or the current price, whichever is less. The maximum they are allowed to buy at these prices is 15 percent of their yearly compensation. "I've only worked here for a year," Kathryn says, "but my sister worked here for eight years, and she's wealthy now."

Kathryn proudly clips any mention of Genentech from the San Francisco newspapers and tacks them to the temporary walls. A handmade sign near her desk announces: "Genentech sweatshirts on sale today, 3 p.m., $23. Checks only, no cash." An employee who arrives at three-thirty learns they are already sold out.

Just outside, the visitor parking spaces always seem full, while employee parking sports the occasional Jaguar or Porsche. White-smocked technicians with Genentech I.D. badges stroll the path along the shoreline where a few local fishermen cast their lines against the downtown skyline visible in the distance. During the summer, reports Kathryn, some people windsurf in the bay behind Genentech.

Most Genentech employees are stockholders, and together they own about 25 percent of the company's shares. Swanson's innovative move helped make that percentage so high. He, along with Tom Perkins, Genentech's chairman, invented something called "junior stock," which employees could buy at a big discount. But there was a catch to it. Those shares couldn't be traded unless Genentech reached set goals, thus providing a built-in incentive.

The idea caught on, but it had to be eliminated in 1984 when new business accounting standards forced companies to count the discount as a salary expense to the corporation. So Swanson turned to other methods instead. Stock ownership is just one thing that has made Genentech's employee turnover rate uncharacteristically low.

Swanson's goal, however, wasn't simply to make a lot of his employees wealthy. Instead, he carefully created a risk-taking atmosphere at Genentech that could still be compatible with the corporation's obligations to outside shareholders as a public company. Swanson described it in a conversation: "I think there is a major difference between a company that you own yourself 100 percent, and one that is public or has venture capital investors or outside investors. One of the things that we work at very hard at Genentech is creating an atmosphere for people to take risks, to maintain the sense of creativity and excitement and innovation that got us to where we are, even as we grow bigger. I think our long-term success will depend on providing the kind of atmosphere where those people can flourish and allow them to grow and develop, take risks and be innovative."

How close is that link between risk taking and innovation? Swanson sees both as highly personal things, that risk and risk taker are one, that innovator and innovation are the same. To Swanson, innovation is a *somebody*. "When you talk about innovation," he says, "you can't separate it from an individual. Innovation is somebody who sees something clearly that other people haven't yet seen, and is driven to accomplish it—to make it happen, if you will." The risks are greatest, he contends, if other people don't agree with you. In that case, you have to have much greater confidence that it's going to work out. That description, of course, fits Swanson himself.

How has he gone about perpetuating that risk-taking, innovation-seeking atmosphere? "I guess part of it is just worrying about it," he says. "That alone gets you maybe halfway there." He worries that the drive for change and creation of something new will diminish "once you've decided you've arrived." To illustrate, Swanson points to the rarity of repeat Nobel Prizes. His solution: *Create other goals.* "You know, a lot of people say Genentech is there. Well, I don't think we're there at all. We've got a long way to go to build a major, profitable, independent pharmaceutical company, which has been my goal from the beginning. I think continuing to take risks is an important part of the whole risk-taking equation."

Swanson sees himself as an informal manager, providing direction, excitement and an atmosphere for his people to achieve and take risks with Genentech: "One of the things that we felt was most important, and we describe this in our corporate philosophy, is to have minimum guidelines and procedures, giving employees a great deal of freedom within the company to apply their skills and knowledge. We make sure the goals of the company are very clear, and that people within the company know what has to be done. And then you give them a lot of flexibility to use their own creativity and skills to figure out the best way to get there, including taking risks, coming up with new ideas, different ways of approaching things. Then people who take reasonable risks that don't work out are rewarded instead of punished. The risks aren't all going to work out, so if your batting average is good enough that's all that matters." For Swanson, the important thing is that his people have taken intelligent risks to make something happen. If the result wasn't the one desired, so be it. It is initiative that earns rewards here.

Swanson describes his researchers as entrepreneurial. "And how do you manage such a crew?" He asks the question, and answers it himself: "It's easy. We don't work on any projects we can't get someone excited about. Sometimes it takes longer than others, but we never change the rule. Almost 70 percent of Genentech's resources are focused on our top five projects."

At Genentech, science and business have been blended like two fine coffees to create an even better brew. And Swanson continues to incubate cooperation between the two polarized endeavors in subtle ways. In one instance, early in the company's history, he placed his marketing department adjacent to the research department to increase the odds of constructive interaction. "If people are bumping into each other in the bathroom," he told *Technology Review* magazine, "they've got to talk to each other." *Technology Review*, edited at MIT, calls Genentech the Hertz of the biotechnology industry: "Swanson may dress and think like a hard-nosed executive, but he shares many of the egalitarian attitudes that his scientific recruits brought with them from

133

academia. And he has used that dualism in his own personality to create an environment at Genentech that encourages scientists to do creative work, while adhering to concrete business goals."

As Genentech grew larger, Swanson started to think more about the concept of leadership, and his role in heading an increasingly large population of employees. It's an area he became especially interested in after a visit to the Air Force Academy. "Having grown up in the anti-military Vietnam era," he says, "I really had a change of heart after that visit. It's a military kind of leadership, but I gained real respect for the Academy because there is really an effort to teach leadership. It was really impressive. I think there is some element of risk taking in leadership. What does it take to be a leader? Where do you learn how to be a leader? It isn't taught in business school."

The troops at Genentech rallied behind Swanson's goal of a billion-dollar company by the 1990s. Perhaps by sheer force of intellect, he showed them how their own constructive risk taking could put the company at the forefront of biotechnology's limitless vistas—vistas that their leader was one of the first to recognize. Swanson's ability to think differently, like a risk taker, and to continue building an ever-changing major corporation on the basis of a risk-taking corporate culture, helped create a new commercial industry that will affect millions of lives, altering forever the way we treat diseases. He wasn't the first to be awed by the potential of recombinant DNA technology. He wasn't the first to dream of the medical potential and financial riches possible from new genetically engineered drugs.

But he *was* first to risk proving that science *had* progressed far enough to produce a commercial product, and to *act* on that knowledge once he had it. The rewards of biotechnology are now coming true in part because the ARTist in Bob Swanson was willing to take those risks.

THE SPIRIT OF WEALTH
CREATION

*"If the animal spirits are dimmed and the
spontaneous optimism falters, leaving us to
depend on nothing but a mathematical
expectation, enterprise will falter and die."*

—JOHN MAYNARD KEYNES,
father of "Keynesian" economics

Risk taking in enterprise has gathered some momentum in recent
years. Business celebrities now talk more freely about the value
of taking chances. Lee Iacocca, for example, put his advice to the
next generation of business leaders in three words: *Think for
yourself.* "You might find it tough advice to take these days," the
Chrysler chairman told a graduating class at Duke University,
"because thinking for yourself doesn't seem to have much status
anymore. Today, no matter what the problem, somebody has already worked out the solution, and packaged it. . . .

"I've been talking to a lot of college presidents and professors
lately, and I always ask them, what do college kids want most
today? And they usually say, security—a nice safe, secure, pros-

135

perous future—and there's nothing wrong with that. But then I ask, what's their biggest hang-up? And they tell me it's the fear of screwing up—the fear of failure. Apparently, a lot of you aren't too crazy about the idea of taking risks. If that's true, you've got a problem, because you're never going to get what you want out of life without taking some risks. . . . Remember, everything worthwhile carries the risk of failure. I *have* to take risks every day. I'd rather not, but the world doesn't give you or me that option. . . .

"I gotta tell you, I just love people who work for me who take chances, make mistakes, learn from them, and then get back up and dust themselves off and move on. . . . So don't be afraid of a few risks," said Iacocca.

Even when it comes to simply finding and holding a job in the business sector, thinking has shifted as corporate CEOs embrace new standards. For example, no longer is simple "company loyalty" a desirable trait by itself. In the past, loyalty by veteran employees was considered a major virtue. It avoided the high cost of job turnovers and provided continuity for the corporate family. Fierce company/employee loyalty—in both directions—is one component that has made the Japanese system so different from American business.

Many American CEOs now think blind loyalty is overrated. Staunch loyalists are too often simple order-takers who contribute few leadership skills and even less innovative drive. They are risk averters, and companies are recognizing more often that they lack crucial leadership skills exemplified by risk takers. Corporate chiefs and the headhunters who supply warm executive bodies are placing greater emphasis on talent and willingness to take risks than on how long the person is likely to stick around. They'd rather have somebody do a great job for a short period than a mediocre job long-term. Many firms are nudging employees into taking more risks by linking their pay to performance. When the Hay Group, a Philadelphia consulting firm, surveyed five hundred medium and large companies, it found that nearly a hundred of them were broadening their use of incentive, risk-taking pay over straight salaries. "What this means—for more and more managers, professionals and technical workers—is that the days of a guaranteed salary that rose almost automatically every year are over," reported *The New York Times* in commenting on the trend.

It's a shift cheered by entrepreneurial-minded executives such as former Treasury Secretary William Simon, who now heads his own firm, Wesray. "Give them equity, not fat paychecks," Simon once told *Newsweek*. "You run the business differently when you think of it as your own money, not somebody else's," added William Farley, chairman of Farley Industries, a firm specializing in leveraged buyouts.

An Entrepreneurial Backlash

Lately, however, a backlash movement has developed. Its proponents argue that some American industries are being hurt by too many talented individuals leaving to start their own companies. Two outspoken advocates of this view are Charles Ferguson, a political scientist at MIT, and Robert Reich, a political economics professor at Harvard. They maintain that larger corporations are discouraged from making long-term investments in innovation if their best risk-taking talent is constantly leaving to form competitive start-up firms. The American semiconductor industry is said to have suffered the most.

Entrepreneurship is healthy in general, the argument goes, but it also has pitfalls that may have been overlooked during America's entrepreneurial love affair in the 1980s. In the high-technology field, the pitfall is too much fragmentation. The burden of change falls to existing, larger corporations. *They* are the ones that must devise internal risk-taking cultures within which their people can thrive and help foster a more *collective* innovation. Sharing the rewards of what is created with those who helped create it could also go a long way toward that goal.

Sparking the risk spirit is a continuous struggle. Children are still taught to always select the "safest" alternatives. From the time we learn the word, "risk" is most often used pejoratively. At the same time, we unabashedly glorify wealth and material success. But here's the paradox: *How is that wealth created?* Every great fortune can be traced to someone who took risks to create the original wealth—even if successive generations had nothing to do with it. If society fails to recognize that the price of creating wealth is risk, the result will be generations of individuals unable

137

to see, let alone comprehend, the unbreakable bonds between risk, uncertainty and payoff. The spirit of wealth creation—risk—will die.

Even business managers tend to see risk primarily in a negative context. A study of managerial risk taking conducted by two professors at the University of British Columbia asked hundreds of executives to define risky business situations. Their responses described risk as including these elements: "Limited knowledge . . . little or no effective control . . . lack of time . . . lack of sources of research . . . lack of experience . . . lack of proper planning or market research . . . high probability of failure not offset by commensurate rewards . . . "

Of the responses reported by the researchers as typical, *not one described risk in terms of its wealth creation potential.* Risk represented the possibility of loss first; anything else was secondary or ignored. That's a backwards view of risk taking. By definition, risk must involve only the *possibility* of loss, not the certainty of loss. If the loss is certain it's not a risk. But it's the possibility of *gain*—the very core of the risk—that gives it life, purpose, spirit.

Risk seems useless, even destructive, to the security-minded. They can't see that risk has more to do with ideas, innovation, change, new applications and procedures—in short, new ways of looking at things—than with simply finding the safest way to bet $10 in hopes of getting back $15. While governments are good at *shifting* wealth among different segments of a society, they generally fail to promote the one ingredient crucial to creating wealth —risk taking. The secret to *creating* wealth, rather than merely shifting it, is no secret at all—in enterprise, only through risk is wealth created. Risk taking is the one brand of economic exercise that routinely discovers *unanticipated* knowledge, services or goods. We often call it innovation. Innovation pays companies back sometimes in cash, other times in increased knowledge (from failure). Using innovation to develop skills or products provides a high "yield of understanding."

The Casino Fallacy

A preoccupation with gambling also thwarts our understanding of real wealth creation. Business is sometimes misleadingly compared to casino gambling. In gambling, lumps of money shift owners depending on the luck or skill of the players. But gambling *creates* nothing; many people must lose so that a few can win. Profit produced by risk taking in enterprise, however, *does* create something new. Here, winning is not predicated on somebody else *losing*. And when risk in enterprise succeeds, the whole society comes out ahead.

Still, there are semantics problems in understanding this. The English language does not distinguish between the dollars "at risk" in a casino and those "at risk" in enterprise, though the two are very different. Gambling is essentially entertainment, at times a disease. It is also highly *specific*. The amount at risk is precisely known; the potential gain is directly related to that amount. The rules are clear, the odds fixed. Gambling is based for the most part on random chance.

Risk in enterprise and investment has none of those set characteristics. It is imprecise, even messy, as we've already seen. Yet unlike gambling, an enterprising risk is based on—or is itself—a hypothesis that *can* be tested in the economic marketplace. In gambling no testable hypothesis exists, only random chance. The casino-gambling variety of risk takers pursue the thrill of simple participation to a far greater extent than do risk takers in enterprise. Gamblers are fond of saying that in a supercharged casino atmosphere, the next best thing to winning is losing. Either way, they still get a rush.

But investing in new high-tech companies, for example, is not like spinning the roulette wheel. Spotting a market niche and launching a new company, committing millions of dollars to an untried new technology, backing an entrepreneur with a good idea, taking a lower salary in return for an equity interest, signing a business loan guarantee that puts your house on the line—these are unique enterprise risks that present themselves one by one. When venture capitalists finance new businesses they aren't just sitting with a stack of quarters, dropping them one by one into the entrepreneurial slot machine. The nature of enterprise permits them to *calculate* their risks by research, experience or just plain intuition. They risk money on uncertain prospects. But when it works the way it's supposed to, the process results in a *contribution* to economic growth, not a dent in a casino's balance sheet.

Casino operators bank on the knowledge that even though they

139

may suffer periodic short-term losses, the long term will always be in their favor. The gambler, however, cannot bank on any such long-term probabilities. He's interested in only a few tosses of the dice. Insurance companies take a long-term view similar to the casino operator's. Like gambling, buying insurance is a transaction where you pay out money but get no goods or services back. Like gambling, what you have bought is a fixed payback later if an uncertain event occurs.

In business, the two types of risk—gambling and insurance—look the same on paper. Money is paid out and nothing is received in return unless specified unpredictable events occur. Insurance, however, seeks to avert risk, while the gambler generates the risk. As risk expert Peter Moore, a professor at the London Business School, has described it, the gambler risks losing a small amount of money for the chance of gaining a larger amount. Buying insurance, on the other hand, accepts a specified loss (the premium and perhaps a deductible) in return for avoiding the chance of a much greater loss. With a gamble, you pay to acquire risk. With insurance, you pay to avoid risk.

SETTING COURSE AT GENENTECH

"We are prone to forget that risk is an inseparable component of individual liberty."

—WILLIAM E. SIMON

Bob Swanson maintains that the essence of successful risk taking is having the courage to pursue a course that nobody else has yet tried, or even believes is possible. The course he set was lined with superlatives: It had to be the best; it had to be first; it had to be the biggest, fastest and most innovative. That's the only way it could survive. Other companies would surely flood the biotechnology field once the technology was proven, he thought—once *Swanson's* company had proven that commercial products from gene-splicing were possible.

Swanson describes himself as a *calculated* risk taker: "One of

140

the things that seemed to be clear from my venture capital days was that successful entrepreneurs have a number of common characteristics. One is that they take *calculated* risks." According to Genentech's founder, the successful entrepreneur stands back just far enough from the problem—takes just enough risk—to make it challenging, but not impossible. Swanson says that's his brand of risk taking.

Some risk takers talk about the need to have information before taking risks. Others talk about deep pockets, or patience, or control, or thinking differently. But according to Swanson, "successful risk taking comes down to this: making the risks *reasonable and achievable* with the assets and resources that you've got." In other words, ART is a question of balance—of having confidence in your own judgment, but not blindness, and being willing to stand up for the judgments, even if that results in a loss later on. And if taking calculated risks is one part of the formula for Swanson, watching his backside is another. He sets aggressive but achievable goals, and then keeps a close eye on what might happen if something goes wrong.

How does Swanson go about assessing his risks? "My judgments are more intuitive than not," he says. "On the other hand, there's a lot of research that goes into making those decisions, and whether there's outside expertise or raw data. But the judgment call usually comes down to being intuitive rather than someone that writes lists of pluses and minuses on a sheet of paper and says, 'Hey, this number is greater than that number.' Any time you want to do something different from the status quo means taking a risk, because you're doing something different from what everybody else is doing. And for whatever reason, that's more risky."

Bob Swanson is an intensely private man. He accepts his "Biotech Superstar" role with resignation, not great relish. If *Fortune* selects him as one of the year's most fascinating businessmen (as it did in 1986), Swanson sees it as part of heading a high-profile public company. That's his public role; his personal life is kept separate.

The roots of his risk-taking drive extend at least as far back as his student days at the Massachusetts Institute of Technology in the late 1960s. Swanson says he went to MIT because he was

141

interested in science "and they were willing to accept me." He studied chemistry first, earned enough credits for a BS degree, then switched over to MIT's highly regarded business school, the Alfred P. Sloan School of Management. If Swanson's future had been predictable, there could have been no better place for him than MIT. Unlike competing business schools at venerable institutions such as Stanford or Harvard, MIT stresses the links between technology and business. Whether learned at MIT or not, it was Swanson's ability to successfully juggle the needs of both disciplines that made Genentech the world leader in biotechnology. In June 1970 he was simultaneously awarded his BS in chemistry and a master's degree in management from Sloan.

An MIT course on entrepreneurship greatly influenced Swanson's thinking. That's when he first became interested in the *process* of enterprise, its dynamics—how a new product idea is germinated, translated into reality, and then becomes a real product that somebody buys. "That was my interest in business school," he says, "focusing on that *transition from concept to reality* [my emphasis]. And then I had a course on venture capital, and that was even more interesting. Because not only were you taking a new concept and turning it into a product, but you were doing it in the context of building a whole new company." The theoretical study of how products and companies emerge, and the risks involved, fascinated Swanson, and planted the seeds of entrepreneurial discontent.

When Swanson left MIT he went to work for Citicorp Venture Capital, Ltd., in New York, "one of the few places at the time that was hiring newly minted MBAs," he says. There he stayed for four years, scouting investment opportunities, negotiating terms, and helping direct small, rapidly growing companies at the board of directors level. Citicorp Venture Capital, apparently impressed, packed him off all alone to establish a branch office in San Francisco. There he caught the eye of another venture capital firm, Kleiner & Perkins (now Kleiner Perkins Caufield & Byers, one of America's premier venture firms), where he soon became a partner. His new task: invest the firm's money in small high-technology companies.

"I was working only at the board level, to help those companies direct their growth and avoid typical small company mistakes. I was also gathering valuable experience about the right things to do in starting a company," says Swanson. But he quickly became a malcontent. Making investments and watching companies grow wasn't satisfying his hunger for a more hands-on form of risk taking. "It was really interesting, and I guess it was that interest in how companies get started and how new products get from the idea stage into reality that got me here," recalls Swanson. "But, you know, eventually venture capital wasn't enough. Being involved at the director level is one thing and doing it yourself in another.

"Why risk starting something yourself?" asks Swanson, now warming to the subject. "Maybe that's the answer to look for. I guess I've always been excited about building and creating things." It was an itch that Swanson eventually scratched by starting Genentech, with his scientist partner Dr. Herbert Boyer, a professor of biochemistry at the University of California, San Francisco (UCSF).

Swanson feels the decision to risk jumping out of a relatively secure venture capital partnership into a "wild" idea of his own was "more a desire to do something different. While venture capital was a lot of fun, and was a good learning experience for me, it was at that point in my life a little frustrating because I wasn't doing the things myself. It was exciting to be involved with entrepreneurs—people who were out to change the way the world was. But it wasn't as if you were doing it yourself. And I missed that direct interaction." Since he had only a little of his own money to invest, the item he felt most personally at risk was his reputation in the business. "That's something you live with all your life. You build it every day," he says.

"I compared the risks of starting my own company with the risks our ancestors took when they got on the boat. And suddenly the risks of starting a business or changing jobs really seem pretty small when you think about them in perspective to bigger risks, real risks. That was one thing that helped me through it. . . .

"I think that if someone is very comfortable with the way the world is—at least the piece of the world they deal with—then they are not going to be out taking risks to change it. There has to be something in the person that *wants* to risk changing something." And Swanson had always been a little uncomfortable.

143

"I wanted to build something. I wanted to create something. It wasn't clear to me what that was, but as I look back I see there was always that element, that desire," he says.

Ironically, Swanson first tasted biotechnology's sweet potential in 1975 through a company that Kleiner & Perkins had backed. That firm was Cetus Corporation—one of the earliest biotechnology start-ups and now a chief Genentech rival. Through Cetus, Swanson learned of this new technique for manipulating life's basic building blocks, and its potential for creating useful pharmaceutical products. The young venture capitalist was astonished by it all. Here was a radical new technology capable of creating biological products that had never existed before. To Swanson, the commercial potential seemed no less than awesome. What's more, the methods of producing those new substances appeared far superior to the clumsy (by comparison) way most conventional pharmaceuticals are still manufactured today. He read everything he could find on the topic. Each fact seemed to add to his perception that there was tremendous commercial opportunity embedded in this radical technology.

Genetic engineering could produce unlimited quantities of substances, usually drugs, in short supply. It could copy the human body's own manufacturing abilities—even improve upon them—to create medically useful natural substances that would be much safer than "artificially" manufactured drugs. And it could use raw materials that were both plentiful and cheap.

At the urging of his Kleiner & Perkins partners, Swanson nearly went to work for Cetus, but the company's managers weren't interested in him. The folks at Cetus, like other scientists in the field at the time, maintained that commercialization of gene-splicing was still light-years away. Their efforts were all research-oriented, and they had little use for a bottom-line-minded businessman at this point. No effort was directed at marketing. Why should it? There was no product to market, and most likely there wouldn't be for many years.

Looking through the ARTist's prism, Swanson saw it differently. He was on the verge of being hooked. The technical papers he devoured on the subject included one written by Boyer, of UCSF. It was Boyer, along with fellow scientist Stanley Cohen, who had reported a key discovery in 1973—the splicing of genes from different organisms to form a new organism that had not existed before. Boyer had figured out a way to "snip" out segments of DNA (genes) from a cell by using chemical tools called restriction enzymes. Cohen knew how to splice those snatches of DNA—with their vital genetic programming—into other living cells, such as bacteria. Those cells, thus reprogrammed, would then produce the desired substance. One example is interferon, a natural disease-fighting substance manufactured by the human body in tiny amounts. To produce larger amounts outside the body, scientists now have taken the genetic code for interferon and inserted it into bacterial "factories" that dutifully produce lots of human interferon. The same process has been accomplished with a variety of other useful substances. Some are far more complex, however, and infinitely more difficult for scientists to "clone."

By the mid-1970s, manipulation of life's very building blocks had become possible. In that ability, Swanson saw the potential to create an entirely new industry. He also saw dollar signs. "It seemed to me that genetic engineering was ripe for commercial application," he says.

Then came the scary, risk-taking part. Nobody else seemed to agree. Other businessmen and scientists Swanson talked to about the idea thought he was grossly premature in his assumptions. The more excited Swanson became about the commercial potential of the technology he'd read about, and the more certain he became that it could be done *now*, not ten or twenty years from now, the more difficult it was to find anyone who'd agree. He kept asking the same question of each person he called: Can rDNA technology be used anytime soon to produce commercial products? And he kept getting the same answer: "No way."

What bothered him most was that there seemed to be no reasons the experts all felt that way—at least no *good* reasons, in Swanson's mind. "They didn't say, 'Well, gee, if only this element of the technology could just be solved, then maybe it could be used to produce products,'" recalls Swanson. "They'd just say that commercialization was ten to twenty years down the road. Period. And when I pressed them for reasons no one had any good answers."

Swanson employed the same philosophy he would use years later managing a staff of thousands. If an employee didn't have a

145

watertight reason for why something couldn't be done, Swanson would ask, politely, that he or she please find a way to do it. So Swanson groped on his own for the missing links. "If you say it can't be done today," he told those he questioned, "what's missing?" The answers were still vague. No one could tell him what pieces were missing or when it might be technologically possible to put them in place. "Is there something today that is missing that *has* to be developed to make it possible?" he asked. "Is there a breakthrough that has to be made in order for this technology to be useful in producing products?" Answers were hazy. Swanson, a nonscientist although he had studied chemistry, concluded that all of the essential pieces already existed to turn gene-splicing toward producing commercial products. It was just that nobody had yet done it. "It became a matter of constantly telling myself, 'Well, if all of the elements *can* be done today, and I can really put them all together in the right order, then I can accomplish this,' " he says. Then the risk was worth taking.

Negative answers digested poorly in Swanson's stomach. "I mean, it was just a case of my being really stubborn . . . and not getting the right answers about why something *couldn't* be done other than the pat answer 'It's going to take a long time for the technology to develop.' " Swanson was still convinced, and the naysayers only made him more determined.

The scientists working in the field seemed motivated by modest goals themselves. Their plan was initially to use genetic engineering techniques to help increase the supply of certain human substances for further study—substances that were normally in short supply. Swanson's view, as an outsider and as a businessman, was far more ambitious and long-term. Instead of a tiny lab producing gene-spliced products in test tubes, he envisioned a manufacturing plant churning out the stuff in huge vats like so much beer. "By January 1976," he remembers, "I was really impatient. Dr. Boyer was clearly at the forefront of the research, so I decided to call him, cold. We'd never met before. He told me he was very busy—he was friendly, but busy. He agreed to give me ten minutes of his time on a Friday afternoon."

Swanson says it was part luck and good timing that he had called Boyer just then. Boyer at that moment had been working on one of the key pieces of the technology, showing that synthetic DNA could be planted inside a microorganism and would behave

146

just like natural DNA. In Boyer's mind, though still unknown to Swanson, that opened up the opportunities to produce the new substances commercially. The next part of the story, as they say, is history. Swanson and Boyer met at a local watering hole in San Francisco near UCSF. At last, Swanson had found somebody who agreed with him. Yes, Boyer told him, he thought commercializing the technology *was* within grasp.

"The ten minutes extended into three hours, and at least as many beers," recalls Swanson. It ended in an agreement by the two new acquaintances to form a partnership that would investigate the commercial feasibility of recombinant DNA technology. Each man put in $500 to cement the deal.

The two partners' talents struck a balance: Boyer the scientific genius, Swanson the business vision. They became entrepreneurs, but as Boyer would later tell *Business Week*, "The first time somebody called me that I had to look up the word. I didn't know if it was a compliment or an insult." Boyer kept his university position while Swanson formed the company, incorporated in April 1976 in California. They searched for a name. Swanson, not known for his wit, suggested HerBob Corporation, an uninspired combination of their given names. Boyer gagged. He countered with Genentech, short for genetic engineering technology.

Swanson knew the biggest risks facing the company immediately would be in the laboratory: Could they produce a genetically engineered product, even on a crude scale? If not, or if it took too long, and cost too much money, the company would quickly be out of business. Those were the first risks, and Swanson felt they were enough to handle at one time so he kept the new company's finances as lean as possible. They rented office space and furniture, and hired a part-time secretary. Boyer remained at UCSF, devoting only part of his time to the new company—a pattern still in force today. Swanson left Kleiner & Perkins to devote full time to Genentech, and his former partners agreed to put up the first $100,000 to fund the company. The money would last about nine months.

"Our first order of business at Genentech was to prove that it was possible *and* commercially feasible to induce bacteria to make a human protein," says Swanson. "Nobody had done it before." This was "basic" research that Swanson was talking about —a semi-dirty word to most of corporate America. *Basic* research,

147

to business, means research at its very earliest stages, far removed from real life, commercial applications—and profits. The words "basic research" are always said with a special sneer. Even businesses fond of R&D hate basic research for two key reasons: It is expensive, and results won't likely be seen on the corporate bottom line for many years.

Genentech was worse than pathetically equipped to conduct any such research. It had no multimillion-dollar labs, one scientist, and precious little money. How could Swanson hope to achieve what leading research universities around the world with huge equipment and brainpower resources hadn't yet achieved? His venture experience, though brief, had at least taught him some of the risk-taking mistakes to avoid. Spreading too thin—trying to do everything yourself—was one of them. So Genentech's first move was to contract out that first research to labs that *did* have the right facilities and scientists.

A Crucial Choice

According to Swanson, the next decision, and the experiments it produced, was the single most important event that helped spawn today's multibillion-dollar biotechnology industry. He also lists it as one of the biggest risks he took in launching Genentech. The company had to demonstrate to the world that the basic idea behind it worked. Genentech had to perform science that nobody, including Cetus, had yet done, commercially or otherwise.

But what substance would Swanson choose first to clone by this new process? He'd probably have only one chance, so he had to make the right choice. Swanson and Boyer knew their company needed to score quickly to survive. Delays could prove Swanson's hunch wrong. Funding would evaporate quickly. The choice had to be something simple enough to be technologically possible, yet not so simple that it was a useless test.

They selected somatostatin, a hormone produced naturally by the human brain in minute amounts. Scientists didn't really know its function, but were interested in studying it. There would be a market in selling the substance to the research community for those studies—if they could clone and manufacture it in quantity using the rDNA technology.

Three labs were involved: Boyer's at UCSF, City of Hope National Medical Center (Duarte, California) and Cal Tech. Within seven months—a compression of years' worth of work—Swanson, Boyer and the scientists working on the contract project made their breakthrough. Or so they thought. They had correctly synthesized the gene for the protein somatostatin, and had spliced it, together with various genetic control elements, into the DNA of ordinary bacteria. Those bacteria were then supposed to manufacture the protein, thus becoming the first microscopic factories of the future that would produce humankind's next generation of super-pure pharmaceuticals. The initial batch of what they hoped to announce to the world as the first "useful" product made by genetic engineering was sent to City of Hope. There they'd test it to see if the substance they sought was really present in the genetic brew they had concocted.

All were present when the test showed . . . absolutely nothing. Their experiment had flopped. At that moment, the risks of launching a business based on so precarious an assumption fell in on Swanson. "Here I saw my whole career and everything else pass before my eyes." All indications said it should work, but it didn't. The elation of breakthrough crumbled. "I was *worried* then," recalled Swanson.

But not *too* worried. "A risk taker is obviously worried about failure, but you really don't think about it much," he says. "In that sense, you just start asking yourself, 'What is the next step to make this thing work?' You're already committed to taking the risk and solving the problem, so it becomes more a matter of just deciding what to do next than anything else. Even so, people had been spending over a year and a half of time; investors had committed substantial money that would have gone down the drain if we'd given up then."

Swanson didn't worry too much because he was supremely confident he was right. "You always have doubts," he concedes. "They pop up occasionally. But I never let it occupy a major part of my time or thinking. I mean, it was always pretty clear to me that it was going to work. Aside from those brief moments where you say, 'Oh my God,' it was always clear. It was just going to work."

Actually, he *was* right. The scientists working on the experiment discovered a flaw. Their mini-factories were producing a

149

second substance that was gobbling up the somatostatin before they could test for its presence. After some adjustments the next test came in positive. In 1977, only one year after its founding, Genentech was able to announce a scientific first that Swanson had been told wouldn't occur for a decade: the successful production of the human brain hormone somatostatin by genetically engineered bacteria. Philip Handler, president of the National Academy of Sciences, called it "a scientific triumph of the first order." And Stanford University's Paul Berg, who later became a Nobel laureate, called it "astonishing."

Still, it was a tiny stone in the great wall Swanson was planning to build. The blueprint to this point had been clear compared to the hurdles ahead. Now he would have to begin the complex and mind-blowing expense of building, from scratch, a corporation capable of taking a new pharmaceutical product from discovery into the hands of the ultimate consumer.

Genentech had scored a coup with the somatostatin breakthrough. By squeezing the time frame and holding expenses low, they had made their breakthrough without much venture financing and, more importantly, without giving up any large pieces of their company.

The early risks were already paying off. "That caught many by surprise," recalls Swanson, "especially the venture capitalists who wanted an opportunity to invest more money at a low price." It was the first proof that Swanson was for real. Genentech now commanded respect and could raise money more easily without giving away too much in return.

Genetically engineering the obscure brain hormone may have been scientifically astonishing, but it marked only the opening gun in what most investors viewed as a marathon. Early leaders often fade. And with Genentech's startling announcement, new biotechnology companies would begin multiplying like the bacterial agents their science depended on. The impression of leadership in the field would be crucial since Swanson's puny business was still far from becoming a real pharmaceutical company with real products.

But the risk-taking Swanson had on his ARTist's marathon shoes. Genentech rammed home its point that the technology had arrived, following its initial milestone by successfully cloning

150

thirteen other important substances within four years: human insulin in 1978, human growth hormone in 1979, interferon and ten others in 1980. Each substance became more complex. In an industry that measures complexity of its products by molecular weight, aspirin weighs in at 180, while TPA, a genetically produced clot-dissolving substance hailed as Genentech's first blockbuster product, tips the molecular scales at a plump 60,000. That's the difference between a bicycle and a jet plane.

Swanson had no interest in being merely a historical footnote to the beginnings of biotechnology. He had gained a quick lead and intended to keep it. The former venture capitalist knew that being recognized as the industry's premier firm could be a multi-million-dollar edge for his company. The only thing investors like better than winners is leaders, and Swanson recognized Genentech would command leverage if it were viewed as the premier company in a soon-to-be-crowded field.

Swanson began making moves that others in the industry considered outlandish, risky, even a bit cocky. One shrewd maneuver that would later prove invaluable was to establish and fund a Genentech marketing department and sales force *long before the company even had a product that it could market*. The scientists that Swanson had recruited were flabbergasted. Why was this upstart shelling out money to market something that didn't yet exist, and probably wouldn't for years?

It was one of Swanson's calculated risks. This savvy marketing man and financier calculated that a marketing department would give his company and its employees a psychological edge over the competition. He was, in effect, using the marketing department *not* to market a product, but to sell the company itself to Wall Street and the rest of the scientific community. What's more, the marketing expertise Swanson brought in so prematurely would pay for itself many times over by helping Swanson correctly make some of the riskiest choices of the company's early existence: *which of the thousands of possible genetic products to select for commercial development*. Time and money were limited. If Swanson chose the wrong products to pursue the entire company would be in jeopardy. It would fall behind competitors in the genetic patents race, and would most likely never make it up.

151

Genentech's CEO began developing unusual strategies to face the unusual risks. He used what he called a focused business approach. "Biotechnology offers promising opportunities in so many fields that it is easy to be like a kid in the candy store," observes Swanson, "doing a little of this and a little of that. But as Dave Packard [of Hewlett-Packard] reminds me at our board meetings, not many companies run into problems because of starvation. It's the indigestion that gets them. We have taken this advice. Bringing a product from the laboratory to the marketplace takes enormous energy, and concentration of both human and capital resources. We recognized early on that it is important to focus on doing a *few* things well—first developing products in one area before expanding into another."

The risk of deciding which "few" things to do in those early formative stages was that a single wrong move could easily have doomed the company. With choices of many industrial, agricultural and health-care applications of the new technology, Swanson channeled his limited resources into health-care products. Within that category, he ignored the booming field of diagnostics and focused on ethical (prescription) drugs. But not just any prescription drugs. Genentech would pursue only products that would be prescribed by medical specialists, most of whom are based at about nine hundred hospitals nationwide. Since there are fewer such specialists to reach, the company's marketing expense could be held low. Says Swanson, "A salesperson could visit a hospital, see an endocrinologist about human growth hormone, then walk upstairs to see a cardiologist about tissue-type plasminogen activator, and go down the hall to see an internist about gamma interferon." When Genentech scientists did make discoveries outside the area of human ethical drugs, they were quickly licensed to other companies for cash payments plus royalties on future product sales.

Meanwhile, other biotech companies were hedging their risks by diversifying into many different areas of research, including related health sciences such as monoclonal antibodies. In later years, those firms suffered as the young industry slumped and raising new capital to keep all those avenues active became more difficult. They were overdiversified against risk.

Swanson preferred to take fewer, well-chosen risks. He chose human insulin as Genentech's next challenge, its first real product. Insulin, a hormone produced in the pancreas, is needed by the body to metabolize sugars and carbohydrates. Diabetes is caused by the body's inability to produce enough of it. The treatment for the disease is insulin, which drugmakers were then obtaining from the pancreas glands of cows and pigs. Animal insulin, however, isn't quite the same as human insulin, nor as pure, and some people are allergic.

Immediately after the somatostatin experiments had proven the technology, Genentech tackled production of *human* insulin. But there were obstacles. On the scientific side, insulin was far more complex and difficult to clone than the simple somatostatin protein. Could Genentech match the swiftness of its earlier breakthrough? Being first would be another coup for the company, but knowledge of gene-splicing's potential was now rapidly spreading, and others would be seeking the same goals.

On the business side, the first product Swanson chose already violated some of his product selection criteria. Chief among them would be marketing of genetically produced human insulin, should Genentech succeed in producing, testing and receiving government approval to sell it. Genentech was still a dismally tiny operation compared to the pharmaceutical Goliath, Eli Lilly, which had the U.S. insulin market locked up.

Recognizing the futility of trying to compete with the likes of a Lilly, Swanson did the next best thing: He made a deal. He brazenly convinced Lilly that Genentech could quickly develop human insulin and that Lilly should help fund the effort and license the product from Genentech if it succeeded. Swanson would get the credit and some money, Lilly could manufacture and market what would probably be the first genetically engineered human drug sold.

Early in 1978, amidst the feverish push to clone human insulin, Genentech first moved to its location overlooking San Francisco Bay on Point San Bruno Boulevard, in South San Francisco. Within one year of the somatostatin success, Genentech's crash program succeeded in genetically engineering human insulin. But Swanson initially kept this breakthrough under wraps. Lilly, which had been dragging its feet on completing the terms of an exclusive licensing agreement, now had to jump at Swanson's command. If they wanted to share the spotlight of this discovery, they'd have to sign *his* deal. Genentech was first again, and on its way.

Four years later, in the fall of 1982, human insulin became the first pharmaceutical product of genetic engineering to receive final clearance from the federal Food and Drug Administration (FDA). It was introduced, under the trade name Humulin, by Lilly early the next year. As Swanson says, that was "lightning speed" for a pharmaceutical to go from discovery to market.

Genentech continued to move with uncanny speed in an industry notorious for lengthy development times. Interferon, for example, took only a year from the time it was cloned to reach human clinical testing. With two product successes under its belt, however, Genentech hadn't yet run the complete pharmaceutical gauntlet: develop, manufacture, test and market a drug, all by itself. Swanson selected human growth hormone—a drug with a very limited market—to be his next designated hitter. It was needed to treat dwarfism, which strikes about 11,000 children yearly—a minuscule market in the pharmaceuticals business, and one hardly worth the huge expense of developing a drug to serve. The disorder was then being treated with extremely limited supplies of growth hormone obtained from cadavers.

Genentech scientists succeeded in cloning human growth hormone in 1979, and clinical testing began in 1981. With a nod of approval from the FDA in October 1985, Protropin, Genentech's trade name for the drug, became the world's first recombinant pharmaceutical product to be developed, manufactured and marketed by a biotechnology company.

Genentech's grand coming of age was cause for celebration. A party tent rose on the bayside parking lot behind Genentech, and fireworks lit the sky on the night of October 26. To cap it off, Swanson offered every Genentech employee options on a hundred shares of stock at the price the day Protropin was approved.

That December the company received more good news. Because the disorder it treated was so rare, Protropin was granted special "orphan drug" status by the FDA, giving Genentech seven years of marketing exclusivity plus special tax breaks.

By 1980, the Genentech caterpillar had blossomed into a more fully integrated corporate butterfly. "We now had the ability to complete each phase of product development," says Swanson, "laboratory research, process development, commercial production [fermentation, purification and sterile packaging], quality assurance, clinical testing, regulatory affairs and marketing." His firm had grown to 112 employees, fifty-seven of whom either had PhDs or other advanced scientific degrees.

The time was ripe, he thought, for taking the company public. He would be the first biotechnology company to do so—another first; another risk. "We had two motives for going public when we did," Swanson explains. "First, we knew we would need more money than venture capital could supply—and long before we had products to sell. Second, Genentech *was* setting standards in the industry, and we wanted to establish a record of business accomplishments [including a successful public stock offering] that other biotechnology companies would have to match" in order to keep up.

Swanson devoted much of his time during early 1980 to helping prepare the company's public stock offering. He was now thirty-two, earning a salary of $68,000 as the company's president, and holding about one million Genentech shares, obtained when he formed the company with Boyer. Two months before the offering, *The Wall Street Journal*'s "Heard on the Street" column observed that while manipulation of living cells to mass-produce specific microorganisms still seemed futuristic, the technology was moving rapidly out of the lab and into commercial pathways. The *Journal* detected strong interest in advance of the offering, "even though the fledgling company, in existence only since 1976, has been required to warn that its stock involves a high degree of risk."

Investors proved more than interested. They were ravenous. When Genentech offered a million shares (13.4 percent of the company) for sale to the public on October 14, 1980, at $35 per share, the stock exploded to $88 in the first half hour of trading—the fastest rise of any new stock issue in history. The story of Genentech's rise remains legend on Wall Street. Although the price settled back to $71 that day, Swanson and Boyer, who each owned about 14 percent of the company, were suddenly multimillionaires on paper. Other major owners of Genentech at the time it went public included Lubrizol Corporation, Kleiner & Perkins, and a company owned by Pittsburgh venture capitalist

155

Henry Hillman. These shareholders collectively had acquired their 86.6 percent portion of Genentech at an average cost of $1.85 per share. By 1988, after stock splits, Swanson's 4.2 million shares were worth close to $200 million.

The original stock-offering prospectus spelled out some of the business risks facing Genentech in its struggle to build a company based on new science:

(1) No money: Genentech would have to borrow money or sell more securities to keep itself going years before any of its own products could be expected to produce significant revenues.

(2) Even the small revenues the company was earning from contract work were tied to performance "benchmarks," and continued payments were uncertain.

(3) Any product Genentech produced would first have to obtain FDA approval before it could be marketed.

(4) Competition would intensify. Although Genentech was first to demonstrate the commercial potential of the technology, the giant pharmaceutical and chemical companies were jumping into the field and backing their efforts with huge financial, human and marketing resources.

(5) Technological changes would be rapid. Another company's breakthrough could force Genentech into the background overnight. Said Genentech: "Success will depend on the company's ability to continue on the leading edge of this technology and its ability to attract and retain scientific and technical personnel."

The Patent Minefield

Yet another risk, and potentially one of the most critical, involved patents. In short, Genentech had to patent every advance it made to protect its ability to profit from those inventions later on. Without maximum patent protection, other firms could easily copy their innovation. But this was new ground, and the extent to which Swanson could obtain secure patent protection was uncertain. Also unsettling: Other companies or universities might be first to patent discoveries critical to Genentech's success. That would force Genentech to license the rights at whatever price the patent holders demanded, or do without.

156

The legal uncertainties Genentech faced over the issue of patents were enough to shake the steadiest executive. The entire rDNA technology involved altering life-forms, creating new ones. Was that patentable? It took the Supreme Court to decide. In mid-1980 the Court ruled, in the case of *Diamond* v. *Chakrabarty*, that patents on living organisms were indeed permissible. The decision was welcomed by the biotechnology industry, but it was a rather narrow victory that left open the question of whether the *processes* associated with creating the new substances could also be protected with patents. The biotech firms were constantly nervous about how well their patents would hold up in court. Should they fail, a firm like Genentech could be left with a menu of fantastic, nonproprietary commodities that everybody else was free to copy.

Genentech characteristically took a more liberal view toward the issue than most other biotech firms. Although it took precautions to protect any patentable discoveries coming out of its labs, its scientists were allotted the ability to publish their research in a way that approximated the freedom they would enjoy in a university setting. If that freedom jeopardized proprietary knowledge it was a risk Swanson willingly took in order to strike an amicable balance between the sensibilities of his scientists and the needs of management. It's a volatile brew that Swanson, as ARTist and brewmeister since the beginning, has been masterful at tapping for its maximum value.

Capital Injections

To continue building his billion-dollar empire, Swanson needed a steady supply of capital, and that's where he turned his innovative juices. Where other growth industries can reinvest revenues to grow, biotechnology was simply too young to do so. There weren't yet any products, and only paltry revenues. "That's where a little innovation in the financial area helps," says Swanson. The solution: "Rather than use equity capital to fund our R&D, we financed our day-to-day operating expenses primarily with revenues from collaborative research, licensing fees and product sales to our corporate partners for clinical use." In 1985, for example, Genentech managed to attract $90 million in revenues from a

157

temporary line of business the company didn't intend to pursue. Like the actor working as a waiter while pursuing his real vocation, Genentech earned pocket money by selling contract research while its scientists were at work developing the products that would be the company's future bread and butter.

It was unconventional, but so was Swanson's company. Shortly after Genentech went public, Swanson said publicly that the goal of his financial maneuvering was simply to keep the firm on a break-even basis, *while more than doubling his investment in high-risk research and development.* The barriers are huge, admits Swanson, but once you're over them first, you know the competition won't have an easy time catching up.

By now, Swanson's personal stake in these goings-on had increased markedly. He was no longer just another obscure venture capitalist scrambling to launch a high-tech company in California. He now had millions of dollars of his own money—the value of his stake in Genentech—on the line whenever he rolled Genentech's dice. And he had a public profile, with its risk baggage, where none had existed before.

A much larger piece of financing came from the innovative private R&D limited partnerships Swanson invented to subsidize the high costs of clinically testing a new drug. Giant pharmaceutical companies fund that testing themselves. Smaller firms must improvise others ways, often sacrificing a share of future profits to obtain the financing. The ingenious partnership financing method Swanson devised for his company "allowed Genentech to raise the funds required for clinical testing while retaining control over the product's manufacturing and marketing. Like the Colt .45 was to the old West, they are a great equalizer when competing with large, well-financed pharmaceutical companies," said the company's CEO. Some biotech industry analysts thought they were a gimmick Swanson could never pull off. They were proved wrong.

The first such partnership, Genentech Clinical Partners, Ltd. (GCP), raised $55 million in 1982 to develop and test two Genentech products. In 1983, GCP II raised another $34 million to test the highly touted drug Activase (TPA) for treating heart attack victims, and in 1984 another $33 million to sponsor human clinical testing and development of tumor necrosis factor (TNF), an anti-cancer drug. Genentech gave up certain rights to the drugs, but retained the critical ability to buy out the partnership later if it wanted. Swanson exercised that buyback option early, at the end of 1986, trading $270 million worth of Genentech stock to reacquire the drug rights from GCP, and $138 million worth of stock to buy back GCP II. "Upon completion of the buyouts," the firm said in a press release at the time, "Genentech will own exclusive U.S. rights to the products now owned by the partnerships—Protropin human growth hormone, gamma interferon, and Activase," the clot dissolver.

The original terms of the second partnership, involving Activase, would have prevented Genentech from buying it back until two years *after* the drug received FDA approval. That would have forced the company to wait until almost 1990. But when Genentech's stock price soared late in 1986, Swanson moved quickly, offering to buy back the partnership with a generous supply of Genentech equity. Swanson was gambling that the predicted riches from Activase would come true. Now all profits from future sales belonged solely to Genentech. By the late 1980s, Swanson proclaimed that "Genentech is now on the threshold of dramatic growth that will propel us into the ranks of the world's leading pharmaceutical companies." A Wall Street analyst agreed, calling Genentech "the most commanding health care story around."

The Pharmaceutical Mother Lode

At Coca-Cola, Roberto Goizueta's big risk was the formula change. For Allen Neuharth at Gannett it was *USA Today*. And for Robert Swanson, the big money gamble came with tissue plasminogen activator, or TPA.

Genentech scientists first succeeded in producing TPA in 1982. They gave it the trade name Activase. It rapidly dissolves blood clots that cause heart attacks—the leading cause of death in the United States, claiming hundreds of thousands of lives every year. Dr. Eugene Braunwald, a Harvard Medical School cardiologist who headed National Institutes of Health testing of TPA, estimated it could save at least 30,000 lives every year if heart attack victims are fortunate enough to receive the drug in time.

This was the Big One, Swanson thought, the product that could

159

make his dream of a $1 billion pharmaceutical company by the 1990s come true. He rolled the dice again, betting that Activase would become Genentech's pharmaceutical mother lode, a product *Fortune* magazine later called a "no-fooling wonder drug," and later still, Genentech's "golden goose." Medical authorities compared its potential to the introduction of the first antibiotics. But years of clinical trials and other testing would first be required to prove the drug's usefulness and uncover any dangerous side effects. Such testing frequently shoots down a company's high hopes for a "wonder" drug when unforeseen side effects develop or the drug simply doesn't prove as effective as expected. Activase still had to clear those difficult hurdles.

But the ARTist in Swanson was impatient. He believed that if Genentech's manufacturing and marketing divisions sat and twiddled their thumbs during those years of trials—if they waited until all the lights were green—they could lose a valuable edge against the competition lurking close behind.

Pharmaceutical industry giant SmithKline Beckman Corporation, for example—which had the industry's first billion-dollar-a-year drug with Tagamet in the 1970s—struck a deal to market in the United States a conventionally produced clot-dissolver called streptokinase that would compete directly against TPA. And SmithKline president Henry Wendt would later disclose that his company was developing its own version of TPA. If he hoped to beat out giants like SmithKline, among others, Swanson knew he'd have to take some chances. So he invested heavily to build $45 million worth of new plant space dedicated to manufacturing Activase—if, and when, it was approved by the federal government. "It's easy to focus on discovery science and overlook the critical role manufacturing plays in a company's success," he says.

Finished in May 1986, the plant was the size of two football fields, contained eight miles of stainless steel pipe and more than 118 major pieces of process equipment—all of which could be operated by only ten to fifteen people on a shift. Genentech now had the largest multiproduct recombinant DNA manufacturing plant in the world. The firm's manufacturing staff had grown from seventy in 1980 to over four hundred by 1987. *But it still didn't have a major product to manufacture in those costly new facilities.*

* * *

Swanson also had plans to quickly expand his sales force five-fold to handle Activase. "By the time we launch Activase," he told a health-care conference in 1987, "Genentech will be in the top ten in the U.S. pharmaceutical industry in terms of hospital-based sales force. Within a year we'll be in the top five. . . . We will be able to compete with the biggest companies in our target markets." Analysts predicted TPA sales for Genentech could quickly reach $500 million to $1 billion *per year*. And the drug received a big unexpected boost when the popular talk show host Larry King suffered a heart attack and was treated with the drug during part of the testing period. King later told the world that TPA had saved his life.

A Genentech research official put the total price tag for developing TPA (Activase) at "hundreds of millions of dollars." But in the spring of 1987, the worst happened. As investors bid up the price of Genentech stock in anticipation of TPA's approval, the FDA announced its decision: It was *not* approving TPA. Even worse, the FDA *did* approve a competing drug the very same day —streptokinase, developed by Hoechst-Roussel Pharmaceuticals, a unit of the German parent company Hoechst A.G. It would sell for less than one-tenth of the cost of TPA ($200 per dose versus $2,200). It was more than embarrassing for Swanson. It was a disaster in the making.

Genentech's stock price plunged 24 percent in a single day, siphoning off tens of millions of dollars in value for Genentech employees who owned it. Rumors spread that even if the FDA did eventually approve the drug, there would be restrictions on its use. The stock continued to drop, at one point falling eight days in a row.

The FDA wasn't closing the door on TPA, but demanded more information from Genentech on the drug's safety and the survival rates of patients receiving it. Genentech scrambled to provide the information. Meanwhile, Swanson used the time to build inventory of the as-yet-unapproved product and step up advance marketing efforts—continuing to gamble that the FDA would grant TPA its blessing.

Critics said TPA had been overhyped. They still stay that. And indeed, Genentech's predictions of TPA's potential had been highly optimistic. Many pharmaceutical substances are hailed by excited researchers and marketing men as possible "miracle

161

drugs." Few ever gain that status. TPA came close. It clearly *was* highly effective. And doctors involved in clinical testing rated it superior to streptokinase. But it might not be appropriate for some heart attack victims: It might save only 30,000 lives yearly instead of 100,000. Those 30,000 people would hardly complain.

Genentech successfully answered the FDA's concerns. In November 1987, TPA was finally approved. The stock surged back. Euphoria broke out at Genentech's South San Francisco headquarters, where each employee was awarded a hundred more stock options, and fireworks lit the South San Francisco sky once again.

Swanson popped the clutch and Genentech's marketing and manufacturing engines lurched into high gear. By the end of 1987, a mere seven weeks after TPA's approval, Genentech had sold some $58 million worth of the new drug. Product sales increased 225 percent to $141 million, while total company revenues for the year soared 72 percent to $230 million. Net income was $42 million compared to a net loss of $353 million the year before. The payoff for Swanson's risky strategy had begun. "The promise of biotechnology is now a reality," he declared. But he'd have to keep moving fast. With competing drugs close behind, TPA's domination of the market could evaporate quickly. Eminase, for example, a drug made by the British firm Beecham Pharmaceuticals, was to be introduced in late 1989. Swanson would have to keep changing, keep risking money on new product development.

The New York Times commented in an article appearing January 5, 1988, "The strong sales can be credited in good part to a marketing strategy that began years before Genentech could even be sure it would win government approval for the drug. . . . Genentech's marketing effort signifies the first attempted transformation of a biotechnology company from a research and development firm to a major pharmaceutical concern. How well it succeeds could have ramifications for the rest of the fledgling industry as others introduce bioengineered drugs."

Shortly after TPA's approval, Swanson's risk taking looked like a major success. Sales of the drug confounded skeptics. Even the tenfold price spread between TPA and competing products didn't hurt. Because TPA worked so well, many patients cut four to six days off their hospital stay—a savings of up to $5,000 or so, *including* TPA's cost. And in 1988 Genentech offered to provide the drug free to needy, uninsured patients. Genentech was granted a crucial patent for TPA in June 1988, although legal battles over TPA patents were expected to drag on for years.

Said *Fortune*: "TPA should so enrich Genentech's coffers that the company will need no outside capital for at least three years. Genentech seems to have mastered the two disciplines that many biotech startups are forced to turn to big pharmaceutical companies for: marketing and finance. This phenomenal success leaves a lot of analysts wondering whether anyone can catch Genentech, not just in TPA but in all of medical biotechnology. . . . [By 1990] Genentech should be closing in fast on $1 billion in sales, probably becoming the fastest growing major company in the U.S."

And the magazine added that Genentech got there squarely on Swanson's shoulders. "The company's life is as tightly interwoven with his own as two complementary strands of DNA . . . Genentech is building the biggest commercially oriented medical biotech establishment in the world. Even competitors are quick to admit that Genentech's R&D operation towers above the rest." Swanson quickly put cash from TPA sales to work, boosting R&D spending by 50 percent.

Stockholders had every reason to cheer as well. A 1988 *Business Week* survey of executive pay at top U.S. corporations found that Swanson was the executive who gave shareholders the largest return in stock appreciation and dividends for the least pay between 1986 and 1988. During that period the value of Genentech stock more than quadrupled.

Robert Swanson has harnessed a key dynamic of risk: He has kept the risk-taking, change-oriented spirit alive through years of rapid growth from a two-man shell operation to a pharmaceutical giant. In doing so, he borrowed a page from IBM founder Thomas Watson's book. "We changed everything—except our philosophy," Watson had once said. To handle the controlled explosion that characterized IBM's early growth, Watson had stuck to his belief that the worst thing a company can do is go dead in the water.

Genentech has changed radically, but not Swanson's risk-taking philosophy about how to run a company. The firm hasn't been dead in the water yet, and never will be if Swanson has his way.

BOOK

IV

GRASPING RISK'S GEOMETRY

"Far better it is to dare mighty things, to win glorious triumphs, even though checkered by failure, than to take rank with those poor spirits who neither enjoy much nor suffer much, because they live in the gray twilight that knows not victory nor defeat."

—Teddy Roosevelt

RISK DYNAMIC #11

PERCEPTIONS OF CONTROL:
AN ARTist's PARADOX

*"The way to risk intelligently, to reduce risk or
increase risk as the case may be is, in a word,
information."*

*"The only virtue consistency has is
predictability, and too many people use that
simply to avoid taking risks."*

—FRED ADLER,
venture capitalist

Active risk takers (ARTists) themselves, as well as the psychologists who probe them, point to one recurrent risk theme more than any other: The best and brightest riskers have supreme confidence in their own abilities to exercise *control* over the risks they take. Goizueta at Coca-Cola, Neuharth at Gannett, Nicholas at Christian Dior, Swanson at Genentech, all claim their risks are wise because *they* have the necessary information; *they* call the shots; *they* have control.

Executives who *believe* they have at least partial control over

their predicament take more risks and they take them more pro-
ductively—even if they don't *really* have more control. Since a
risk taker in enterprise can never wield absolute power, the *perception* of control is even more important than its reality. This is
the confidence factor in dynamic risk taking.

To hear CEOs at many of America's top corporations tell it,
control has been eroding. But *control* is often confused with *security,* or *unassailability.* They are not the same. Security in the
executive suite breeds a false *illusion* of control. It breeds resistance to change. In 1987, when *Business Week* magazine explored
the changing role of the American CEO, it concluded that the
once well-protected corner CEO office had become far more vulnerable to attack. "Twenty years ago the CEO of a major company
had almost a fiefdom to rule," said James Cotting, CEO of Navistar International, the successor company to International Harvester. "He was unassailable. That's no longer true." Left *unsaid*
in that *BW* assessment was that in most cases, the weakening of
the CEO's armor should be welcomed because it *forces* greater
risk taking where none might otherwise have sprouted. Had International Harvester taken more risks instead of protecting its
fiefdom it might never have encountered the nearly fatal troubles
that plagued the company in the early 1980s.

Don Kelly, then CEO at E-II Holdings, added this thought:
"We are not in total control of our destinies. There is no protection
in size. Some CEOs are pretending it can't happen to them.
They're the most naive of all. They are living in an era that doesn't
exist any more. You can't relax." This erosion of control forces
executives to be more creative in their decision making and risk
taking. Instead of selecting from among the obvious alternatives
presented by a risky situation, they must decipher new alternatives—*adjust* the risk to better fit their company's ability to handle it. Adjusting is another way of battling for greater control.

Part of using control well is recognizing that it is never complete. Tiny and totally unforeseen events can affect the risk. Even
small errors or changes can produce radically different results. In
the science of meteorology they call this the "butterfly effect."
It's a peculiar, half-serious suggestion that something as insignificant as air turbulence created by a butterfly's wings on one side
of the world can somehow, through a series of fantastic chain
reactions, affect the weather weeks later on the other side of the

globe. Is the world's economic system, where once independent domestic economies have become increasingly interdependent, any less complex than the world's weather? There's no reason to think so. This forces enterprise to be increasingly vigilant—to take more risks and to calculate them more carefully.

Control by Illusion

The *perception* of control is important even if that control is not exercised. Behavioral researchers once tested the concentration of two groups of workers who were asked to perform complex tasks while being subjected to annoying background noises. One group could block out the noise by pressing a button. They had *control* of the situation. The other group had no button. Findings: The group with the button performed much better *even though they never actually used it.* By *feeling* more in control, they were able to do their jobs better. ARTists, at times, use control in a similar way. The confidence they accumulate helps them risk continuously to the point where they no longer feel the need to exercise their control.

Psychologists, of course, have a label for this type of personality. People who feel *they* have the determining influence on the outcome of their own lives—who feel what *they* do makes the most difference among life's controlling factors—are called "internals." These folks believe their lives are internally controlled, or self-controlled. The opposite type, those who feel their lives are ruled by luck, chance, astrology, institutions, outside forces or destiny, are generally the risk avoiders. They are the "externals" who ask, why take a risk if it's an out-and-out gamble anyway? One man who has studied this "locus of control" is Dr. Julian Rotter, a psychologist at the University of Connecticut. "The people who are externals," he explains, "will either take very little risks or very big risks. The internals, the ones who feel they can control their environment—who feel that what happens to them is mainly the result of their own actions—take moderate risks."

Since destiny rules for externals, they are the ones who more often play the lottery or go for the long shot, even though they have no control over the outcome. The rest of the time they tend to play things safely. The internals take many more risks, and some large ones, too, but they take them after more careful consideration. They take many more "calculated" risks where they can play a role in the outcome. The feeling of control provides continuing confidence to keep taking risks. The probability of success, even in the face of possible failure, encourages risk taking.

Some entrepreneurs themselves point to a distinction between a "constructive" type of risk and a "destructive" type. Fred Smith, the risk-taking founder of Federal Express, once told *INC.* magazine, "There are different types of risk and risk takers. One type of risk taker is very self-destructive, and he is characterized more by the mad-inventor type—somebody for whom the risk itself is the end. For him the risk is a high—the equivalent of those people who leap off the cliffs of Maui with those little hang gliders. Frankly, there are a lot of people in business like that, including many whom we've come to think of as entrepreneurs. And then there are those people who recognize that if you want to accomplish anything, then by definition you must take risks. And that is the sort of risk that more often is associated with lasting and important innovation."

"That makes sense," observes Farley, the University of Wisconsin psychologist. "An entrepreneur must be somebody who feels that he can take action in the world *and be a success.*" The focus is on accomplishment. "An entrepreneur is trying to make a good life for himself. He's also trying to find who he is; to feel a sense of competence in this world that he can act and bring about changes, and to know that his mind can lead him to accomplish things. And risk taking is enormously important to that. If you don't take a risk, there are many consequences. You're not going to come to know yourself so well," says Farley. His Type T personalities are not crazy risk takers with a death wish; they calculate their risks and proceed intelligently, knowing that risks sometimes fail even if they are calculated. "Entrepreneurs are tremendous," notes Farley. "They get knocked down, they just pick themselves up and go at it again."

VENTURE CAPITALISTS: AGENTS OF RISK

"The secret is in not *perceiving a risk when*
everyone else perceives that there is one."

—NOLAN BUSHNELL,
founder of Atari

The key risk dynamic of control is by no means limited to entrepreneurs. It is a factor across the spectrum of corporate and individual ARTists, including the breed we know as venture
capitalists (VCs). If American enterprise owes its fertility to any
single group of risk takers, payment for that debt should be directed to the VCs. They bankroll new businesses—thousands of
them yearly—with hundreds of millions of dollars at risk. Sometimes the money is their own, often it is raised from groups of
private or institutional investors who entrust it to the VC. Venture
capitalists gamble money on people and new, unproven ideas.
The concept is hardly new. Even Christopher Columbus used a
form of VC backing to launch his floating fifteenth-century enterprise. And as Columbus showed, when risks deliver results—
even unanticipated ones—the rewards can be huge.

In the past, the classic version of a venture capitalist was a
wealthy individual with an open checkbook, looking for a place
to earn a big payoff and maybe do some good. These "angels" still
exist. But the standard-model venture capitalist is now a group of
men and women organized into a venture capital firm—one that
invests in launching companies, or more likely, helps young existing companies to grow. There are more than six hundred such
firms doing business in America today. From the late 1970s to the
late 1980s their numbers increased by 150 percent, and they now
raise over $4.5 billion to invest yearly.

They do far more than write checks, however. They are impre-
sarios of risk, acting as conductors to an often disorganized orchestra of ideas, companies, entrepreneurs, investors, markets
and money. In risking money, they help push risk toward the goal
of progress and profit by giving the orchestra instruments to work
with, and some direction.

171

Some of the firms involved in this business of launching businesses have themselves become legendary. Among them: Kleiner Perkins Caufield & Byers, in San Francisco, which backed (and made millions on) such start-ups as Cetus, Tandem Computers, Home Health Care, Amdahl and Genentech. Venrock Associates, of New York, launched VisiCorp, a successful computer software maker, and was one of the firms that backed Apple Computer's launch. Sevin-Rosen Management, of New York and Dallas, had early successes in Compaq Computer and Lotus Development. Greylock Management Corporation, of Boston, was a backer of Prime Computer, ROLM and Apollo Computer. And TA Associates, also in Boston, had a risk-taking founder named Peter Brooke who was an original backer of Federal Express.

Today's venture capitalists are institutionalizing the process of risk capital; they are giving it structure, specialization and diversification that it never had before, enlarging the field so that it no longer resembles the private gambling parlor of the idle rich. But that's not all good. Once the booming high-tech years of the early 1980s ended, and more venture money started chasing fewer high-potential ventures, the industry turned cautious. Michael Milken, Drexel Burnham Lambert's high-yield bond maven, suggests a reason for this: The United States has been transformed from an industrial society that is short of capital into a society with lots of money. "In an industrial society, capital is a scarce resource," Milken says. "But in today's information society, there's plenty of capital." The challenge is to move it to the most dynamic uses.

That's where venture capitalists can play a role. Their ART is different from that of corporate executives. They are often conduits, matchmakers, brokers or agents of risk. They introduce entrepreneurs and their innovative ideas and new companies to their necessary partner in marriage—money.

Venture capital riskers are becoming more sophisticated in the way they nurture the companies they back. They increasingly specialize their risk taking. Some, though a dwindling number, provide initial seed money—considered the most risky of all. Others get in on second- or third-round financings. Some venture capitalists have reputations as slavemasters who can take a moribund company and give it new life. Some are focused on high-

172

tech, some on low, and more and more on retail and service sector businesses.

The checks they write are anything but handouts. In return for risking their entire investment, venture capitalists typically grab ownership of 20 to 50 percent of the venture, 20 to 30 percent of any profits (which might take three to seven years to appear, if at all), plus the power to switch management (or step in themselves) if the existing management screws up.

Venture capitalism is arguably the most cyclical of any business. The fat years are phenomenal. But when things cool, there's a mad rush to the lifeboats. Venture capitalists don't earn steady 15 or 20 percent annual returns. They earn 100, 200 or 300 percent one year; perhaps nothing, or worse, the next.

Venture capitalists are bred to be dispassionate risk takers. The best of them have the ability to step back, analyze a business risk with the cold eye of reason, and make a balanced decision. The venture capitalist doesn't have the same emotional baggage of the entrepreneur who, more than likely, has been living and breathing his or her idea for years. That excess baggage is what often contributes heavily to an entrepreneur's failure.

A LEGENDARY AD-VENTURER

"Risk is always present when progress into new fields is made."

—DR. DENTON COOLEY,
surgeon who performed first
U.S. heart transplant

Of the few venture capitalists who have achieved the amorphous rank of "lengendary," one who stands out is Fred Adler, manager of his own New York VC partnership, Adler & Company. Though his tough tactics draw faint praise from some colleagues, Adler is known for a Midas touch in selecting companies to back. His catalogue of fifty-to-one and hundred-to-one payoffs is as extensive as any. And when that touch escapes him, Adler is regarded as a genius at taking a struggling company and whipping it into profitability. He invests millions of dollars of his own money in high-risk ventures—including "seed" ventures (those at the very earliest research stages)—as well as many more millions through a continuous series of venture funds put together by his company.

Ironically, among the dozens of ventures worth hundreds of millions of dollars that Adler has invested in over the years, personally and through his venture funds, the one he selects as representing the most risk had relatively little of his own money at stake. *Reputation*—a commodity more valuable than mere money in the venture capital profession—was on the line.

Early in 1981, William Janeway, head of investment banking at the New York firm Eberstadt & Company (now Eberstadt Fleming, Inc.), came to Fred Adler with a hot deal. The two men had worked together before, and Janeway knew Adler was on the lookout for venture investments in the exploding medical technology field. Adler was offered a chance to invest in Bethesda Research Laboratories (BRL), based just outside Washington, D.C. The company had been launched in 1976 by an entrepreneur named Stephen Turner, and by the end of 1980 was pulling in $5.5 million in yearly sales. BRL was based on a brilliant idea, at precisely the right time.

The company was a supplier of crucial products needed by the genetic engineering industry, which itself was poised to soar. Turner had gambled, correctly at first, that the explosion of activity in genetic engineering would spur immediate demand for the highly specific tools of the trade. One key example: something called "restriction enzymes"—the chemical shears that genetic scientists use to snip out pieces of genes and splice them back together. The beauty of BRL was this: While the genetic engineering companies were still years away from selling *their* products, BRL had real products that could be sold *now* to this industry, for cash. Demand was immense. BRL barreled ahead to meet the demand, not with one product, but with scores of them.

BRL needed ever more cash to finance its breakneck expansion. That's where Eberstadt came in. Other investors, including Citibank's venture capital arm, were more than willing to back the venture. But Adler said no.

Janeway asked again late in 1981. The answer was no again. "I read the presentation, and I was quite friendly with Eberstadt,"

174

says Adler. "But I told him that I thought the deal was overpriced, and that while the business was interesting, it did not seem to be focused." So Adler was out.

Eberstadt's group put in $15 to $18 million to give BRL the push they thought it needed. These were exciting times. Everyone thought BRL was going to be a big winner.

Then, as *The Washington Post* would later say, BRL became a classic example of trying to go too far too fast on too little. Turner took on more than he and BRL could handle. The company undertook an ambitious program to build a major new Genentech-like structure, but ran ahead of itself. "They had more of everything than they could afford," Adler points out.

The concept, however, was sound. "In fact," says Adler, "if Turner had been able to get the sort of financing that Bob Swanson so brilliantly arranged at Genentech, and had gotten the same quality of scientists, he might have been able to pull it off. But he didn't get that much financing." By early 1982, BRL was in deep trouble. Observes Adler, "They went in early, but the industry had not matured. They expanded and found themselves losing a million dollars a month. . . . They were obviously hoping that someone was going to come along and give them another wad of cash."

Adler's phone rang again. This time he was in Florida, trying to get his mind off a painful hip problem. It was Janeway. "You know that company you turned down before," he said, "Bethesda Research Laboratories? Well, it's on the edge of bankruptcy."

Adler's risk instincts had been right. Now he had a new proposition—one that appealed more to those instincts, and one that offered the opportunity of control. This time Janeway didn't want Adler's money. "You were right to turn it down for your venture funds," he said. "Your concerns about the multitude of diverse directions they were going were right. But I believe in the industry, and I think this company can be turned around."

Adler, Janeway thought, was the right man to do it. "I'd like you to meet with the management of the company, and some of the key investors, and we'd like you to come in—not as a venture capitalist, but as a manager to turn it around," Janeway told Adler. "And we're prepared to pay you either a substantial amount of cash, or, if you prefer, you can gamble and take a stock interest."

Just how much cash Eberstadt & Company, and the investors group it represented, was willing to pay Adler was never discussed. Eberstadt had already raised close to $20 million for the company and didn't want to walk away. The firm was obligated to its clients who had put up most of that money to try to salvage the company. Adler was intrigued: "Janeway sent me a mass of material on BRL's situation. I read it, called him back, and told him the company was losing even more money than he thought; that it had about sixty days, at best, to survive; and that he ought to make sure they were paying their withholding taxes because I suspected they were not. And I told him they had taken none of the steps necessary to salvage the company."

The risks changed completely for Adler. It was no longer a question of Adler & Company's venture fund investing in the deal. This was now *personal*. Eberstadt offered to transfer 10 percent of BRL's stock to Adler—860,000 shares. "It was, frankly, worth nothing in my judgment," he says. But he insisted on paying something for the stock anyway. "The reason I did that was I wanted to put my money where my mouth was." So Adler personally put up a quarter of a million dollars for the shares. "I thought that if I really believed I could salvage it, I'd put in the quarter million. If it didn't work I'd lose."

At that point, no outside investor other than Adler was willing to sink another dime into BRL, a company one breath away from Chapter 11 bankruptcy. Eberstadt had convinced the existing investors, however—the ones who'd already tossed in millions— to plow in $7 million more. "Their old investors were already stuck," explains Adler. "This was 'sinkhole' money. They were throwing more money down the sinkhole in the hope that somebody was going to bring in the sump pump and draw it back out."

The pump operator they were betting on was Fred Adler. Janeway had sold the investors on Adler's reputation as a turnaround magician. He had been drawn into turnarounds before, often because existing management had not taken the necessary actions, made the necessary changes, taken the necessary risks. Adler brought instant credibility to the BRL bailout plan. That was also a big risk for Adler. If he failed, he would no longer have that credibility. There might not be a "next time." The new $7 million was a gamble not on BRL, but on Fred Adler. And he knew it.

"My monetary risk was the quarter million. But far more importantly, my risk included the expectations of a lot of people putting
in a lot more money on the basis of Fred Adler coming in like Sir
Galahad waving his sword." That's what worried Adler far more
than losing cash. He imagined the caustic headlines that would
appear in the business press if ninety days later Sir Galahad was
a bust.

The reason Adler was invited into so many venture deals was
his reputation. That was his, and his firm's, most valuable asset.
That's what would make or break him in years ahead. Putting it
on the line with BRL was something he didn't have to do. He
calculated the risks as high. He also had his own business to run
in New York. But Adler was confident in his own skills—his own
ability to *control* the risk he was taking.

"It would have been stupid for me to risk my reputation like
that—forget the quarter million, forget the bad P.R.—if I didn't
think I could prevent that additional $7 million from disappearing
in ninety to a hundred and twenty days," Adler explains. "The
key for me was knowing that I could make the cuts, reduce the
payroll, and bring the company to cash-flow break-even—forget
profitability—before the clock ran out. I thought the possibility of
salvation was reasonable, even though it looked like a 100 percent
risk to others. Therefore, the likelihood of substantial injury to my
name was less than it appeared on first blush." He tapped the
skills of several close friends and top managers on loan from Eberstadt. "I was willing to take the personal responsibility," says
Adler, "but I didn't want the risk to penalize my venture capital
business."

Was $250,000 a lot of money to Adler at that point? He was
already a multimillionaire. "Yes and no," he answers. "I don't
know what a lot of money is." To Adler, money is something that
runs things, the way gasoline runs a car. He lives simply, even
now that he is far wealthier than in 1981. No limos. No private
planes. He points proudly to the six-year-old sport jacket he's
wearing, the brown flannel pants he bought from Land's End, and
the "very cheap but very good" shirt he bought at the Harvard co-
op on his last trip to Boston. He claims to be completely happy
with his home in New Jersey, a *pied-à-terre* in Manhattan, and

177

his one extravagance, a home in Jamaica where he likes to spend every third weekend during the winter. He's also a generous contributor to charities.

"It *isn't* a lot of money, and it *is* a lot of money," Adler says of the $250,000. "I don't like losing 20 cents . . . $20 to me is a lot of money. The real risk was in doing a bad job; the publicity I'd get from it [Adler is a favorite subject for the business press]; and the personal feeling would be the worst, the feeling that I'd blown it." He worried about those risks: "I'm like anybody else. I hate rejection. I have my pride.

"On the other hand, you know something, I thought it had a shot. I told Eberstadt openly that there was good probability we might not make it. What I thought *could* be done was, if they raised the additional millions, I could at least stabilize the company so that the new money that came in would be safe. . . .

"What I really did was a risk assessment of what the market value of the company would be if I could stop the bloodletting, if I could preserve the assets that were there." Adler figured if he could stabilize the situation another company might be willing to buy out BRL as the entry price to this high-potential market. He particularly had in mind foreign companies.

Adler moved quickly. "I showed up at the company, met with the key managers and told them where I wanted cuts—what areas and what projects." The number of full- and part-time employees was slashed from 650 to 250. Turner was relieved of his duties as president and CEO of the company, and cringed as Adler's meat cleaver hacked away in his attempt to save the young company's life. Turner still held stock in BRL that several years later would make him a rich man.

Adler made his choices of what to keep and what to cut at BRL based on his own appraisals, his idea of the company's future, and opinions from others. He'd already gained a reputation as a high-tech visionary, but says the decisions were business decisions, not technological ones. "I'm *not* a scientist. I'm overrated on my scientific abilities. People think I'm a technologist, but I'm really not. I'm a businessman who's very much of a generalist." Any extended conversation with Adler bears this out. He shifts effortlessly from the economics of the cruise ship industry (one of his funds was considering an investment in this area), to cellular telephones, to integrated circuits, to marketing videos in California.

"In analyzing the company, I tried to break everything into its smallest component. Then I decided whether that particular component made sense," Adler says. If not, it went. "It was a very simplistic approach, and it worked. It seemed to me that the biotech industry was going to take off. And that if you could develop a prime supplier of real quality products to that industry—products they needed to develop and make their products—you really had a hell of a company."

Some insiders blasted Adler for being too heavy-handed, for dumping worthwhile projects. Turner was bitter. He told a reporter two years later, "There was a lot of wreckage. Many good things the company was doing should have been salvaged, but Adler was in too much of a hurry." Adler agrees that some of Turner's babies went out with the bathwater. "I haven't the slightest doubt that I cut out some projects that were worthwhile," he says, knowing it was either that or Chapter 11.

After cutting loose all except what Adler considered BRL's core business, he threw all the company's resources into a massive effort at improving quality in the firm's key products—a gamble on positioning BRL as the company customers would look to first. By the summer of 1982—four months after picking up the gauntlet Janeway had thrown down—Adler had brought BRL back to a cash-flow break-even point. It wasn't yet profitable, but at least the company had enough money coming in to continue operating. Investors in Adler's venture fund were allowed to buy in, and would later profit handsomely from their leader's personal risk taking. Adler himself invested another $2 million in the company.

In September 1983, Adler merged BRL with GIBCO Corporation, a subsidiary of Dexter Chemical Corporation. Dexter had one major condition before the merger: Adler must remain as principal executive officer and chairman of the combined companies for at least two years. BRL's owners received 36 percent of the new company, diluting Adler's holdings considerably; Dexter's interest was 64 percent. The new company became known as Life Technologies.

Adler stayed on, and the company continued to improve each year: Profits soared 116 percent in 1985, jumped another 37 per-

179

cent in 1986, still another 46 percent in 1987. In October 1986, Life Technologies sold a small part of its shares to the public for the first time. By 1987, the company had captured 50 percent of the U.S. market for cell biology products and an even larger percentage in Europe, according to a Shearson Lehman research report. Shearson rated Life Tech's R&D program as extremely promising.

By 1988, Adler still reigned as chairman and principal executive officer. Sales had passed $110 million; after-tax profits were $10 million. The company employed 1,100 people and had no debt. Adler's combined investment of about $2.3 million was worth about $9 million—not a fantastic gain by VC standards, "but a reasonable gain," says Adler. He now believes his biggest payoff came from other opportunities that arose along the way as a result of the contacts he made in the BRL/Life Technologies risk.

Pro-Active Risking

Adler describes himself as a "pro-active" investor—"somebody who is not just passive, but who gets involved and tries to help management of the company to do better; somebody who does more than read the annual report and quarterly statements."

Wall Street, a passive arena according to Adler, is not this VC's bag. When most Americans think about the financing mechanism that builds corporations in America, they think of Wall Street. To Adler, that's bunk: "Wall Street plays an insignificant part" in raising capital for new American enterprise. Adler contends the real risk spadework is done in the venture capital trenches, long before Wall Street ever hears of these companies. Nine out of ten may be gone before they reach the "going public" stage—when they arrive on Wall Street. Even then it's often with just a small piece of the company, and much of that money goes to compensate the original venturers who took the biggest risks.

"Wall Street is a pipeline," Adler observes. "That's all it is. It is *not* pro-active. That's the critical difference. It's people trying to hustle a buck." They play an important role, he concedes, but have little interest in building an enterprise for the future. *They* are the quick-buck artists, he contends, *not* the VC.

"Although I do some open market [Wall Street, stock market]

180

investing, I'm really not a good open market investor," he says. "I don't have time for it."

Adler was a forty-year-old Brooklyn-born, Harvard-trained lawyer working for the New York law firm Reavis & McGrath in the mid-1960s when he began to sour on being a hired gun for people he mostly despised. Helping one client turn around a flagging business gave him his first push toward venture capital, as did a developing interest in the potential of computers.

His first big chance to do something about it came along in 1968 with the opportunity to help back Data General Corporation, a new minicomputer company being launched by a group of former Digital Equipment engineers. So Adler kicked in $150,000 of his own money, some of it borrowed. The risk paid off, and Adler was soon hooked on his new profession. By the time the Boston-based Data General became a $1 billion company in 1984, Adler's original stake in it had swelled to better than $20 million.

By 1978 he had formed his own firm, Adler & Company, as a more organized method of risking money on new ventures. The firm has operated highly successful venture capital funds worth hundreds of millions of dollars, with investors that have included Merrill Lynch, Sears Roebuck, Citibank and Prudential-Bache. Adler's influence reached cross-country to dozens of the high-technology firms sprouting in California's risk-fertile Silicon Valley during the late 1970s and early 80s. Among the scores of companies he has backed are MicroPro International, Daisy Systems Corporation, Intersil, Biotechnology General, Medical 21, Control Automation, Purification Engineering and Graftek Technology Corporation—some of which were later sold to larger corporations for huge profits.

A child of the mid-1920s whose father's restaurant business went broke in the Great Depression, Adler operates from an office within Reavis & McGrath. Twice married, the hard-driving Adler is still a senior partner in the firm that he joined in 1951, but has long pursued his own venture capital interests exclusively. Even in a profession full of uncertainty and change, Adler is considered a maverick. Often described as a daring visionary, he juggles an intense involvement in dozens of companies simultaneously, constantly pouring over technical materials to stay ahead of his risks.

Unlike most other venturers these days, Adler still backs companies at their earliest stages with "seed capital," and for fun he likes to revive troubled firms he calls the "living dead." Seed investing has been a hallmark of Adler's for years. Most of those investments are his own. He wants to avoid objections from venture fund partners unwilling to foot the even higher risks and longer payback periods of seed deals. "I pay the going rate on the seed investments. And I pay the going rate if it looks good and there are additional rounds," says Adler. "I take the risk. And for what it's worth, my seed money investments to date have been my biggest losers."

But he keeps making them. Why? Partly because he hopes his efforts can make a difference to society. "If somebody has a nutty idea in cancer or other health-care area, if it looks interesting and the people are good, I'll put some money in," explains Adler. "But I have to be candid with you. For the most part, I've lost my shirt in them." He has invested about $3 million of his own money on seed companies in Israel, none of which have worked out. Adler won't invest his *company's* money in the seed deals until later. "It shows you how somebody with their personal investments will take risks that make no sense because they've added an emotional value to them," says Adler. "My own conclusion is that you need specialized funds to do seed financings, and the best thing people like myself can do is invest in those funds."

Adler, his slim leathery-looking face parked behind a desk stacked high with papers, holds court in his forty-second-floor Park Avenue office as streams of people flow in and out. He is talking about risk taking; how to do it ARTfully, intelligently. For him, knowledge is the key. "You have to know the *limits* [his emphasis] of the risk," he says. "What are you *really* risking? What's the upside? Like a lot of people in my field, I read tremendously. I try to have enough background to essentially understand what's going on. I take a case of work home practically every night, and two or three cases home every weekend—technical journals, analyst reports, just a mass of materials. The way to risk intelligently, to reduce risk or increase risk as the case may be, is, in a word, information."

Adler has been reading up on tissue plasminogen activator (TPA), a then experimental, genetically engineered drug that can stop heart attacks by dissolving the blood clots that cause them. A company he has backed, called Biotechnology General, is developing another new substance, called SOD (superoxide dismutase). Some experts believe SOD can be used in conjunction with TPA to help limit the damage to the heart muscle caused during a heart attack and its subsequent treatment with TPA. Adler's research has convinced him that TPA and similar products will receive government approval and reach the market much sooner than some people think. Thus, he reasons, "the odds of our getting SOD to the market rapidly as well will be up substantially."

He contemplates sinking more money into the venture to accelerate development. "Just by reading about TPA," Adler explains, "it raises questions in my mind as to whether our work on SOD should be accelerated. So I'm plugging this into the business plan." Now he says he can risk more money on Biotechnology General more intelligently. The information, Adler believes, has given him one additional element of control over the situation.

But constantly seeking information, instead of acting, can slow decision making—a hitch venture capitalists can't afford in a fast-moving field. To avoid that trap, Adler claims to seek only the *essential* information needed to calculate his risk-taking decisions. "The stages of decision are this," he explains, "to first define your objective or problem. Then gather your data. It's what I call 'truth seeking,' because getting data is more than just getting raw information—it is seeking truth. Then once you have your truth, you go through it to reach decisions, and I say decisions, rather than a single decision, because in my world I try to have a preferred decision, and several alternative decisions to back away from it if the risk doesn't work out. *I try to preserve reasonable alternatives, not inconsistent with taking action.*

"Then the next step after reaching a decision is to implement. But at the same time, I believe in reducing risks by continually reviewing every decision you make. There is no virtue, as far as I'm concerned, in consistency if the decision you've made needs either revocation or modification. The only virtue consistency has is predictability, and too many people use that simply to avoid taking risks. If your decision is wrong, so what? Modify it. Move to an alternative.

"In other words, it's not only your decision process and your implementation process that involve risk taking, it's the failure to *further* decide and implement." Adler, a single-minded-type ven-

183

ture capitalist who prefers medical technology companies, is one of his industry's leading apostles of maintaining risk-taking alternatives, control and flexibility—all key ART dynamics. "What I am saying is that a lot of people are too damned rigid," Adler growls. "They make a decision and that's the end of it. They throw it into the hopper, it gets acted on and goes through the machinery, and whatever comes out comes out. Well, bullshit. Whatever comes out, at some point, may not deserve to come out anymore. At some point you may want to truncate the whole process. You may want to void it. Well, *do* it.

"There's nothing sacred about a risk. You keep examining your facts. You keep going into it. That's why risk takers often appear to be big risk takers, but frequently they are not really *big* risk takers. Risk is relative and changing. It's a dynamic, rather than an absolute. You increase real risk by treating it as an absolute. We reduce real opportunity by sometimes not taking a risk, because you treat it as an absolute and overrate the negative, or overweight the negative, because you don't include the ability to modify or abort your risk."

Too Much Talk

According to Adler, today's CEOs talk too much about making changes in their organizations, but do too little about it. He claims that 80 percent of needed corporate fat trimming is obvious and could be done immediately, yet managers make a big deal about each cut and piddle around until it's too late. Adler also believes strongly that companies must take risks by "obsoleting" their own best products to make room for new generations yet to come. "You don't milk new products for the *earnings,* but rather for the next generation of products that will replace the ones you've got," he says, drawing a bead squarely on economist Joseph Schumpeter's process of creative destruction.

Adler puts little stock in being consistent in running a business. He's more attuned to change and surprise—the fodder of risk. He despises corporate raiders, and the so-called greenmailers, who make obscene sums by threatening hostile takeovers, or by purchasing companies and then selling them off in pieces for big profits. "The procedure of taking apart companies and making a quick profit by selling them in pieces is not for me," says Adler. "You can *always*, at a given point in a company's history, make more by breaking it up than by building it. The real question is whether the longer-term building makes a great deal of sense," even if it does require greater risk taking, greater long-term commitment. "And it's a balance. I understand the interests of the shareholder are paramount. But they're not the only interests. The interests of the employees count, too. I don't like what I call the pirates operating out there because they strip, they wreck companies. Greenmail is the worst part of it. Being paid off like that is just wrong."

Still, Adler maintains that the wave of corporate restructurings in the 1980s—at times prodded by the raiders—is a positive force. His own company now has a special fund investing in leveraged buyouts (LBOs), run largely by Adler's partner, Leonard Shaykin. Shaykin structures the financial assets of the LBO deals while Adler looks at the broader picture: Will the company's line of business make money? Does it have the right direction for the future? Can it continue to meet the needs of its customers?

But Adler's heart is elsewhere. "LBOs have much less risk than pure ventures," he says. "Turnarounds and ventures have much greater risk because what you are aiming for there are much higher returns, based upon your ability to enter a new field and beat out the competition, when you don't even know yet what competition is out there."

LBOs are different. "When you go into a leveraged buyout situation you have the advantage of a management team that has experience you can look at so you can judge it. You have the data on the industry showing in great, great detail the competitive companies anywhere near the size of your operation and bigger. And you have enormous product information showing the direction of the product. You have a history of *need*."

Venture financing offers none of that, according to Adler. "When you start a new company, or invest in the early stages of a company in classic technology investing, your risk is enormous. And in many cases, you can be totally *right* about the industry, and totally *wrong* about the timing."

Just trying to bring a company public involves great risk for the venture capitalist. If the market sours the VC investors might have to pump more of their own money into the company to keep

185

building it until they can realize some profit in a public stock offering.

But even though Adler doesn't consider the LBOs to be high risk, he makes a distinction: "We still *plan* them as if they are high risk. And by that I mean the analysis is a heavy-risk analysis —we make judgments on what we will have to do if the *probable* events don't work out. If we do encounter problems we're situated to handle them."

If flexibility and adaptability are Fred Adler's Rule Number One for successful risk taking, then self-reliance—control—constitutes success Rule Number Two. "People who are risk takers tend to have heavy reliance on themselves," he says. "In my own case, I find that when we have a successful enterprise, in 75 percent of the cases it is directly proportional to my involvement. I have a reputation in venture capital for probably being more involved in management than most others."

SHARING RISK: OPM AND OPB

*"Everyone has a 'risk muscle.' You keep it in
shape by trying new things. If you don't, it
atrophies. Make a point of using it at least
once a day. . . ."*

—ROGER VON OECH,
A Whack on the Side of the Head

If risk taking is valuable, does that make risk reduction harmful?
Not at all. Many situations call for avoiding a risk, or at least
reducing it. Executives who take *every* risk are not intelligent,
calculated risk takers. They are attempting economic suicide.
This is a troublesome ARTistic trip wire. The critical distinction
that helps vault that trip wire is this: *There is a difference between reducing risk itself, and reducing or spreading the possible
negative effects of a risk.* By taking separate steps to dampen
the impact of a failure, should that happen, managers can keep
the positive potential of risk moving forward, while reducing
only the impact of potential harm. Avoiding the risk altogether
would have avoided the danger, but also the potential gain.

Risk-taking companies do this in many ways. One is the joint venture—drawing on another firm's or individual's resources to better the odds and spread the risk. Constant review and flexibility help tremendously, too. If conditions change, that pliancy permits the risk taker to change his or her plans as well, thus softening the negative blow; or, under happier circumstances, leveraging unanticipated gains.

Market studies are one of the most common tools, if used correctly. Coca-Cola used its exhaustive market studies to support a hugely risky move, and—*it thought*—to reduce the potentially negative results, even though it didn't work out that way. The trouble is, market studies are often used simply to postpone decisions, and as an excuse *not* to take action. Herbert Allen, a Coke board member and CEO of Allen & Company, which owned Columbia Pictures before Coke bought it, says Coke executives used their market studies the right way: "Obviously, changing the formula was more risky than anything else Coke has done. I would call [Goizueta] an intelligent risk taker. The difference is the level and depth of thought involved. He thinks things out as much as possible, plans as much as possible, and does as much research as possible in depth. *Then he's willing to take a chance.* While most companies use their research as an excuse for why not to take a risk, Roberto uses it as a positive experience."

"Cautious risking" is not an oxymoron. The potential trap is this: Risk reduction is often nothing more than risk rearrangement. Managers who aim to modify their risks must be certain that's what they are really doing. Venture capitalists like Adler are always sharing risks. Adler likes to have other risk takers on his side. "The ultimate leverage in my business is to find other people who are very good," he points out. "I want them to take intelligent risks, absolutely." He believes strongly in having the managers of companies he invests in take risks along with him. Getting those individuals to put their own money and their own futures on the line "makes for a better company," he says. It's one of the VC's basic operating rules: Make sure the entrepreneur you are backing has his rear end on the line as much as or more so than you do.

That philosophy isn't limited to the venture game. Even a conglomerate builder like J.B. Fuqua, of Fuqua Industries, uses it. When he began acquiring companies for his stable, Fuqua had little cash. He looked for private companies with entrepreneurial-minded owners willing to exchange everything they had for stock in Fuqua Industries. "I surrounded myself with a lot of other risk takers," he recalls, "as opposed to the professional management types. That's the reason this company did so well in the early years. Everybody had something at risk, and a number of people had their entire fortune at risk. We bought private companies founded by their managements and offered them large ownership incentives that tied them to the company. The ownership arrangements ensured that these people had a continuing interest in profitable growth, since the number of shares they received was linked to performance. At one time, using this technique, we had twenty-three millionaires on our payroll."

The key, says Fuqua, is OPM and OPB—his acronyms for "Other People's Money" and "Other People's Brains." He listens to others. He nudges people into sharing the risks. And that, to Fuqua, is what has made all the difference in building his corporate empire.

Fuqua claims most CEOs lack courage. "American business may be experiencing an entrepreneurial revival," he argued in *Chief Executive* magazine, "but in my view the corporate suite today is wall to wall fear. Despite ample evidence that new management methods are vital to progress, entrenched businesses are digging in further and dragging American industry down." In Fuqua's view, too many top managers have risen by avoiding risks. Or, as Rosabeth Kanter, a Harvard business professor, once described it to *Business Week*, top corporate executives frequently "manage to their résumé." That means they choose their projects based on how it will look on paper. Risky projects are avoided. The result, contends Fuqua, produces executives who can't take risks now because they never learned how to do it in the past.

By taking risks himself, Fuqua tries to set the example for others. And he delegates responsibility easily. "That's one of the things that makes us different in how we manage this company," he says. "We have a highly decentralized management operation. We don't want to manage anything in this building [Fuqua's corporate headquarters in downtown Atlanta]. The subsidiaries are encouraged to make their own decisions. That's always been the way."

189

If there's a solution to corporate stagnation that J. B. Fuqua has to offer, it's simply this: Start taking risks and things will happen. "Once having taken a risk, it's easier to take a risk down the road as you do other things," he advises. "A lot of that's a matter of getting started taking risks. Just like the dark. If you're afraid of the dark, you go out there and walk a little in the dark, and you find out there's nothing in it that's going to hurt you. So you're able to walk further. Once you get started taking risks, it's easier."

THE STANLEY STEAMER:
FAILED FOR LACK OF RISKING

"There's as much risk in doing nothing as in doing something."

—TRAMMELL CROW

The fear of risk that J.B. Fuqua talks about is not unique to recent times. Consider the intriguing story of an earlier American high-tech industry—the beginnings of the automobile business. We take it on faith that today's rendition of auto locomotion—the internal-combustion engine—was somehow the best technology, because it's the one that survived.

Not necessarily. VHS wasn't technologically superior to Sony's Betamax VCR, but Sony blinked and VHS won. If the risk takers had been switched, Betamax would be the VCR standard today. Similarly, there are convincing arguments that if twin brothers Freelan and Francis Stanley had been ARTists instead of risk avoiders at their Stanley Motor Carriage Company, of Newton, Massachusetts, the auto industry's standard-setting technology might be radically different.

In 1900, with autos in their infancy, there were no industry standards about what an auto should look like, or how it ought to be powered—just as there were as yet no standards in the 1970s when personal computer makers first unearthed that massive market, or when VCRs and HD-TV were young. There was only a large body of profit-seeking inventors and promoters who, as a

190

Harvard University historian noted in the 1950s, "had more faith in, than knowledge of, their innovations."

Steam propulsion offered huge advantages that even by today's standards sound attractive:

• Steam-powered autos were simple and easy to control. Later models of the Stanley Steamer had only twenty-two moving parts (including the four wheels), less than the gasoline engine's self-start mechanism alone.

• Compared to early combustion engines, steam was smooth and could be flexibly adapted to a road vehicle. It also had greater range, power and speed than the electric cars of that day.

• Unlike early gas engines, the steamer did not have to be cranked to start (an arduous and dangerous task), and there were no gears that required manual shifting.

The Stanley Steamer offered consumers of the day the tremendous competitive advantage of shift-free driving, first touted in the company's 1902 catalogue. Stanley's competitors, who were developing the gasoline engine, spent years of research trying to win back that advantage for their version of the auto—research that ultimately resulted in the automatic transmission we know today.

During the era of the Stanley Steamer, the gasoline-powered internal-combustion engine was in its first stages of development. Inventors hadn't yet figured out how to "gear down" this constant speed engine for variable speed operation. Says Charles C. McLaughlin, the Harvard historian, "To operate without stalling, the gasoline engine had to turn over at a rate of at least 900 revolutions a minute, and to gain maximum efficiency it had to run at three times that speed. The transmission of this power at a controllable speed to the wheels of the vehicle became a complex technological problem." Engineers still are finding ways to refine this transmission.

According to McLaughlin's study, the Stanley brothers were hardly alone in their belief in steam. Over a hundred entrepreneurial auto companies focused their efforts on steam technology in the early 1900s, fearful of the gasoline engine's complexity. Ransom Olds, whose Oldsmobiles live on in name today, first worked with steam-powered cars. And the Doble steam car, of the

191

1920s and early 30s, was considered unsurpassed in trouble-free operation and performance among all cars of its time, says the Harvard study.

The Stanley brothers were constantly adding innovations to their designs. But, according to McLaughlin, "Despite the constant improvements and simplifications which they lavished on their product, the Stanley twins did little to improve their methods of production, financing or selling." There was no spirit of creative destruction at Stanley. The company's product quality and early innovations had made it the largest and longest-surviving of the steam-powered automakers. But a failure to keep taking business risks and expand the company ultimately fueled Stanley's demise. With it perished steam's chances to develop further technologically and perhaps remain a force in the auto industry's future.

In an entrepreneurial pattern familiar to this day, the Stanleys distinguished themselves as inventors, not ARTists. As businessmen they failed to take the risks that could have prevented their company's downfall. They operated their company—one of the more prosperous of the time—on hand-to-mouth financing. They were afraid to borrow money, a minor risk taken for granted today, but something taken less lightly back then.

Their cars were popular and commanded premium prices. By 1920, the Stanley Company had a large backlog of orders waiting to be filled. But since the Stanley twins were so unadventurous, so averse to taking risks with their enterprise to allow it to grow, their failure to keep up with new production, financing and marketing techniques started to leave them behind. Rather than challenge the market with risk and innovation, they made a classic, blind-spot error of belittling the movement in Detroit toward gasoline. In calling gasoline power "an engineering fashion," the Stanleys were blind to their own company's complacency. Had the Stanleys been less risk-averse, the history of one of America's greatest industries *might* have been different.

OPB for Adler

In venture capital, Fred Adler follows his own version of conglomerateur J.B. Fuqua's OPB technique: "What we try to do is get young managers. I happen to like a lot of young managers because the better ones are more open-minded. Later on, they get too involved with it. Their ears get clogged with age. They don't listen anymore. They want to do it their way. Some take risks that are stupid and others take no risks. They forget that information includes more than raw data—*it includes other people's thinking."*

Here's where Adler finds an exception to his own rule. *Too much self-reliance can be a dangerous thing for a risk taker,* according to this self-assured venture capitalist. The narrowly self-reliant individual, in Adler's view, not only believes he can drink his own bathwater, "but considers bottling it as champagne as well." Risks, no longer calculated, become unintelligent risks.

Adler has uncovered a subtle difference between *confidence* and *self-reliance.* Confidence in risk taking is essential, but if it leads to excessive self-reliance—to the exclusion of valuable outside opinions—it becomes a formula for failure. At the same time, when a risk taker begins to doubt his or her own ability to be successful, it can lead to trouble.

That's precisely what Adler theorizes happened to Ivan Boesky, the arbitrage king who was busted by the SEC for illegal insider trading in 1986. Boesky was zapped with the biggest penalty ever imposed for illegal dealings on Wall Street—roughly $100 million. "I don't think Boesky did it out of money greed," observes Adler. "I think it was worse than that. I think the man became insecure about himself and his abilities, and was willing to do almost anything to reduce the risks of arbitrage. He wanted to take the profits of normal risk arbitrage and inflate them by eliminating the risk totally."

Risk Key: Pattern Recognition

In two decades of venturing, Adler has become a maestro of risk and change. He has backed dozens of firms in scores of technological fields, from computers to high-tech skin moisturizers, from nuclear magnetic resonance to materials for artificial limbs. (Adler himself had two artificial hips installed in 1983.) In each case, whenever there was room, Adler would put some of his own money into the companies his venture firm backed. "I put money in because it works for me," he explains. "The rewards from the money that you put in personally are actually much greater than the override that you get on other people's money. Why do I do it? Because I can afford it, and it also makes me think more carefully about the risk of my fiduciary money. Given where I come from—a background where I had no money at all—I think instinctively. The sort of risk assessment that I do for my own money acts to make me more careful when I deal with other people's money."

But to Fred Adler, "instinct" is not the mysterious internal alarm clock that it is often described as. To him, it's a *collection of knowledge,* and an important part of calculated risk taking. "What is instinct?" he asks. "*Instinct is a recognition of patterns.* Each of us takes an information base, consisting of everything we've learned since we began to think well, and that becomes our experience. It becomes a data bank. And what we do is take that information and apply it to everything we do, as long as we're not too tired or too stretched.

"Risk takers reach conclusions, and they call the process instinct only because they don't want to admit they've gone through a thinking process along the way, which they do. Risk takers always go through a thinking process, even if they call it instinct," says Adler.

One reason this venture capitalist has been so successful at taking risks is that he hates to be wrong. And when things go badly, he blames only himself. "Usually my initial risks are okay," he says. "But my risk taking is like everybody else's. If I don't stay on top of it and focus on it, my main risk is myself. My biggest danger in the world is me. I'm the person who makes me lose money; very few others do."

Adler cites the example of Ztel, "a major technology risk" company that his venture firm was backing. It's one risk he now feels he didn't pay close enough attention to. He didn't recognize the patterns.

Ztel, based in Massachusetts, was developing advanced telephone switching technology. According to Adler, it was a top-notch group, with leading-edge technology. Everything seemed to be in place. The idea had drawn big-name investors. In addition to Adler personally (as well as his venture fund), NCR, General Electric and the Hillman family (well known for venture investing) were involved. A similar company based on the West Coast was pursuing the same technology with backing from the venture firm Kleiner Perkins. Expectations were high all around.

"Then something happened," Adler recalls. "The market changed. By the time Ztel developed its product—and it was late, as frequently happens—spending for these large switches" had tailed off. "For both companies, the market that was supposed to materialize, according to every analyst in the world, failed to materialize. And it was a disaster. We lost 100 percent of the $10 million we had invested. At that point we withdrew. The other investors put in another $5 million or more each, and lost all of that, too.

"Still, the largest single loser in Ztel was *me*, personally," a direct result of the Adlerian philosophy of putting his money where his mouth is. "You see," he explains, "I invest with the [Adler & Company] fund in just about every situation where there is room." The trouble is, the deals where there is "room" for him to invest are usually the highest risk deals. The best ones are generally sold out . . . no room for personal money.

"If there's a lot of room, everybody and his mother can invest," says Adler. "And in the case of Ztel, of the $10 million we had invested, $1.5 million or more was mine personally—in addition to my share of the fund's losses. So it was an expensive risk." Adler hadn't spotted the coming slowdown in the capital goods market, nor the shift in the economy that helped kill Ztel.

When the partner handling the project left the firm, Adler went to see the company. What he found angered him. "This is supposed to be an entrepreneurial company," grumbles Adler in recalling his visit, "and the president's office was 25 percent bigger than this office," he says, indicating his own Park Avenue workshop. "The guy had brand-new ultra-expensive furniture. The bulk of *my* furniture was bought in 1964.

"You walk into [a situation like that] and you know it's bad. I'll tell you, I walked out of the office cursing myself, saying, 'Adler, you're a damn fool.' " His visit prompted him to take another look at the firm's business plan, and he began to reconsider his risk. "I decided there was no way this thing would work without a much greater infusion of money than anyone thought." While the other investors lost another $20 million, Adler refused to participate

195

anymore. "We probably could have cut the loss earlier, but we didn't see the turn fast enough. . . . But that's the risk of venture capital."

What Adler lost in Ztel, however, he more than made up with Daisy Systems, a pioneering firm in computer-aided engineering. In 1980 there was plenty of room to invest in the Daisy deal. Adler went in personally, along with his venture fund.

This, too, was a new technology. "But my assessment in this case was that the market would be there quickly," recalls Adler. "We learned something from Ztel. The longer the development period, the greater the risk. There's more time for things to go wrong."

In Daisy, Adler, and his fund, had about $3 million invested. Adler says he personally made about $12 million on Daisy, the fund about $90 million. That was largely due to timing—Adler and his fund took profits on Daisy before the company got into trouble. "We were lucky," he admits.

As the BRL case demonstrated, however, Adler won't hesitate to grab a company by the neck and shake it if that's what he thinks is needed to bring it around. He can be ruthless in taking a company he believes is sick and shocking it back to life. And he won't blink at dumping a chief executive in whom he's lost faith.

In 1984, California-based Daisy Systems Corporation was still riding high. Wall Street loved the firm; the stock was performing nicely. A smiling Aryeh Finegold, Daisy's chief executive, a co-founder and a former Israeli paratrooper, appeared in photos accompanying articles about Fred Adler's venture successes. Adler had backed Daisy when none of the high-tech San Francisco venture capitalists would touch the company, and it made good press. He was able to grasp the commercial value of computer-aided engineering before most people, and was willing to risk his money on it.

By 1986, however, Daisy was in trouble, its stock struggling, and Adler again brought in his ax and fire hose. One of his first moves was to remove Finegold. It was vintage Adler ARTistry. He'd placed his bet on Finegold earlier, but didn't hesitate now to change it. Flexibility. Control. Conditions were different. Adler needed to adapt, to shift to his next available alternative.

With Adler, however, it wasn't anything personal; it rarely is with the men and women he backs. His decisions are tough, but they are all business, and only occasionally emotional. They are, however, intuitive. A short while after Finegold's removal, Adler invested more money in a software company Finegold had moved to as chief executive. With that type of loyalty, Adler demonstrates his commitment to risk taking *and* the inevitability of its periodic failures. For Fred Adler, those periodic failures hurt, but he has the ability to analyze them and make them stepping-stones, not roadblocks.

He faced a similar situation with MicroPro International, the computer software company that created the wildly successful WordStar word-processing software package. Adler became a major investor in 1980, and two years later took over as company chairman when the firm started losing money. Within ninety days under the Adler scalpel in 1983, the firm went from losing $1.5 million in one quarter to making that much the next, before the venture capitalist backed off. His ready alternative in that case was to rely on his own considerable skill in turning a situation around. Armed with that dispassionate venture capitalist's aura, Adler could easily take new risks, eliminate old ones that had gone wrong, and *move the company forward.*

"Whenever you take the chance on developing a new market," Adler concludes, "the upside is fantastic, à la Daisy, and the downside is just as fantastic, à la Ztel."

Adler takes another in the unrelenting wave of phone calls pouring into his office, sets up a business meeting for Sunday, and hangs up. "Now that was a risk," he says. The phone call had been from a Greek friend of his who a year earlier had called Adler asking him if he'd be willing to help bankroll a new technology company in Greece—a socialist nation antithetical to Adler's economic views. Adler is a strong believer in America's brand of enterprise, and feels that venture capitalist risk taking has contributed more than any other profession to moving American business ahead, helping instill a spirit of progress in the nation along the way. The rewards of backing raw start-up companies can be huge, but he feels they are well deserved, since they involve taking risks few are willing to take.

"I couldn't justify investing in Greece out of my venture capital fund," continues Adler, "so I said I would put in $500,000 of my own money and take 55 percent of the company. That made the risk very simple: half a million dollars. Plus, I know myself, and it would be another $300,000. But I decided that the bulk of it would be deductible if it went bad, and therefore I could cut my loss to half. So I decided my real out-of-pocket risk was $400,000.

"And since I wasn't taking anybody else's money, the biggest risk I worry about, which is my reputation, couldn't be attacked, only my own money," he says. "So it's a $400,000 risk. I view the upside of it—my share—as perhaps $10 million, and there's at least a 50 percent chance I can get out whole."

It's not the first time Adler had risked money on a friend's word. As the story is told, Adler once sent $50,000 to a friend who called with no time to explain why he needed it. As it turned out, Adler had just invested in a hospital chain, and his $50,000 became $1 million three years later.

Taking responsibility for risks? Adler sometimes takes it to extremes. Shortly after he took Biotechnology General public in 1983, for example, the market for high-tech stocks crumbled and the price dropped from the $13 it was initially sold at to about $7 per share. Investors who bought at the offering price were staring at a 46 percent loss. They weren't amused. But in the high-risk market for IPOs (initial public stock offerings), that happens all the time. The standard response: tough luck.

Not Adler. He felt responsible. He'd nursed the company, brought it public, offered it to investors. So Adler tried to make up the losses to the investors who had bought at the offering price by convincing insider shareholders (company officers, directors and major shareholders) to grant a special dividend of more stock to make up for the original stock's bad showing—an unheard-of company giveback. They had no obligation to do it, but Adler insisted.

Why Companies Stumble

According to this veteran of the enterprise gridiron, CEOs wouldn't find their companies in trouble so often if they paid more attention to basics such as intelligent risk taking and cash flow. "A human body lives on blood," he says. "Without blood you're dead. Cash is the blood flow of corporations. You *must* take

198

risks in a company that's growing in line with your ability to support those risks. And that doesn't depend on recorded profit—it depends on real cash flow. Companies typically get into trouble when their spending gets out of proportion with cash flow. That's the largest single cause of failure they have.

"Of course, there are other situations where executives don't take intelligent risks. One of my own companies, Data General, is an example. A number of years ago I proposed to them that they go into the business of on-line transaction reporting [a cash management service for banks and corporations]. But we were spread thin, and the management at the time made a decision that made no sense. The market was small and even though they thought I might be right about prospective growth, they didn't do it.

"Well, Tandem Computers [the Cupertino, California, firm that *did* move into the field] is likely to reach $1 billion in the next year or two," says Adler. Tandem had received funding from Kleiner Perkins after other venture capitalists rejected its founder, James Treybig, and his idea for a fail-safe computer to use in electronic money transactions. "Was management right or were they wrong?" asks Adler. "You never know, really, because if the company really wouldn't have been able to handle the expansion within the scope of its cash flow or other interior resources, they probably were right. Similarly, we at Data General accented office automation over scientific work stations a couple of years ago. And given what has happened to those that went the other direction, it was probably a wrong decision. We've been playing catch-up ever since.

"Those are examples of not taking risks of developing new areas or new pieces of equipment when we should have. But those are comparatively rare cases since most of the companies I'm involved with are essentially entrepreneurial. They take risks fairly well."

As a venture capitalist, Adler sees his role, in part, as helping nudge entrepreneurs into a position where they can begin taking *more* calculated risks. The way Adler sees it, in the early stages of a company, entrepreneurs often are *not* taking as many risks as they should be, nor are they taking wise risks. That's where Adler believes his ARTist's palette can lend expertise, in addition to financing.

199

"The risks entrepreneurial companies take are more often the market risks rather than the technology risks," he says. "The only thing that's worse than being late to the market in terms of a new product is being too early. In the sales cycle, the early bird does *not* catch the worm, he starves to death."

Being well-informed is still another ingredient in Fred Adler's formula for successful risk taking. Simply recognizing what risk is, and what it is not, is crucial. "Definition of risk is important to success," he says. You have to know what risk is. "What's the up? What's the down? What are the points at which the risk starts operating? Is the downside *all* the money you're putting into it? Not necessarily. There may be safe elements to it. You have to define the whole degree of the risk you're taking."

While some business risks are less then they appear, Adler points out that others can be greater than anyone thinks. Nowhere is it illustrated better than in the debilitating venture capitalist's disease called *throwing good money after bad*. "Here's an example," says Adler. "A company with which I'm involved, against my very vehement advice, put about $10 million into buying a minority position in a company with an option [to buy more]. I said, 'Hey, fellas. You really haven't done two things in my judgment: a really careful analysis of the cash needs of this company over the next twelve months, on a probable scenario, a worst case and a best case. You really haven't taken apart these managers to see whether you can live with them on the basis of the cash flow you define. And you don't have any fail-safe plan, either in your contract of investment or in how you're going to operate if it starts to fall apart unexpectedly.' I said you can't do it. You're making an error.

"And they said, 'Well, Fred, we don't have more than $10 million in this thing.' And I said, 'That assumes, my friend, that you don't make the mistake of putting in more money as it goes along. Because you will. You always do. *Your period between decision and cutback is always slower than you think*, except for the few people who are really on top of it. And I make that mistake, too, if I'm not personally on top of it, and I'm pretty experienced. You people will definitely make mistakes. Aside from all the bullshit, the risk is really $30 million, maybe $40 million, real risk.' "

To Adler, who has been through it countless times in the real world of venture capital, it was common sense. To the academic world, the point he was making is called the "escalation dilemma"—the tendency of a business to continue sinking money into a project that to any outsider would already appear to be unsalvageable. Risk takers looking for ways to avoid that age-old trap set limits going in and listen well to outside opinions along the way in case their view of the impending failure is shrouded in rose-colored mist.

That blinding mist has caught many venture capitalist risk takers, including low-key Pittsburgh billionaire Henry Hillman, by surprise. *The Wall Street Journal* estimated that for five years, ending in 1986, Hillman's venture risks had piled up losses of some $80 million. "Instead of cutting losses, as most venture investors would have done, Mr. Hillman often threw good money after bad," reported the *Journal*. "Some wonder, only half-jokingly, whether he is more a philanthropist than a venture capitalist." In contrast to Adler's quick moves to ax bad management, Hillman himself admitted, "Our greatest weakness has been in going along with management too readily and not being the tough guy."

More Risks Today

Like all venture capitalists, Adler remembers well the ones that got away—the risks he wishes he had taken, but didn't. He passed up an opportunity to invest in Seagate Technology when he failed to obey his own risk-taking rules—he said no because its founder, Alan Shugart, had already been fired from one firm. On one of his better days, Adler would not have done that. The risk takers who backed Seagate and got out in time made fifty times their money. He also passed up opportunities to buy into Home Health Care and Genentech—two fabulously successful ventures.

"I was offered pieces of the Genentech limited partnership," laments Adler. "I should have bought it. Profits have been enormous and the write-offs have been great. I did a poor evaluation on the upside of the product [human growth hormone in this case]. I didn't do enough analysis. Bad fact gathering . . . too busy."

But making investment selections won't get any easier. Adler now finds himself in a field where risk is steadily increasing.

201

"Venture capitalists must take hugely more risks today than they did even two, three or five years ago," he says. "It's because you don't have any major technology changes on the horizon today, and the costs are much higher. Data General, which cost less than $750,000 to get going [in 1968], would cost $15 million today. The risk has been increasing in recent years, in part because of America's slow growth economy."

THE FLIP SIDE OF FLOPS

"A man of genius makes no mistakes. His errors are volitional and are the portals of discovery."

—JAMES JOYCE

"If you play tennis, you know that if all of your first serves are going in, then you're not making the most of your first serve. The same is true in business. You have to take reasonable risks. If you never fail, you are probably not taking them."

—JOHN F. AKERS,
chairman and CEO, IBM

"The littlest novel effort feels like a huge risk to most, and it traditionally has been. We must, then, especially on the front lines, become 'failure fanatics,' constantly in search of a little mistake to applaud, even a dumb one made in an effort to improve something."

—TOM PETERS,
Thriving on Chaos

Bob Swanson cheers internal failures by scientists at Genentech. Why? Because it is proof that great things are being attempted. But let's be honest. Failure, in this land of success worship, just doesn't get the attention it deserves . . . especially business failures. Enterprise today is inundated with the rhetoric of success. News that over 60,000 companies now fail each year in the United States causes brows to furl. The broader, positive significance of those failures is lost. *Periods of growth and progress often produce more business failures than stagnant periods when little is happening.*

By definition, there would be no risk without the possibility of failure. Risk takers themselves often point out that risk taking is a process of trial *and error.* If one choice is wrong, they try another. Studies show that entrepreneurs have an extremely high restart rate—nine of ten who fail will pick themselves up and risk again. A large and rising number of business failures can mean that Americans feel optimistic enough to take more chances. It means the system is working well. That's the flip side of flops.

Why, then, does enterprise so often neglect the dynamic lessons of failure? Simple human nature, say leading business psychologists. There's an anxiety over failure that runs deep in the American business psyche. We tend to fear failure as something subversive. We see it as the *antithesis* of success, rather than one ingredient in the complex brew that eventually *produces* success.

Put bluntly, success sells. But who will buy failure? As John Diebold, the management consultant, attests, most companies prefer to buy optimism from consultants, not warnings of failure. Diebold says it's a risk his profession faces all the time and cites an example. When he was asked to evaluate a potential megabuck investment being considered by a division of a major U.S. corporation (he declines to name the firm), he concluded that it was a very bad idea. But even though he'd done ten projects or more for that corporation, he knew this would probably be his last if he came out against the proposed deal. "That's the risk of truthfulness," Diebold explains. "It's a great risk, but you have to take the position that you believe in." Diebold did, and says he next saw work from that corporation ten years later.

The fear of failure works against risk in two ways. It prevents managers from taking risks in the first place; and perhaps more insidiously, it keeps them from pulling the plug early on a risk that has already failed even though they haven't recognized that yet. Often the more severe damage is done by executives who won't risk admitting a failure.

Fortunately, however, humans *do* have the ability to try again once they've failed. The cat who jumps on a hot stove once probably won't repeat his mistake. Then again, the cat won't jump on a *cold* stove either. And there's the dynamic linking risk and failure. We keep testing, experimenting, calculating in enterprise. If the stove is too hot one day we'll try it the next. If one enterprising risk becomes too hot to hold we've learned something from it. Failures, in the words of James Joyce, are "portals of discovery." Regrets should come *not* from the taking of risks and losing, but only from failing to take the risks in the first place.

Failure is one reason perfectionists make poor risk takers. Perfectionists strive for an impossible goal. And because they often measure their own self-worth by how much perfection they achieve, they don't handle failure well.

America tends to define failure as everything short of the absolute top. That's admirable in some cases. The danger is that we create more people who view each failure as a disaster—an excuse to quit and not risk again. Ironically, American society sees itself as a group composed largely of risk takers. We believe we are *supposed* to take risks—as long as nothing ever goes wrong. If it does, reactions generally center around pity. Consider John Connally, the former U.S. Treasury secretary and Texas governor. He lost his entire personal fortune of $8 to $12 million—plus tens of millions more that he had borrowed with his partner, Ben Barnes—in Texas real estate ventures. The public's reaction to his bankruptcy auction was part pity, part amazement, and part fear that if Connally could blow it so could anybody else. Connally had rolled the dice during the early 1980s boom years of Texas real estate, and went bust when collapsing oil prices K.O.'d the real estate market. Texans at least admired his guts for throwing the dice in the first place.

Connally, who was wounded in John F. Kennedy's assassination, had started life with nothing and learned that to get somewhere you sometimes had to borrow money. OPM. When he jumped into the real estate game with Barnes, he was already in his mid-sixties. Nevertheless, he attacked his new career with

205

zeal, taking a classic entrepreneurial risk of borrowing money against his personal signature. That means if you can't pay back the money you could lose everything you own personally—which is exactly what happened to Connally and his wife, Nellie. At age seventy, however, and after bankruptcy left him with only his house and about $30,000 in personal possessions, Connally vowed that he would pick up the pieces and start over again.

Francis Ford Coppola, a filmmaker with five Oscars to his credit, has always been a daring visionary who prefers to buck movie industry convention and do things his own way. He put up $16 million of his own to finish *Apocalypse Now* during the 1970s when Hollywood studios backing the project refused to spend more.

Coppola, who had polio as a child and says he was fascinated by the concept of ingenuity, takes risks and makes up new rules as he goes. His film credits include *Patton* (co-author), *The Godfather, The Godfather, Part II, The Conversation, The Cotton Club, One from the Heart, Peggy Sue Got Married, Gardens of Stone,* and *Tucker.* Perhaps his boldest move was a business, rather than an artistic, decision. He bought his own movie company, Hollywood General Studios, and took daring steps to make it a revolutionary high-tech outfit that would reinvent the business of movie making.

But even though he sank millions of his own dollars into the venture, Coppola made a classic risk taker's mistake after his early successes. He believed he could do no wrong. He succumbed to the illusion that "the bigger the risk, the better the idea." The studio tried to do too much it couldn't afford. It was auctioned off in 1984 to pay debts of some $50 million. Coppola barely salvaged his homes and a small production company, now Zoetrope Studios, in San Francisco. Within a few years, however, Coppola was back in the game, making movies, taking risks and saying his best work was yet to come.

J. Fred Risk, a man whose name alone sets him apart, is also the risk-taking chairman of a company called Forum Group, Inc., which operates nursing homes and retirement centers. During the first half of the 1980s, it ranked as one of the country's fastest-growing small public companies. Fred Risk sees the ability to accept failure as a critical risk-taking component. Says Risk, "Some people can't stand the thought of failure. Those are the people who can never be the risk takers. If you're going to take aggressive risks—even major ones that you've thought out carefully—you're going to have failures. Some people are just not constituted to live that life, to admit that they've undertaken something that failed. The only essential ingredient I know is that people who are going to be risk takers must be able to stand failure."

Success Littered with Failure

The careers of many successful risk-taking individuals and companies are littered with failures and frustrations. Successful risk takers will naturally have dealt with failure and frustration. It's part of the bargain. They do not make the mistake of believing that each risk is a potential Armageddon. Opportunity *does* knock more than once.

Failure is actually a far better teacher than success. Its lessons are more poignant. The key questions, according to John Diebold, are these: "Do you want a society where people find it easy to engage in risk? Do you want to provide an incentive and disincentive structure such that a young person will be willing to undertake the risks of a new enterprise? I think in that sense you get a considerable contrast between Europe and the United States. Bankruptcy laws are such in Europe that you get a considerable cooling factor on people taking risks. Whereas in this country, I think that we are much more oriented to a willingness to take risks because the stigma attached to failure is less, as long as there's not been any dishonesty. . . . We're in a period where the virtues of being an entrepreneur are trumpeted from the rooftops, and presumably that encourages the taking of risks. But I don't know how many politicians really understand what being an entrepreneur is all about. They think it's glamorous, and they just don't have much of an understanding."

The perceived mission of bureaucracies—be they government or corporate—is to minimize or eliminate failure, through a process of eliminating risk. Failures are embarrassing to governments and corporations. Avoiding risk is equated with avoiding possible embarrassment. But Diebold believes it's important for a society to acknowledge the role of failure in building toward progress, and to have tax and bankruptcy laws that encourage people to continue taking the risks that produce progress as well as failure along the way. Centrally controlled economies fare much worse on the topics of risk and failure. The Soviet Union, for example, carries fear of failure to an extreme on a national scale. The pre-*glasnost* Soviet obsession with secrecy was based on the ruling powers' fear that a failure—any failure—would make the Russian state appear weak. An entrepreneurial economy grants people the freedom to fail, get up, and start again. It encourages them to "fail successfully."

PRESIDING OVER FAILURE

> *"If all else fails, immortality can always be assured by spectacular failure."*
>
> —JOHN KENNETH GALBRAITH

Adam Osborne is a risk taker who presided over one of the most explosive high-tech business failures of recent times. His firm, the Osborne Computer Corporation, manufactured a lap-top computer that made Osborne the fastest-growing company in Silicon Valley during the early 1980s. Osborne tallied $100 million in sales by the time its first full fiscal year ended in 1982. Everybody associated with the firm was planning to become immensely rich with a public stock offering in 1983. Before that year was out, however, Osborne Computer Corporation had gone bust in what Osborne himself later described as a "flaming disaster."

Osborne, who had earned a PhD in chemical engineering, took it in stride. "If you're an entrepreneur, you have to expect to fail sometimes," he told *SUCCESS!* magazine. Within a year he was involved in launching a new computer software company. "It was an event, something to cope with," he said. "You can't take failure too hard if you're an entrepreneur . . . you can't be the kind of person who is embarrassed by a failure."

Though Osborne's was among the more spectacular business blowouts, it has not been lonely at the bottom. People Express

208

Airlines, hailed as one of the great entrepreneurial start-ups of the eighties, ran itself dry by 1986 and was absorbed by Texas Air. International Harvester, Financial Corporation of America, Chrysler, Lockheed, Continental Illinois and Braniff are but a few of the well-known companies that have tasted failure within recent memory. Other big firms took their licks, but had pockets so deep the damage was slight. Time Inc., for example, lost an estimated $47 million on an ill-fated magazine venture called *TV Cable Week,* though the publishing giant's pantry was well-enough stocked to shake that one off.

Convergent Technologies, Inc. was one casualty of 1985's computer industry slump. On the strength of its minicomputers, Convergent had been a high flyer, and went public in 1982. Its founder, Allen Michels, then presided over a deadly foray into personal computers which brought down the company. When Michels was interviewed by *The Wall Street Journal* about the failure, the conversation went like this:

Question: When you first started Convergent, did the prospect of failing worry you?

Michels: Constantly. It hung over my head like an ax. I felt terribly responsible for the people who worked for me. I remember watching them with their wives and children at one of our first Christmas parties; they look up to you, like you're in charge and everything will be fine, and I felt that the shame of letting them down, of having them trust me and then screwing up their lives, would be appalling.

Question: Starting Convergent, how much did you personally have at risk?

Michels: I bet everything. I went into debt. And I loved to see my senior managers go into hock, too. "Go ahead," I'd tell them, "buy that house." They'd say they couldn't afford the mortgage. I'd say, "Buy it anyway." That kind of burden helps maintain a focus on business.

Question: What was it like at the top when Convergent was flying high? Did success go to your head?

Michels: I started worrying about how to maintain that success. We called a management meeting in Carmel; we set schedules, cost objectives, everything. I felt absolutely euphoric. It was the first time my stomach had stopped churning in a long time. Ben

[Wegbreit, an associate] and I sang Beethoven's Ninth, the First Chorale, all the way home in the original German, and really made fools of ourselves.

Yes, it was heady. In retrospect, I can see what was happening; a guy who always questioned what he did, who wanted to sleep on decisions, suddenly began to believe that all his decisions were right—because they were his. The normal apprehension that goes with decision making gave way to a dangerous conviction that we were always right. In fact, invincible.

Question: Then you spent $20 million trying to break into personal computers. Your engineers got out a laptop machine, the Workslate, in record time, and it got rave reviews when you introduced it early in 1984. When did you get your first inkling that the computer was in trouble?

Michels: The orders weren't materializing, so I decided to give a Mercedes SL to every salesperson who sold something like two hundred units in three or four months. I knew that if they didn't get the car, their wives would kill them. Everyone was excited. I was getting calls from wives specifying the color they wanted. I even called a dealer to tell him I'd need at least fifty Mercedes.

But nobody won one. And I said to myself, "Oh, [expletive deleted]."

Question: Your instinct was right about that. Workslate was a flop. How long did it take you to do something about it?

Michels: Within six months of its introduction, we shut down production. In fact, we shut down the division and got out of the business. Rather than let the company hemorrhage, we pulled the plug fast, and there was no looking back. But I still wonder where we went wrong.

Question: Even after dropping Workslate, Convergent was in trouble. Your new minicomputer was stalled in development and the company had grown in such a helter-skelter way that management had lost control of it. How did you feel at this point?

Michels: I realized that someone else ought to be running the company. Clearly the wrong guy was in the job. I remembered the time years before when I'd taken my daughter—she was fourteen months old then—for a walk in New York. I glanced away for just a moment and when I looked back she'd fallen and cut her face. She had to have stitches and everything, and I thought my carelessness had disfigured her.

That was the same feeling I had in October, 1984, when I decided someone else had to take over the company. I felt I'd horribly disfigured the jewel of my life. If there had been a gun in the house, I would have had the barrel in my mouth. My wife was heartbroken. She cried and cried. I felt awful for months.

Question: In retrospect, do you think you handled the crisis well?

Michels: I'm proud that I acted objectively, not defensively, and that I moved on. This valley is filled with people who can't accept defeat.

Question: You've just started up another company, Dana Computer, Inc., with $31 million in venture capital. Having failed once, is the fear of failure any less this time around?

Michels: The word is terror. My fear of failure may be greater in some respects. People say adversity is good for you. Well, that's not exactly true. I'm not the same person I was.

Question: What did you learn from what happened at Convergent?

Michels: I learned—painfully—that I'll never be a successful manager. Some people are good at operating big companies; I'm good at starting companies, creating life where there was none. I've told investors here that at some point they'll have to bring in a professional manager. My job is to make sure he's here soon enough. I'm not fighting a war here, trying to make up for the last failure.

And I no longer feel that I'm putting the careers of people at risk just so little Allen Michels can start yet another company. They'll have the opportunity to control their own destinies. We're all going to do this together. If we're right, we're winners, if we're wrong, we lose. If we're half-right, we join the ranks of the living dead. And what the hell, there are a lot of them in Silicon Valley.

Question: If your son or daughter were to launch a business today, what advice would you give him or her about handling failure and success?

Michels: Take pleasure in the genesis. Try not to mourn the losses; I'll be damned if I'm going to dwell on my failures. Know what you can and can't do. Get out if you must. Start again.

211

Beware the "Near-Success"

One of the great fears haunting Allen Michels, as he risked launching another company, was being half-right—of joining the many living-dead companies that suck up more money without giving any clear signals of impending success, or failure. It's a danger venture capitalists such as Fred Adler guard against diligently. Similarly, management expert Peter Drucker warns that near-success is more dangerous than failure itself. He contends that knowing *when* to bail out of an effort could be even more important than deciding which risks to take in the first place.

In a near-success, human nature urges us to hang on, to make it over that last hump. Business lore is filled with inspirational tales of innovators who "hung on" and persevered until their dream came true. Those fairy-tale-come-true stories make for great speeches, but bad advice. Looking back to original expectations on entering a risk often proves the most helpful technique when deciding whether to pull out of a risk or proceed. Risk takers often find that their "near-successes" really weren't so near as they thought. Tracking original expectations can provide them with the further courage to abandon an effort that is fully deserving of abandonment. Veterans of the entrepreneurial wars counsel neophytes to sell off the near-successes as rapidly as possible.

And, so we don't become *too* enamored of failure, Drucker also observes that "a good many failures are, of course, nothing but mistakes, the results of greed, stupidity, thoughtless bandwagon-climbing or incompetence whether in design or execution." Big, well-run corporations have been guilty of much bandwagon jumping, and plain silliness. General Mills, for example, tried long and hard to get into the restaurant business—an admittedly high-risk field sometimes compared to mounting a Broadway play. One flop General Mills bankrolled was a chain of Betty Crocker Treehouses, where the idea was to serve customers pie on elevated tables, with tape-recorded bird chirping in the background.

DERAILING AMERICA'S BULLET TRAIN

> *"Behold the turtle. He makes progress only when his neck is out!"*
>
> —DEL DE WINDT,
> chairman, Eaton Corporation

Some ambitious failures just couldn't quite fit all the pieces together. Consider how one attempt to build America's first high-speed "bullet train" ran off the track.

Big projects with a capital "B" are normally the province of governments and big business. When entrepreneurs set their sights on such ventures they take on additional layers of risk. Building a new railroad is such a Big project. Building it in a high-density urban area is even more tricky. And making it America's first high-speed train would be icing on the cake. This was the vision behind American High Speed Rail Corporation and its chairman, Alan S. Boyd. Boyd was no stranger to railroading, or to transport in general. He was America's first secretary of transportation, helping form that Cabinet department in 1967. He was president of a freight railroad company, and also president and chairman of Amtrak.

Later, as chairman of Airbus Industrie of North America, an affiliate of the European aircraft manufacturer, Boyd reclined in his thirty-fourth-floor office overlooking the skating rink at New York's Rockefeller Center, and reflected on risk taking: "If you believe in the capitalistic economic system you've got to take some risks. If you deal only with sure things there will be no progress, there will be no money spent on research, no money spent on development. But you don't take risks just because they are out there. You take risks where you think you have a vision of being able to accomplish something. It doesn't happen every day."

The spark for American High Speed Rail was ignited in Japan. When Boyd took the Amtrak job in 1978, America's rail system was, as he puts it, "in the ditch." His first priorities were some of the basics: resurrect at least a semblance of a time schedule, get

213

heat in the cars, and fix the bathrooms. Nothing fancy. But as he watched Amtrak's budget being whittled away by Congress, Boyd began to think there was no real future for rail passenger service in the United States unless something could be done to change the public's perception of what rail passenger service was all about.

"I was casting about to see what could be done," Boyd recalls. One cast took him to Japan as guest of the Japanese National Railroads, another monumental money-losing operation. But Japan's high-speed train—known as the bullet train, or Shinkansen —caught Boyd's attention.

Like most others in the rail business, Boyd had believed the bullet train, despite hauling 100 million passengers a year, was a money loser. After gaining access to Japan National Railroads' books, he was startled to find out otherwise. The bullet train was not a money loser at all, says Boyd, it was a "cash cow"—a fact that had been completely obscured because the proof was lost in a morass of other money-losing operations at Japan National Railroads. Because the giant JNR was losing money by the billions, the bullet train's billions in revenues were instantly gobbled up, Boyd explains. "If you knew the railroad business, you could look at their investment and see that it was really a cash cow. Load factors, yields per kilometer—you didn't have to be a genius to do that."

Meanwhile, Congress had permitted Amtrak to study America's top twenty-one rail markets for the feasibility of establishing a high-speed rail service in some region of this country. To no one's surprise, the study found that the most likely place was the Northeast Corridor—the Boston to New York to Washington, D.C., route. But Uncle Sam had already committed $2.5 billion to upgrade that rail corridor. Convincing Congress to scrap that project and build a high-speed train instead was out of the question, according to Boyd.

The number two prospect on the list was San Diego to Los Angeles—an auto trip that takes some two and a half hours on traffic-choked freeways. Existing Amtrak service was glacial, building new freeways doubtful, and population density in the region continuing to grow. Boyd's first idea was to create a separate Amtrak subsidiary to explore the project on a free enterprise basis. The year was 1981, and a fresh-faced Reagan administration

—unconvinced a bullet train could be economically feasible, and bent on reducing government spending—squashed the idea. "Forget it," Boyd was told.

Japanese investors were more optimistic. Further studies they financed concluded that creating a private corporation to undertake the massive project was feasible. According to Boyd, a "back of the envelope" estimate of total construction costs was $3 billion. In 1987 bullet trains were to begin speeding their human cargo along a 131-mile stretch of the Pacific coast.

Boyd could feel his vision gaining momentum. When the project was nixed by Transportation Secretary Drew Lewis, Boyd asked, "Okay, do you have any objection to us setting it up as a separate corporation?" There was no objection. Boyd knew that meant he would have to leave Amtrak shortly to avoid conflict of interest, but he could get things rolling.

Boyd, along with Lawrence Gilson, Amtrak's vice president for governmental affairs, and three other buddies, formed the American High Speed Rail Corporation in January 1982 and funded it with "minimal" capital. They received initial backing from Japanese firms that stood to benefit by selling engineering technology for the bullet train to the American firm, and they also borrowed $750,000 from Amtrak. They lined up First Boston Corporation for the daunting task of putting together a financing package for the risky venture.

A few months later Gilson quit Amtrak to be president of High Speed Rail; Boyd also quit and took a position with Airbus, on the condition that he could also spend time as chairman of the bullet train project. By early 1984, one business magazine said of American High Speed Rail, "The story of this new railroad is a modern-day tale of how entrepreneurs, propelled by their own great visions, attempt to bring their projects to life in a society that thirsts for visionaries, yet not always welcomes them."

Feasibility studies were completed and cross-checked by several high-powered outfits. First Boston wasn't about to sell snake oil to firms it was seeking millions of dollars from. The studies all said the bullet train company could work *and* make a profit. The California legislature was enthusiastic—perhaps too enthusiastic. Lawmakers rushed through legislation allowing the train to use public highway system rights-of-way (although that later proved not to be feasible) and creating authority to issue industrial revenue bonds for the project. They did it, however, without holding public hearings. High Speed Rail's visionaries were pleased with the swift legislative action. Potential investors "would see that we were serious, and not just a bunch of guys running around with some plans," says Boyd. Others didn't see it that way. They concluded the uncharacteristically smooth legislative path was not just the result of enthusiasm for the project.

Boyd explains, "The problem was, *The Los Angeles Times* concluded that there was some funny business, and they became an enemy of the project. The *Times* was convinced there had been some chicanery in getting the legislation through," even though they did not really object to the project itself. Boyd now believes the biggest mistake was forcing favorable legislation through too fast, without public hearings, and incurring the wrath of public opinion. Another mistake: keeping the corporation's plans secret. On top of the other suspicions, that only made matters worse for Boyd and Gilson. "Once that aura is created, you are in deep trouble. And we were in deep trouble." The rail entrepreneurs hadn't properly calculated their risks.

Still, the financing package came within an eyelash of launching American High Speed Rail. "It's like the old story of the $5 million hotel deal that failed to go because the buyer could not raise $5,000 in cash," says Boyd. In order to trigger the overall financing package, American High Speed Rail Corporation needed to come up with $50 million in equity. Spirits were high when commitments reached $43 million. But then disaster struck again. A $20 million commitment fell through. That money was supposed to come from the building trades unions. They were enthusiastic about the project. It would mean a lot of jobs, and the unions wanted to invest. The money they wanted to use, however, was in their pension fund. And the pension fund is managed jointly by union and management. The union guys said yes. The management representatives said, "No way." And "No way" won.

"When the union commitment fell through, I knew it was over," recalls Boyd. The kind of money High Speed Rail needed had to come from corporate and institutional investors. And, notes Gilson, who went on to form Venture Associates Inc., which advises business start-ups, "they aren't organized to evaluate such high-risk investments. . . . We knew it was an all-or-nothing proposition, and we fell short."

The first-round financing was enough to pay off the company's bills, without forcing bankruptcy. And, says Boyd, the temptation was great to prolong the effort by borrowing more money. They opted to take the advice of many others who've been involved in failed ventures. They remembered their original expectations and closed down.

Boyd says there are no regrets, but that he would do some things differently. "I would spend some money on public relations. We did not spend any, and that was a great mistake." And he would put local business leaders on the corporation's board of directors, to avoid being seen as "carpetbaggers."

He'd also be bolder about believing in and selling the concept as an out-and-out profitable enterprise to investors. "Nobody has ever made money in the railroad business in this country, at least not since World War II," First Boston told Boyd. So their scheme was to sell it the way Peter Ueberroth had sold the 1984 Los Angeles Olympics—as a civic affair. According to Boyd, First Boston said, "You'll never sell it as a pure business investment." But American High Speed Rail wasn't the Olympics, and Boyd believes the "civic affair" route was a mistake. Better to sell the idea as a potential profitmaker to a few monied investors who were willing to take on the risks of creating America's first bullet train. "It was honest, it was aboveboard, and it was well worth the risk," concludes Boyd of his fling at High Speed Rail. "It would have been very profitable."

BOOK
V

RISK-TAKING TACTICS

"I believe that great deeds are usually wrought at great risks. I have been asked many times what the secret of my success is. Without a doubt, I attribute it to hard work, good luck and my willingness to take risks. . . . People don't always know how to take advantage of opportunities. You have to be willing to take risks."

—ARMAND HAMMER,
chairman, Occidental Petroleum

"Never succumb to the illusion that the greater the risk the better the idea."

—ROBERT HELLER,
The Supermanagers

QUICK ON THE OODA LOOP

"All good ideas involve risk."

—ROBERT J. WOOD,
Confessions of a P.R. Man

The U.S. Air Force was curious: Why was it that under combat conditions certain fighter pilots consistently came out winners in aerial dogfights, even though they flew planes technologically comparable to those of their equally skilled adversaries? So air force brass sent a team to study the matter. They found out that, all other things being equal, the most successful pilots analyzed situations—involving both danger *and* opportunity—more quickly and reacted more quickly as well.

The victors completed the necessary steps faster than the vanquished: (1) observation, (2) orientation, (3) decision, (4) action. That's the OODA loop. Successful, dynamic risk takers follow the same OODA loop as they calculate their risks. They scout opportunity constantly. When they find something they quickly set their plans, make their go/no-go decision, and act. Fighter pilots do it in seconds, or less. And while it may involve days, weeks or months for a corporation, the calculation loop is the same.

In making the fighter pilot analogy, Thomas Hout and Mark

Blaxill of the Boston Consulting Group contend that American companies must become "fast-response" firms to compete in years ahead. "Business competition has become more like an encounter between fighter planes than a chess game, which had been our prevailing analogy. Product life cycles are much shorter." Indeed, the twin concepts of *speed* and *acceleration* are critical common denominators linking today's perceptions of business risk. An innovative Japanese electronics company like Sony, which pioneered VCRs and the Walkman, once expected market exclusivity, or at least leadership, for two or three years. Now technological leads are measured in months.

The two Boston consultants believe fast-response companies must gather sales data more quickly, personally visit the centers of advanced research in their field, and speed decisions by making more of them at lower levels. In the action stage, they suggest that "a few, multi-functional working teams perform better than many departments that separately handle and slow down information."

Management expert John Diebold contends that corporate risk taking faces an even more difficult time ahead because economic and social changes are so rapid. "The rules change so quickly that it's difficult even knowing what risk is, or isn't. . . . It makes risks difficult to assess." Then how do corporate executives take risks and still protect themselves? Says Diebold, "I think the only way is to be extremely sensitive to the social and economic changes. I think you can't assume any longer that knowing all there is to know about the statistics of a particular business, or the technology of a particular business, is adequate. I think that today's CEOs are more and more in a world where social and economic value changes have at least as much to do with the bottom line as the more conventional factors such as profit and loss."

The problem, he says, is that "the American business community doesn't have good mechanisms for spotting changes. There is very little effort, as far as I can see, to create mechanisms to better understand this." And even if there were an effort, Diebold is uncertain that large corporations yet have the know-how to translate the knowledge into a greater willingness among line officers to take calculated risks. A few companies are at least trying . . .

SPEEDING UP BIG BLUE

> *"Entrepreneurial risk taking is inversely*
> *proportional to the size of an organization."*
>
> —HIGHMAN DE LIMUT hypothesis

Well . . . not always. Take IBM. In a sweeping 1988 restructuring —its most dramatic in thirty years—Big Blue focused directly on the "fast-response" concept. By pushing decision making and risk taking down the corporate ladder, John Akers, IBM's chairman, CEO and a former fighter pilot, said his most urgent objective was to speed the process of developing and introducing new products. By forcing important decisions into IBM's middle ranks, he hoped to spur his managers into taking greater responsibilities and more dynamic risks. At the same time, Akers was setting an example for thousands of other corporate managers who have long admired IBM for its management prowess. The message was that risk taking belonged throughout all levels of a company, not just the executive suite.

Speed had become a major problem at Big Blue, and Akers was forced to spend much of his time unsticking corporate logjams. Akers, who took on the CEO title in 1985, spent the first two years of his tenure in a frustrating effort to revitalize a company that had become sluggish. When business started booming again at other computer companies, such as Digital Equipment, Compaq and Apple, revenue growth at IBM was stalled . . . even declining slightly at times. IBM's stock, the quintessential blue chip issue, had lagged the market average considerably in 1986 and 1987.

Akers trimmed some of Big Blue's fat the hard way—by reducing staff levels *without* a single layoff, through attrition and an attractive early retirement program. He began reinventing IBM around a crop of younger managers who were invited to attack their jobs with greater risk-taking zeal. The main goal of Akers's risk orchestrations was to find new products and improve old ones.

Long before he implemented the changes, Akers had given risk taking at lower levels, by younger managers, a pat on the back.

223

"If the management of a large company wants to encourage entrepreneurship," he said shortly after donning the CEO cap, "it has to be willing to give other people the ball and let them run with it, knowing they might fail; knowing that inevitably some of them will fail; and be ready to manage and digest that failure. In fact, a certain small amount of failure is an essential by-product of entrepreneurship." Then, describing his restructuring three years later, he declared, "If it works, it will make our employees more entrepreneurial, more accountable and more independent."

What Akers tried to do, in fact, was create more "intrapreneurs" at IBM. Intrapreneurship—the name applied to entrepreneurship that occurs within the corporate structure—is actually more a description of the *organization* than the *individual*. Once CEOs set the tone by taking real risks themselves, and by signaling clearly that others should do the same, it sets up a trickle-down effect that pushes risk taking into the rest of the organization. It sets up intrapreneurship.

Managers adjust the degree to which that takes root by the type of people they hire. Dynamic risk is infectious. Risk-averse individuals exposed to it often enough can even acquire greater willingness to take risks themselves. John Diebold, the management consultant, agrees: "Some people find risk taking easier by nature, and that must come from a lot of things. But I also think you can learn an awful lot about taking risks in an art sense, in a skilled sense. If you take up tightrope walking, for example, there must be a lot to know about wind conditions, or what types of rope and tension to use. It seems to me that part of risk taking is what you can do mathematically, and part of it is a question of art, and part of it may be your own orientation."

As intrapreneurship matures, more companies are fostering it the same way that venture capitalists handle entrepreneurs. They expect their risk takers to have something at stake in the projects themselves. If the weight falls only on the corporation, there is no real entrepreneurship involved in the venture. It might even be dangerous for a corporation *not* to ask its intrapreneurs to share risk. That avoids ill feeling among other workers who see the intrapreneur profiting without risking anything tangible in exchange. At the same time, aggressive individuals who want to be intrapreneurs must be prepared to ask for something in return for assuming those risks . . . or take their ideas elsewhere. They'll have to display one of the key attributes of intrapreneurship: A willingness to ask *forgiveness* tomorrow gets things done faster than asking for *permission* today. This, too, will help force an entirely new mix of corporate compensation structures in the near future.

SETTING AN INTRAPRENEURIAL TONE

"Preserving the status quo is riskier than change."

—CHRISTIE HEFNER,
CEO, Playboy Enterprises, Inc.

Intrapreneurship can thrive in all kinds of corporate soil—from a real estate development company to the nation's largest diversified corporation. It was Texas real estate developer Trammell Crow who first turned the phrase "Debt is the path to wealth." Trammell Crow Company (TCC) is now the largest real estate developer in the United States. But Crow no longer controls the private company himself—a payment to some of the debt risks that failed him in a slumping 1970s real estate market. TCC, however, was built on Crow's courageous risk taking, and the spirit of ART survives. Even its competitors say that TCC became the biggest and best in its field because its founder had the most courage to take risks.

Crow started out borrowing money to build office buildings on speculation—an unheard-of risk at the time. Control of the company passed to a group of real estate partnerships in 1977. And from its troubles in the 1970s grew what *The Wall Street Journal* called "one of the most unusually-structured companies in American business: an ever-expanding nationwide partnership controlled by an oligarchy of intensely competitive, semi-autonomous entrepreneurs—all fundamentally driven by a risk-reward corporate culture . . . a culture dedicated to creation of wealth through sweat equity." The formula for success at Crow was simple: decentralize authority and give everyone the opportunity to earn equity participations in their own real estate deals.

225

Partners at Crow may draw less than $20,000 salaries, but can earn many times that if they are willing to roll the dice.

Other developers later mimicked the approach. One firm's press release announced a new willingness to set free its "action oriented, free wheeling, risk taking businessmen . . . to respond to market demands with innovative ideas that could make the company millions or flop miserably." That's how Phoenix-based real estate giant Del E. Webb Corporation described its move to create separate subsidiaries, hand the keys to a corporate intrapreneur, and watch the sparks fly.

Webb risks the assets used to capitalize the new entity, and the intrapreneur gets the chance to succeed or fail. The company claims to have found this brand of risking profitable, and sees it as a chance to recapture some innovative energy from the high-tech industry. The firm initially projected first-year profits for one such commercial properties' spin-off at $75,000. But in less than a year profits hit $1 million, and within eighteen months they passed $3 million.

Even a company as massive and diverse as the restructured General Electric Corporation can foster intrapreneurship if the right signals come down from on top. The top in this case is Jack Welch, who in 1981, at age forty-five, took over the firm that Thomas Edison had founded a century earlier. The question facing Welch was how to spark life into the $40 billion GE behemoth, America's largest diversified corporation. Welch's answer was radical change. He sold off many of the corporation's traditional lines of business and took it into newer, riskier areas. At the same time, Welch, like his counterpart at IBM, encouraged authority taking and risk taking at ever lower levels within the corporation. Welch had a simple, dynamic goal that would require dynamic risks: to make GE the world's most competitive enterprise.

From Stability to Turmoil at GE

Welch took a stable corporation and introduced an element it hadn't experienced in years: turmoil. Much of it was unwelcome, especially the elimination of jobs. Unlike IBM, GE made cuts.

The company employed over 400,000 people when Welch became CEO; less than 300,000 seven years later. Welch became known as "Neutron Jack"—when he finished his work, physical facilities remained, but the people disappeared. At least it wasn't just rank-and-file jobs that suffered. While GE's overall work force dropped 25 percent, its bloated corporate staff—the top managerial ranks—was slashed an even deeper 40 percent. Welch's aim was to push decision making and risk taking down the ladder, and one way of doing it was to saw off the top rungs.

In Welch's first seven years GE's revenues rose nearly 50 percent. The total return to GE stockholders (stock appreciation plus dividends) was nearly 275 percent for that period, more than double the average for companies in Standard & Poor's 500.

Welch had risen through GE's bureaucratic ranks and saw a glaring need to encourage individual initiative within the corporation's many divisions. Now GE runs its own training school for managers, aimed, in part at least, at making them better risk takers. Welch preaches the gospel of change. When he acquired NBC as part of the RCA purchase in 1986, Welch told the network's executives point-blank he felt they were too attached to the past, and had better start changing—or else. His divisional leaders are told to run their units as if they were running separate companies. The chairman, meanwhile, handles the broad-scale, strategic risk taking.

The intrapreneurship GE encourages was at least partly responsible for helping the company's jet engine division capture the lead in that industry away from longtime engine champ Pratt & Whitney, a division of United Technologies. One reason for GE's victory, which *The Wall Street Journal* called "a stunning reversal of industrial fortunes," was the fast-response ability Welch had created through lower-level risk taking/decision making. Pratt had dominated the market for two decades or more—a market now estimated at $160 *billion.*

Ironically, Welch's aggressive engine makers had forced Harry Gray, then chairman of United Technologies, into taking a $1 billion risk to try to catch up again—a risk he wasn't in a good position to pursue. Nimble GE technicians had surpassed Pratt in some areas of engine design, reported the *Journal,* making GE's engines cheaper to build. Pratt even bought one of GE's engines to tear apart and see how they were doing it.

227

Gray decided to invest $1 billion developing a superior jet engine. "We didn't have much choice," he said. "GE had left Pratt in the dust." To pay for it, Gray canceled development of a smaller jet engine. Several years later sales of the new Pratt engine were weak, while the market for smaller engines soared—a market GE had by then taken over.

Welch has been a fearless buyer and seller of companies, a strategy much criticized. In his first five years at the helm he scrutinized thousands of buyout possibilities and bought over three hundred firms for $11 billion. Welch sold off another two hundred companies that GE had owned. He wouldn't make a hostile purchase, so any target would have to be willing to go along. His biggest catch—and the largest non-oil takeover in corporate history to that point—was the $6 billion purchase of RCA. Welch's counterpart at RCA was Thornton F. Bradshaw. Bradshaw had become a CEO the same year as Welch and had succeeded at reviving his company. RCA's finances were healthy, its future bright. So when Bradshaw opened the door to Jack Welch and GE late in 1985, critics of the deal were abundant. It wasn't "necessary" for RCA to sell out, they argued. The company was too healthy. An exposé in *The New York Times Magazine* titled "Did RCA Have to Be Sold?" answered its own question in the negative.

Bradshaw, however, believed in creative destruction—in systematically dismantling the old and replacing it with a new order, even when it didn't seem "necessary" with things going well. "All of business is making changes in anticipation of changes being shoved down your throat," he said when asked for his views on taking business risks.

Welch and GE, however, aptly embody another key tenet of regular corporate risk taking: They sometimes screw up. In 1986, for example, GE paid $600 million for the investment banking firm Kidder Peabody, in a celebrated march on Wall Street. Two years later the value of the company was pegged at roughly $200 million and Welch was battling to salvage a risk gone awry.

Business Week came up with the best conclusion about the strange goings-on Welch produced at GE: "Like him or not, Jack Welch has succeeded in sweeping a major American company clean of the bureaucratic excesses of the past and transforming a paternalistic culture into one that puts winning in the marketplace above all other concerns. Like it or not, the management styles of more and more U.S. companies are going to look a lot more like GE's."

A CABLE TV FIGHTER PILOT

"Despite the threat of audience erosion from the new technologies, we see the networks scrambling —not to innovate, but to imitate, because innovation requires risk-taking, and risk-taking is antithetical to winning in the short term."

—NORMAN LEAR,
television producer

When *Advertising Age* named its top ten newsmakers of 1981 the list included such notables as Prince Charles, Princess Diana and NBC's programming wizard, Grant Tinker. Also making the list that year was Kay Koplovitz.

Every industry, it seems, has at least one celebrity executive whose name is widely known to American consumers. In the cable television biz that name is Ted Turner. But industry *insiders* often go by a different list of who's who in their field. And the name Kay Koplovitz figures high on any such list in cable.

Koplovitz is president and CEO of USA Network, a cable television outlet that reaches into some 40 million U.S. households— one of the largest advertiser-based cable networks in the country, with yearly revenues close to $100 million. As a thirty-year-old in 1977, she had helped found its predecessor company, Madison Square Garden Network. Cable television was then in its infancy. Ten years later Koplovitz was considered one of the most respected and powerful figures in the business—and one of its premier risk takers. By the time she was forty, the New York–based cable executive had more experience under her TV-risk-taking belt than anyone else in the business, except perhaps Turner.

*   *   *

"I guess I subscribe to the old golf adage, 'Never up, never in,'" says Koplovitz. "If you don't take risks your business doesn't progress quickly enough to take you to the plateaus that you need to get to. . . . What motivates me is the chance for the big win—the chance that when you take the big risks you will have pulled your company to a new plateau. That's very exciting to me. I think it's an enormous challenge."

Her trip to each successive cable plateau began deep in the valley—at the industry's beginnings. Koplovitz started as an apprentice television producer at a station in Milwaukee—her hometown. But she quickly realized producing wasn't her bag. "I discovered I was more interested in the business side," she explains. So she went back to grad school, picked up an MA in communications from Michigan State University, and went to work for Communications Satellite Corporation, in Washington, D.C. Four years later, in the early 1970s, she moved on to UA-Columbia Satellite Services, Inc., where she was involved in franchising. By 1975, Koplovitz decided to take the advice she now gives to other women—she started her own company. While still in her twenties she formed Koplovitz Communications, a consulting, public relations and publishing firm in New York City. Her client list reached over a hundred companies, including Home Box Office.

According to Koplovitz, one of her contacts, the president of UA-Columbia Cablevision, Inc., began to see the attractiveness of forming another program network to compete with HBO. "So we began to work on the concept of developing another network, and sports was the logical departure from movies. We felt there would be a wide audience for sports." So Koplovitz left her own firm to become, in 1977, a founder of Madison Square Garden (MSG) Network, which, in turn, became a partnership of MSG Sports and UA-Columbia.

Suddenly, a woman with no previous experience in sports was running the nation's first cable television sports network. "I had worked in the cable industry, I knew the right people, I knew about satellite technology [the topic of her master's thesis], and I knew programming production. It was the right combination of experience," she says in explaining her coup. The new sporting network introduced itself to the world at a cable convention in Chicago in April 1977.

Koplovitz wired her future to the new cable industry, convinced that the broadcast giants, locked into a comfortable growth phase, would ignore the new technology that was about to radically alter the industry. "I think the biggest risk that I took was going into cable in the first place," says Koplovitz, who likes to ski, play tennis, go backpacking, or do just about anything outdoors in her free time. "But to be a risk taker you have to at least have enough knowledge to know where you're going to take your risks, enough experience to say this risk is worth taking. Historically, women have not had the experience in business to help them decide which risks to take."

Koplovitz then took a series of steps that later would make her, in the words of one industry publication, "the unsung pioneer of sports on cable," the first person to negotiate national cable deals with major league sports. MSG was in business cablecasting live sports. But the network had only a few events, and many nights it was dark. In an effort to bring in more games, Koplovitz made a deal with George Steinbrenner, principal owner of the New York Yankees. "My reasoning was that people love the Yankees, and they hate the Yankees. But they watch the Yankees," she explains. "We thought the team would have a national interest." The first game, against the Boston Red Sox in 1978, went into extra innings.

"It was a very exciting game," recalls Koplovitz, who thought her deal with Steinbrenner was going to pay off. But her excitement ended the next day when she received a call from Bowie Kuhn, commissioner of major league baseball. He told her the cable network was violating the agreement each team signs regarding rights to televise games in their home areas. Kuhn said she'd have to stop carrying the games or be sued. "Well, I'd like to come in and talk to you about that," Koplovitz told Kuhn. So she went to Kuhn's office in New York, and, as she now tells it, "We traded in the Yankees contract for a contract with major league baseball to carry *all* the teams. And that was the beginning of major league sports on cable television. Shortly thereafter, we negotiated with the NBA and NHL, and by 1979 we had them all."

By the end of the 1970s, the cable business was jumping. New cable networks were being formed so quickly, "it was like having a new network of the week," says Koplovitz. Competition to gain affiliates around the country—local cable systems that would

231

agree to take the network's programs—heated up. And the cost of obtaining cable rights to sporting events began to skyrocket. In 1980 the network took its next risky move, expanding into other costly programming in addition to sports. The name was changed to USA Network, to reflect its new, broader scope. Koplovitz now began establishing "brand identity" for her new company.

New Owners

From 1977 to 1980 the network had been breaking even. But the switch to broader programming pushed it into the red. It needed more capital. Familiar story. In October 1981, USA Network was acquired jointly by Time Inc., Paramount Pictures Corporation and MCA Inc. Koplovitz felt the new ownership—with its infusion of money—was necessary to keep the network alive, but she was dismayed. Before the sale USA Network had explored going public. But there was little interest at the time in a tiny, unknown cable company that would be hard for Wall Street to put a price tag on. "And I would have liked to buy it myself," says Koplovitz, "but I didn't have the wherewithal to put together the kind of money it would have needed at the time."

Although the three new owners sometimes clashed, Koplovitz found the ownership arrangement oddly liberating. A single corporate owner, or even two, might be inclined to meddle in network affairs. But three owners tended to cancel each other out, leaving Koplovitz the latitude she needed to build the business and take her risks.

"I'm definitely a risk taker," she declares. "I'm very much of an entrepreneur in my attitude. But I've learned how to move from an *entrepreneurial* attitude to an *operational* one, and that's a bridge that's not easy for many people to cross. I have definite instincts for what must be done in this business, and I feel strongly about pursuing those instincts."

She spent over $3 million to acquire a second transponder (the satellite link) for USA Network—"a substantial amount of our total revenue at the time." Without the transponder, West Coast viewers were receiving programs at the same time as East Coast viewers (that is, three hours earlier by the clock). That meant they were getting the network's programs at the wrong time. The second network feed allowed Koplovitz to service those viewers bet-ter, and western viewership more than doubled in the first year. "That calculated risk has proven to be well worth it," she says.

"We are also investing enormous amounts of money in program production," Koplovitz continues. "Programming is very high risk, as the three broadcast networks can tell you. When you spend $20 to $30 million on programming you're risking a lot of money, especially in such a fledgling business." And the pro-gramming decisions are always uncertain, always risky. "In our business, research is *not* going to give you a definite answer—not about programs. You can test, and see how the audience reacts, but in the end it's not going to make the decision for you. . . . In the programming business, you fail all the time. You know from the outset that every show you produce isn't going to be success-ful. And the margin of failure is larger than 50 percent."

Her aim is to make USA into a major, national, independent TV network before others, such as Rupert Murdoch's Fox Television, can do the same. According to Koplovitz, it will take "a lot of money and effort to promote the network," and a lot of risk taking. Things are looking up. After years of scraping for every revenue dollar, the cable industry as a whole seemed to finally hit its stride in the late 1980s, when cable company revenues were soaring from 20 to 50 percent per year. USA Network ranked fourth among cable networks in ad revenues.

"I've been involved in the bottom line ever since the begin-ning. We've gone through all the classic entrepreneurial stages, from initial growth, to a period of very rapid growth and compe-tition, to establishing a day-to-day operating company in a high-risk business like television programming," says Koplovitz. "My experience in this industry is that risk taking is essential to sur-vive—you have to make calculated choices, and take risks with those choices." But for Koplovitz, knowing when to pull out of a risk is equally important. "When you're in a battlefield, as we have been and still are with many contenders, the winners some-times are those who didn't make the big mistakes. But that's not to say they didn't take risks to get there." They took successful risks, she adds, and when they saw mistakes in the making they changed direction before it became too damaging.

"What I have learned is this: You have to know what your bot-tom line is, what your base is, where you need to cut it to survive.

When you take risks, what you have to know is where to cut your losses. If I were to give anyone advice about risk I would say to definitely take risks, act on your convictions, but know where you have to stop the risk in order to survive. You've got to have the conviction to stop a risk as well as start it."

RISK DYNAMIC #15
RISKING FROM STRENGTH

"Why aren't big-company CEOs leaders?
Because they stopped taking chances when
they got in line for the top job."

—ROBERT TOWNSEND

Creative corporate risk taking doesn't always require a plunge into unknown territory. Corporations often risk best where they have *existing expertise*. Risking wisely also means risking with strength.

Like the dynamic of control, however, risking from strength is not an absolute. No matter how much experience a business has in its area of specialty—from silicon chips to chocolate chips—it can't rely on that experience completely to pull it through in the future. The reason is simple. Conditions change. No risk repeats itself identically, not even a calculated risk.

Risking from strength is precisely how Allen Neuharth, chairman of Gannett, says he plays the game of newspaper acquisitions. At times he has paid what media analysts considered outrageous prices—gambling on his own perception that newspaper properties would one day be valued much more highly. And with his acquisitions, as in launching *USA Today*, Neuharth has been willing to suffer a little at the short-term earnings window on the expectation of later gains, perhaps years away.

Neuharth calls one shopping spree, from early 1985 to the following spring, his "triple crown." That's when he, with smoking checkbook in hand, doled out $1.2 billion to nab three of the nation's premier newspaper properties in a series of spirited bidding wars. The three journalistic thoroughbreds were *The Des Moines Register, The Detroit Evening News* and *The Louisville Courier-Journal.*

The rich price tags represented a marked change of attitude within the publishing industry from a few years earlier, and a major economic shift in America. Throughout the 1970s and early 1980s, scores of unprofitable papers folded, many more were on the brink, and still others were able to survive only through federally sanctioned joint operating agreements. JOAs permit competing newspapers to combine forces in every way except their editorial coverage. Common wisdom held that the growth of electronic news delivery, via cable, computers and videotex, had made newspapers the dinosaurs of the communications industry.

Gannett, perhaps more so than any other media company, with its new "can-do" attitude and hunger for growth, proved the conventional wisdom wrong. Says Neuharth: "We in the newspaper business need to quit worrying about cable or television or radio or two-way electronic systems and recognize that if we run our newspapers properly, we will benefit—not suffer from—the technology that makes this information age possible."

In Iowa, the battle started when a group of *Des Moines Register* insiders, with backing from Dow Jones & Company, tried to buy their company for $112 million. The package was to include several small papers, as well as television and radio stations. The ensuing battle for the *Register* ended when Gannett paid much more—$200 million, for the group of four newspapers alone. Gannett was still unwrapping its new Iowa acquisition when another opportunity arose. A company called L.P. Media Inc., controlled by Hollywood producers Norman Lear and A. Jerrold Perenchio, was preparing to make a bid for Detroit's Evening News Association (ENA), which counted among its print and broadcast properties the *Detroit News* and WDVM-TV, the top-rated television station in Washington, D.C. Both were properties that Neuharth coveted—the *News* for its prestige, and WDVM for its powerful earnings and Washington location.

Two years earlier shares of the closely held ENA were valued at under $50 per share. Dissident shareholders, believing the stock was woefully underpriced, started looking for a buyout candidate without the company's consent. In December 1984, ENA began buying back its own shares for $250. By the time Lear and Perenchio made their hostile tender offer for the company in 1985, the bid was $566 million, or *$1,250 per share.*

Meanwhile, ENA chairman Peter Clark invited others to bid. One of his phone calls was to Allen Neuharth. Entrepreneur Jack Kent Cooke, a media investor who also owned the Washington Redskins football team, was the only other bidder.

On August 29, Gannett emerged victorious, with a $717 million, *$1,583-per-share* offer—the largest acquisition in its history. The purchase included *The Detroit Evening News,* four smaller daily papers, five television stations and two radio stations. Gannett immediately sold the radio stations and three TV stations for about $200 million, bringing its net cost down to $517 million.

The Detroit Evening News, founded in 1873, the nation's sixth largest paper (with a daily circulation of 650,000 and Sunday circulation of 840,000), became Gannett's eighty-sixth and largest local newspaper. One of the television stations Gannett kept was WDVM in Washington, D.C., a CBS affiliate that was renamed WUSA.

Detroit was one of the few markets where Gannett would have to compete with a rival paper—the *Detroit Free Press,* owned by Knight-Ridder. In one of the few remaining big-city newspaper wars, both the *News* and the *Free Press* had been losing money. For Gannett it was a textbook case of risking from strength. The company had just spent half a billion dollars to buy the new properties, but Neuharth was supremely confident his team could make it pay. The paper's ridiculously low newsstand price of 15 cents could be raised. And since both papers showed a financial loss ($35 million for the *Free Press* and $20 million for the *News* over the previous five years), Neuharth figured he could join Knight-Ridder and seek government approval for a joint operating agreement that could quickly push both into the black. The JOA

237

is, in essence, a partial waiver of government antitrust laws intended to preserve newspaper competition. In every city where Gannett competes with another newspaper, it has such a joint operating agreement to boost profits.

Before submitting their bid, in fact, Gannett officials had probed Knight-Ridder's interest in such an agreement. The skids were greased. After the *News* deal was struck, Neuharth powwowed with his counterpart at Knight-Ridder, Alvah H. Chapman, Jr., and within weeks of the purchase the chairmen of America's two largest newspaper chains announced a truce, and a hundred-year JOA—subject to government okay—that would be Gannett's eighth and largest JOA, and the twentieth such agreement in the United States.

When the investment banking firm Drexel Burnham Lambert examined the Detroit deal, it concluded that Neuharth had actually negotiated quite a bargain. New revenue from a joint operating agreement, plus the cash flow from the broadcasting properties, "would make this purchase a super deal instead of just a good one," concluded a Drexel analyst. John Morton, a respected newspaper industry analyst with the firm Lynch Jones & Ryan, estimated that operating profits under the joint deal would reach $57 million by the third year. With the JOA, he said, Neuharth's purchase was actually "dirt cheap."

Everybody expected quick approval from the U.S. Justice Department; no JOA had ever been turned down. Until this one. When Justice said no to the JOA it highlighted a critical risk-taking point: Even risking with strength can bring surprises. Expect the unexpected.

A high-stakes battle ensued, dragging on for years. Just days before he left office in August 1988, the embattled Attorney General Edwin Meese overruled his own department and approved the Detroit JOA. In pinball-like fashion, one federal judge blocked the merger eight days later, and another subsequently approved it a few weeks after that. The whole JOA affair was dizzying for Gannett and Knight-Ridder.

The last leg of Neuharth's risk triumvirate began when Robert Worth Bingham's superrich wife, Mary Lily Kenan Flagler, died suspiciously in 1917. Bingham, a former judge, mayor of Louisville, Kentucky, and later ambassador to Great Britain, was never charged with any wrongdoing. He inherited $5 million of his wife's $100 million estate and used part of it in 1918 to buy control of *The Louisville Courier-Journal* and *The Louisville Times*. Thus was born the Bingham family media empire that would reign for the next sixty-eight years.

When controlling family members announced their decision to sell in 1986, at least six potential buyers examined the goods— the Hearst Corporation; the Tribune Company of Chicago; the Washington Post Company; the New York Times Company; Jack Kent Cooke, who had also bid against Neuharth in Detroit; and Gannett. Neuharth's winning bid of $305 million for the Courier-Journal and the Louisville Times Company topped the next closest bid by $40 million. The huge gap reignited decades-old criticism that Neuharth overpays for his acquisitions. It was the highest price ever paid for a newspaper property alone. Although the total price was higher in the Evening News Association deal, it had included television and other properties. But Neuharth bristles at incessant criticism that he overpays: "In my twenty years there has not been an acquisition that in someone's opinion —usually in the opinion of every media critic—has not been overpriced. But there has not been an acquisition we've made that has not turned out to have been either a good buy, a bargain or a steal."

Neuharth's gamble that the value of newspaper companies would increase proved a bull's-eye. Still, he concedes, "The criticism is understandable to me, because you have Wall Street analysts and critics who come and go, and while some of them follow a company for a period of time, very few of them follow a company for ten years or fifteen. So they don't have the benefit of the *historical pattern*. We have that benefit.

"The risks in acquiring newspapers and broadcast stations are easy for us to assess because we now operate broadcast stations and newspapers of almost every size in almost every market. Certainly, the financial risk is a formula. You can overlay something you are already doing on any acquisition you're looking at. That makes it simple to assess the investment, the financial risk and the financial reward. There are always non-economic factors to consider. But strictly from the standpoint of the numbers on the financial end, it's a formula."

Neuharth says he made a bid that he was "pretty sure would be the winning price, but we arrived at that by carefully analyzing what we think we can do with it under our ownership. We don't get too concerned with what it has earned in the past." Instead, Neuharth wants to know about general revenues—how much money flows through the till—and then makes up his own mind about how much of it Gannett can make stick to its own fingers. That's where he and his chief financial officer use their "overlays" from other Gannett papers. While others tended to fix prices based on current cash flow, Neuharth bought for the long-term earnings potential, and his company's ability to make management decisions good enough to make it work, at the price they've paid.

Fortune magazine, for one, didn't buy Neuharth's formula. "Gannett is the freest spending, most voracious acquisitor in the business," reported *Fortune,* which likened the firm's predicament to that of a drug addict. "The acquisition game has become vastly more expensive at a time when the company's internal growth is slowing significantly. To ensure strong, steady growth, Gannett is virtually forced to make major acquisitions, even at prices that may seem exorbitant to sober-minded bystanders . . . An acquisition may provide a quick earnings fix, but before long the company must go looking for the next fix, and the next. And Gannett has reached the size where only very large acquisitions can provide the fix."

The Los Angeles Times, however, sided with Gannett: "Neuharth foresaw that newspapers would soar in value and Gannett has grown because it has been willing to pay more than many had thought prudent. One key reason is that Gannett has the wherewithal to wait four or five years before recovering its investment."

240

SHEARSON'S WALL STREET JUGGERNAUT

*"Those who live in the midst of democratic
fluctuations have always before their eyes the
image of chance; and they end by liking all
undertakings in which chance plays a part. They
are therefore all led to engage in commerce, not
only for the sake of the profit it holds out to them,
but for the love of the constant excitement
occasioned by that pursuit."*

—ALEXIS DE TOCQUEVILLE,
Democracy in America

Shearson Lehman's December 1987 acquisition of E. F. Hutton
for just under $1 billion was an ARTist's paradigm. It elegantly
illustrated at least four risk-taking dynamics: It was a contrarian
play, it was a risk from strength, it was an action carried out under
severe time limits, and it ignored short-term problems to get at
the big picture.

A key figure in Shearson's gamble was Peter Cohen, the Wall
Street firm's young, aggressive chief, who had taken over as CEO
in 1983 at the tender age (for the head of a major financial firm) of
thirty-seven. He assumed the chairman's post in 1984.

In the brokerage industry, the big story of 1987 was the stock
market crash. It forced a painfully abrupt turnaround for an
industry that had been romping through expansion and profits in
a five-year global bull market. The October meltdown, however,
obliterated hundreds of billions of dollars in assets. Retail investors bailed out. Their departure, among other dark financial
clouds, pointed squarely to a major squeeze on brokerage firm
earnings—on top of the beatings those firms had already taken on
trading losses. Fewer investors would mean fewer trades, fewer
commissions, less business. The pessimistic outlook that gripped
the brokerage world pointed to less of a need for the huge retail
broker networks that belonged to both Shearson and Hutton.

Shearson had taken a $70 million after-tax loss for the crash
month of October. The mood in brokerage house boardrooms was

241

cautious. Expensive projects were being dumped. Cutbacks quickly replaced expansion plans. Jobs disappeared. A slightly different tone prevailed in Peter Cohen's ART (active risk taking) shop. "Since Black Monday, most of Wall Street has lost its financial nerve," wrote *The Wall Street Journal* in a front-page story December 3, 1987. "Not Shearson. In one of the securities industry's boldest and perhaps riskiest maneuvers, the aggressive firm is moving to dethrone Merrill Lynch as the nation's top retail broker."

Under Cohen, Shearson had spent heavily during the mid-1980s on new computer technology, building a $260 million facility in Manhattan to handle the company's immense and growing recordkeeping and order processing demands. Says Cohen, "Every transaction prompts as many as eight separate bookkeeping entries which must be processed that same day. The fact that [all Wall Street firms combined] can process hundreds of billions of dollars in transactions day in and day out stands in my mind as one of the greatest technological, organizational and management feats of recent times." During the good times Cohen gambled that Wall Street's head-over-heels expansion would be followed by a period of consolidation, and that Shearson would have an edge with its high-tech back office and lean overall operation. He was exactly right.

Cohen's view of risk taking evolved over time. In his earlier years at the firm he'd been most concerned with the impact of short-term changes. As CEO, he took a new view—a big-picture view—of how using Shearson's strengths to take new risks could transform it into one of the world's premier investment houses. When he looked at Hutton he saw a gamble, a huge consolidation job. But most of all he saw that buying Hutton would make him commander in chief of the largest retail brokerage army in the business, larger even than Merrill Lynch's. Shearson had 5,600 brokers, Hutton 6,500 and Merrill about 11,500.

In the short run, following the stock market crash, the prospect of a major merger wasn't tasty at all. But Cohen, looking broad scope, believed the giant Japanese securities firms would be the future's key competitors. If the opportunity to take the risk presented itself *now, now* is when he'd have to take it. That the rest of his industry was bracing for bad times didn't matter.

Cohen claims that managing a company on Wall Street takes a little more executive chutzpah than running the average enterprise. "What makes securities firms so different is that we can't play the management game by conventional rules," he says. "First and foremost, ours is a business that both attracts and is run by people with strong entrepreneurial instincts. As little as ten years ago most of today's powerhouse firms were small partnerships with very shallow pockets. What the firms lacked in capital they made up for in entrepreneurial talent, the lifeblood of any successful firm.

"A firm that loses its entrepreneurial edge, the ability to take an idea and run with it, might as well close up shop. Stoking the entrepreneurial fire is the fact that our managers both manage the business and produce income for the firm. This dual role can't be emphasized too much. I myself spend half my time producing income for the firm and half my time on management. I suspect my counterparts at the other major firms find themselves in much the same position.

"By way of contrast, imagine, for instance, an auto manufacturer running its business the way we run ours. The company would come to a standstill if the folks in the executive offices, accustomed to handing out marching orders, had to design, make, sell and service millions of cars each year—all by themselves. Our management style is unique to the securities industry. We are not special, but we are different."

As Cohen sees it, one of his toughest challenges is keeping the risk-taking spirit "alive and kicking inside the soul of a very large corporation. Inside a corporation, I might add, in one of the most heavily regulated industries on the face of the earth . . . inside a corporation that demands its managers make split-second decisions in response to ever-changing markets."

What about the securities firms that failed to survive the securities industry shakeout of the 1980s—the "weak sisters," in Cohen's words? "I could go on for a long while listing the reasons some firms made the cut and others didn't. In the end, it all boiled down to whether a company could change with the times. And that, in turn, boiled down to disciplined, forward-looking management."

When the Hutton opportunity arose in November 1987, Shearson was in a better position to gamble than most other Wall Street firms following the crash. But other financial giants were still interested in Hutton, including Merrill Lynch, which was twice Shearson's size; Dean Witter, the Sears unit; PaineWebber; Commercial Credit; Equitable Life Assurance; Transamerica Corporation; and even Chrysler Corporation. Most had their eye on what Wall Street considered Hutton's key strength: its 6,500-strong network of retail brokers around the country, and the huge client base they handled. Owning Hutton would have made any one of these firms an instant powerhouse in the retail brokerage business. By adding Hutton's force, Shearson, Dean Witter or PaineWebber could instantly challenge Merrill Lynch for supremacy in the field.

Beyond their lust for Hutton, these suitors faced frightening problems. The effort needed to smoothly integrate an operation the size of an E. F. Hutton would be herculean. Conflicting computer systems, overlapping staffs, redundant branch office networks, and big egos to go along with the equally big paychecks of the firm's superstar brokers and executives—all posed problems an acquiring company would have to solve, and solve quickly.

Then there were Hutton's legal woes. Just two years earlier Hutton had pleaded guilty to fraud charges in a check-kiting scam, and the firm was still overwhelmed with regulatory and legal paperwork, with the possibility of more lawsuits arising from the stock market crash. And just one year earlier Hutton had moved into posh new quarters that were siphoning off cash at an alarming pace. In a business keyed largely to its people, the talent drain at Hutton had already reached red alert status. Standard & Poor's was about to lower Hutton's rating, meaning it would have trouble borrowing money. In 1986, Hutton had lost $90 million—the same year most other brokerage houses were romping in profits.

The proud firm to which everybody had once listened, E. F. Hutton Group Inc., founded by entrepreneur Edward F. Hutton in 1904, was leaderless, demoralized and headed down the financial drain. But Peter Cohen wanted it. His firm, Shearson Lehman Brothers Holdings Inc., had made a career of acquisitions—more than twenty in as many years. The latest big one had been the absorption of Lehman Brothers Kuhn Loeb in 1984, which pushed Shearson into the big-time global securities league. Shearson itself is 62 percent owned by American Express Company; another 13 percent by Nippon Life Insurance Company, a

244

Japanese firm; 18 percent by the public, and another 7 percent by management and employees.

Because of Shearson's relentless acquisitions, many of which Cohen had been involved with, the firm literally had hundreds, if not thousands, of people with experience at making brokerage firm marriages work. The combined firm, Shearson Lehman Hutton, would have total capital of $3.7 billion and more than $100 billion in assets under management. It would serve about 2.9 million active client accounts in the United States, representing another $110 billion in assets, through a network of more than 600 offices and 12,000 financial consultant/brokers. As Cohen described it, "Integrating the two firms will require the precise execution of a thousand simultaneous events." Cohen, and Shearson's president Jeffrey Lane, knew it was the biggest gamble of its kind they'd made, but were confident their strengths could pull it off. Other potential buyers were less confident of taking the gamble.

An internal American Express Company publication's account of the buyout posed the question itself: Was Shearson's $961 million acquisition of Hutton, just six weeks after the market crash and in the face of gloomy economic prospects, a risk? "You bet," they admitted. But Lane said the bold step was consistent with Shearson's track record. "Our greatest moments of opportunity have come at difficult times," he said, including the stormy 1984 acquisition of Lehman Brothers, a move skeptics said wouldn't work.

Though confident, Lane wasn't numb to the risk. "Sure I'm nervous," he conceded. "But I've been nervous as long as I've been in the business." Lane knew that if anyone could digest the Hutton mouthful it would be Shearson.

Cohen ran a highly cost-conscious operation. That, along with his new computers, he thought, would make the risks of integrating Hutton tolerable. If Shearson's estimates of the cost savings it could achieve by eliminating as many as 6,000 of Hutton's 18,000 jobs, as well as other efficiencies, proved right, it could boost the firm's earnings $100 million a year and make the whole deal a phenomenal bargain.

In November 1986, a year before the acquisition was actually made, Cohen had offered to buy Hutton for $1.65 billion, or about

$50 per share. Hutton asked for $55 per share and some sweet-heart deals for its top executives. It fell through.

A year later, in late November 1987, Hutton called back to say it was putting itself up for sale. Led by their point man, Peter Ueberroth, a Hutton director as well as commissioner of major league baseball, Hutton officials contacted Cohen. That was November 23, 1987. At the urging of Salomon Brothers, which was acting as advisor to Hutton, the firm tried to entice interested buyers into an auctionlike bidding war for the company.

A Shearson team headed by chief financial officer Robert Druskin hunkered down in Cohen's personal conference room—temporarily renamed the "combat room." It launched a crash effort to analyze the deal's potential and come up with a price Shearson would be willing to pay for Hutton. They code-named the project Operation Baseball, in honor of Ueberroth's role as head batsman for the other side.

On the afternoon of the day Ueberroth first called Cohen, the American Express board was scheduled to meet. Druskin's group, and another headed by Cohen's assistant, Andrea Farace, scrambled to compile a Hutton acquisition proposal Cohen could put before the board in a matter of hours. Board members gave Cohen the nod to pursue a deal.

Time was short. Cohen's team had only a few days to blast through nightmarish logistical problems and put Hutton's complete financial profile under Shearson's acquisition microscope. Carton upon carton of documents changed hands. But Shearson wasn't alone. Other firms contemplating a bid were trying to get at the same information at the same time.

By the day before Thanksgiving, Shearson had the risk broken down. Separate teams would look at: (1) how to fix a value on Hutton's stock portfolio; (2) an overview of Hutton's operations; (3) Hutton's private client list, and compensation packages Hutton brokers would require to stick around after the buyout; (4) Hutton's investment banking business; (5) how to value Hutton's assets and liabilities, tax benefits, employee benefits, and more.

Some fifty people were involved. Rumors circulated about what the competition was doing. As work proceeded over Thanksgiving weekend, Shearson operatives even checked the sign-in books at Hutton headquarters to try to determine who else was there working, and perhaps by that, how serious they were about bidding for

Hutton. That snooping would later pay off. When Shearson discovered that other bidders had not come as far along in their research, they knew the competition's offers would have to be subject to many more conditions. Shearson, however, could be more confident in its bid.

By now, the potential buyers had balked at what they considered Hutton's brash attempt to establish an auction atmosphere. Forced to choose a pecking order, Hutton officials entered into exclusive negotiations with Shearson. Ueberroth, who had turned down Hutton's request that he take over as chairman, first wanted written proposals from Shearson. But Cohen, like many good deal makers, requested and received a face-to-face meeting with Ueberroth instead. The two men met for the first time on November 30, 1987, along with sundry lawyers and financial advisors for both sides. But no deal resulted and Hutton set a deadline for Shearson's final bid: noon the next day, December 1. If Hutton officials didn't like the deal, they'd look elsewhere.

At 10:30 a.m. Cohen signed the bid letter, but in a bit of risk gamesmanship he had Farace wait right up to the deadline to deliver it. At Hutton's building, Farace held the elevator door to allow in a woman who appeared in a hurry. Farace later learned it was actress Dina Merrill, daughter of Hutton founder Edward Francis Hutton, a Hutton board member (and now a Shearson board member).

Hutton officials read the letter and invited Cohen and his team uptown for further negotiations. By 8 p.m. the deal was struck— they thought. As details were being worked out at the offices of Hutton's law firm, it fell apart. Twenty-four hours later the lid was finally nailed down. Hutton had its buyer.

Within ten days of Hutton's first telephone call, the deal was done. It *had* to be fast. The impending sale was being reported daily in the newspapers, and increasingly nervous Hutton employees were beginning to defect. Cohen finally agreed to pay $961 million, or roughly $30 per share for Hutton in its entirety— almost $700 million less than he'd offered to pay in 1986. A short time later the combined firms became known as Shearson Lehman Hutton Inc.

Ironically, however, while the price was cheap compared to Shearson's first bid, Hutton now opened itself up to lawsuits from disgruntled shareholders claiming the firm should have accepted the earlier $1.65 billion bid. And as the new owner of Hutton, Shearson would assume the liability for any such lawsuits. Despite the seemingly bargain price, *The Wall Street Journal* described Cohen's move to acquire the ailing firm as "a huge gamble."

Cohen went right to his strength, dispatching the team charged with placing Hutton's hand into the Shearson glove. "There is no one grand stroke that does it," Cohen said. "It's a lot of little steps." In two decades of acquisitions, Shearson had devised a step-by-step bible of how to integrate companies. Wall Street might be calling it the biggest gamble of Shearson's life, but for Cohen and his team, that was their strength . . . that was how they took risks best.

COKE'S DARING COLUMBIA MOVE

"Everybody is at risk in this business. There's no security at all. People who were my idols ten years ago are not even working today. You have to be ruthless in your strategy."

OLIVER STONE,
filmmaker, director

Coca-Cola's CEO Roberto Goizueta has earned risk-taking wings in the acquisition league as well. But unlike Gannett and Shearson, this was virgin territory for Coca-Cola until Goizueta came along. When the new CEO of a cautious old-line firm makes a major corporate acquisition, and that acquisition is a movie studio, there's only one term for it: high-risk.

But it was not without purpose, not without a broader plan Goizueta had for Coca-Cola. He wanted the company to be less vulnerable to a single product, and less vulnerable to volatile earnings from foreign sales. The entertainment business, he reasoned, would be a way to achieve that goal.

* * *

Herbert Anthony Allen was twenty-seven when he became president of Allen & Company, a New York investment firm built by his father, Herbert Senior. Herbert Jr. ran Allen & Company with an entrepreneurial zeal, and was himself a willing risk taker. In 1973 he bought control of Columbia Pictures at a time when the moviemaker had just recorded a yearly loss of $50 million and bankruptcy loomed. Under Allen & Company ownership, Columbia reversed course and profits were flowing again four years later.

During the late 1970s, Columbia Pictures was rocked by power struggles, Securities and Exchange Commission investigations, internal psychological warfare among its owners, top executives and board members, and attempted takeovers. It all seemed to arise from allegations that David Begelman, then president of Columbia studio, had embezzled money from the company. After rebuffing a hostile takeover attempt by financier Kirk Kerkorian, and emerging victor in a fierce internal power struggle, Allen privately said that he'd sell Columbia Pictures if someone offered him a "ridiculous" price for the stock, well above its market price. Friendly shoppers who considered acquiring Columbia included Philip Morris (which declined and later bought the 7-Up Company) and Time Inc. (which also passed it by). Time later made a brief, unsuccessful foray into moviemaking through another company, prompting Time's chairman to say of the motion picture industry, "This isn't business, it's rocketry . . . and nine out of ten fizzle."

The other interested party was The Coca-Cola Company. That Coke would even consider such a purchase raised eyebrows. Roberto Goizueta had assumed the chairmanship of the dull, risk-averse, albeit profitable cola-maker only months earlier. But when an outside consulting firm first suggested that Coke consider moving into the entertainment business—the movies specifically— Goizueta listened.

When Coke's CEO first looked at Columbia it hardly seemed the type of company that would fit with his firm's chaste, all-American image. The movie business—and Columbia especially —was, well, less than virtuous. The coals of the Begelman scandal were still warm. What's more, a scathing exposé of the scandal at Columbia—former *Wall Street Journal* reporter David Mc-Clintick's tome *Indecent Exposure: A True Story of Hollywood*

249

and Wall Street—was about to be released. Columbia's image was the antithesis of Coke's. Its high-risk financial structure, filled with "creative accounting" practices and a past besmirched by criminal charges, clashed with puritanical Coke.

In pursuing Columbia aggressively, not only did Goizueta ignore the company's scandalous past, but many thought he later paid Allen's "ridiculous" price as well. Coke's initial offer, which amounted to about $69 per share, was almost five times Columbia's book value, and well above the stock's market price of about $40 per share. The price Allen wanted, however, was even more ridiculous: $85 per share. He didn't know Goizueta well, and doubted he'd pay through the nose to take such a risk. But in January 1982, Coke reached an agreement in principle to acquire Columbia for $692 million, or roughly $75 per share, and the board of directors approved the deal that March.

Outsiders thought Coke had popped its cork. Large institutional holders of Coca-Cola's stock feared that the company's earnings would suffer due to the Columbia acquisition. One Wall Street analyst called it "a violent departure" from Coke's traditional style of doing business. Pension and mutual funds that were big owners of Coke shares had bought them for their *conservatism and steady dividends*. They had little desire to invest in motion pictures. Columbia shareholders, on the other hand, were more the riverboat gambler type.

Coke had been one of America's most debt-free corporations. Columbia nearly quadrupled Coke's debt ratio. But that was Goizueta's intent. Upon taking over as chairman, he was determined to *leverage* Coke's economic clout by taking more risks. Unlike his "cash is king" predecessors, Goizueta was willing to assume some debt if he felt it could benefit the company long-term.

Herbert Allen, Jr., personally banked tens of millions in profits on the buyout—plus a share of the millions that Allen & Company realized through handling the investment banking end of the deal. He also landed a post on Coke's board of directors—a venue Allen expected to produce more yawns than risks. He later reversed that opinion. "Columbia was a risk for Roberto because the perception of the film business at the time was that it really didn't fit Coke," says Allen. After the purchase, however, things changed. According to Allen, "When Coke laid its hands on the film business," the industry gained sudden respectability among the Wall Street investment community that had looked askance at the perilous racket of making movies. Allen points to the steady upturn in film company prices after the Coke acquisition as proof.

He also believes Goizueta and his team spotted a key under-valued asset—Columbia's vast film library—well *before* the spread of VCRs into American households made the value of that asset obvious. "People now talk about the value of libraries," says Allen. "But if you look at the press when Coke did the Columbia deal, you'll see that nobody talked about that. The risk was great . . . Roberto is a risk taker.

"I think if there's to be progress there has to be risk. In retro-spect, a good deal of progress appears to have been risk-free—but you have to judge these things at the moment . . . what were the pressures at the time? There has been absolutely no change ever in the history of the world without risk," Allen says. "Roberto is good at risk taking because he is tremendously detail-oriented, and he does a tremendous amount of study before he takes a risk."

Goizueta himself maintains that by researching his moves quickly, though carefully, the risks to *him* seem far less than to outsiders who lack the same perspective. "You hear so much these days about corporate planning," muses Goizueta. "I've never seen so much paperwork as we had before deciding to move into the entertainment business. Piles of paper . . . study after study after study. I don't think we *really* needed any of those studies. If you just open your eyes and look at society, there's an insatiable appetite for human beings to be entertained—and par-ticularly American human beings. Our projections of the video cassette business in this country turned out to be less than half of what the reality has been. But we had to produce all those papers —not to make our decision more right, but it was to make us feel *comfortable* with our decisions. . . . Market research provides a sense of direction, but that's about it. Eventually, *people* make decisions, numbers don't. . . .

"It irked me on the Columbia acquisition that people made it seem like some of us around here went to bed one night and the next morning we woke up and said, 'We want to buy a movie studio and go into the movie business,' " he recalls. The risk was calculated. It was measured against what Goizueta believed would be the benefits to his company, despite critics who said

251

otherwise. The chairman leans forward now, his voice growing perceptibly louder as he emphasizes his words with the special relish of a man having later been proven right: "In the Columbia acquisition, I remember the initial reaction was that our stock dropped 10 percent. And I was thinking all the while, Those dummies do not realize what a good deal we have!"

Specifically, Goizueta's research had tipped him off that the value of Columbia's television properties for syndication, and its film library for the soon-to-boom video cassette business, were worth more than anyone else realized. Coke executives expected the rapidly growing number of independent broadcast and cable television stations to increase demand and drive up prices for the programming. They also anticipated a VCR explosion that would boost the value of Columbia's film library. "But, most unfortunately, people have bad memories," Goizueta reflects, looking back at his roll of the dice on Columbia. "Those who said Columbia was very risky now are saying it was a brilliant move. Well, you know, risk and brilliant moves are not mutually exclusive. You can make a brilliant decision that was risky!

"But the fact is, the Columbia acquisition for $692 million was not that risky. Just think, what's the worst that could have happened? Suppose it would not have worked. The worst that could have happened is that two years later you sell it. That's the worst. And look at what they're paying for movie studios now. Why, Ted Turner has paid more for movie studios that are losing money."

Goizueta's aggressive operating style also bred innovation in the back office. In one particularly adept financial maneuver, Douglas Ivester, Coke's chief financial officer, packaged Columbia's receivables (money owed but not collected) and sold the IOUs for $750 million—$58 million more than Coke had paid for the entire company. Goizueta explains how it worked:

In 1985, owing to its success, Coke's entertainment sector found itself generating increasingly large receivable balances. These receivables come from the extended product life cycle of motion pictures and syndicated television shows as they move through their various market segments. A movie, for example, goes from theaters, to cable, to video cassette, to television. A large chunk of Columbia's value was in the syndication rights it owned on old television programs. TV stations buy the rights to air those programs in advance, but they don't actually *pay* the money until the program is shown. Hence the large amount of money due, but not collected—the receivables.

After Coke's 1985 purchase of Embassy Communications, another $300 million in receivables was sold. Thus, gloats Goizueta, Coca-Cola was able to convert over $1 billion of receivables and contract rights into ready cash for the corporation. "No matter how much you may criticize our television programs and our movies, the fact remains that, unlike Detroit, Hollywood manufactures products that the Japanese haven't yet found a way to improve upon," he says. "That, I think, is very significant for the long pull, and we want to be in that game."

Five years after Coke bought Columbia, and following a string of box office flops for the moviemaker (including *Fast Forward, The Slugger's Wife, Perfect, Leonard Part 6,* and *Ishtar*), and a management shake-up, Goizueta shuffled the cards again. Coke agreed to merge Columbia and other Coke entertainment operations into Tri-Star Pictures, Inc.—another filmmaker already partly owned by Coca-Cola. Coke emerged with a 49 percent interest in Tri-Star.

Goizueta had spent nearly $1.5 billion to build Coke's TV and motion picture holdings, which included Columbia ($692 million), Embassy Communications ($267 million), Tandem Productions ($178 million), Merv Griffin Enterprises ($200 million), and perhaps another $100 million for its original stake as one of the founders of Tri-Star. Media analysts estimated that during those five years, through the sale of some assets picked up in the acquisitions, sales of receivables, and cash flow after expenses, Coca-Cola extracted nearly $2 billion from its entertainment properties. And after the merger with Tri-Star, Coke's 49 percent interest was still worth about $800 million. Media industry superanalyst Paul Kagan, of Paul Kagan Associates, called the whole deal a "spectacular" one for Coca-Cola.

Another Face-off with Pepsi

Goizueta would also have bought the Dr. Pepper Company—the nation's fourth largest soft drink maker—if the federal government's antitrust enforcers hadn't objected. When word that

Pepsi was planning to buy 7-Up from Philip Morris for $380 million reached the executive suite of Coke headquarters early in 1986, Goizueta's team mapped a retaliatory strike. Goizueta enjoyed having 39 to 40 percent of America's soft drink market (including all of its products) to Pepsi's 27 or 28 percent. If Pepsi were able to acquire 7-Up, the combined firm would come perilously close to equaling Coke's total market size, boosting Pepsi to 34 percent.

In the United States, the normal corporate reaction to such a threat is to call in the lawyers and claim restraint of trade. Instead of turning to his legal department, however, Goizueta called in his financial crew. What came next was a brilliant strategic move by Goizueta: He set out to acquire the next largest soft drink maker in America, the Dallas-based Dr. Pepper Company, to thwart Pepsi's newest challenge. In late February, Coke announced a $470 million bid for Dr. Pepper.

Advantages were twofold: Buying Dr. Pepper would permit Coke to retain a sizable lead over a combined Pepsi/7-Up. Mixing Dr. Pepper with Coke would have placed control of 46 percent of the American soft drink market in Coca-Cola's hands. In many major markets, Coke would control better than 50 percent of sales. And, more important perhaps, if the federal government objected to the marriage of Dr. Pepper and Coca-Cola, it would have little choice but to quash the Pepsi/7-Up deal as well.

Confidential internal Coca-Cola memos that surfaced later in court proceedings revealed Coke's strategy. Its first objective in bidding for Dr. Pepper was to stir up public as well as government sentiment against further consolidation of power in the soft drink business. When the Federal Trade Commission decided to oppose both acquisitions early in 1986, Pepsi dropped its bid for 7-Up. But Coke executives decided to challenge the FTC in court —perhaps so that it wouldn't appear too obvious they weren't really interested in owning Dr. Pepper but had only wanted the 7-Up acquisition blocked. U.S. District Court Judge Gerhard Gesell blasted the proposed buyout as a "stark, unvarnished" attempt at eliminating competition, totally lacking "any apparent redeeming feature." Coca-Cola lost the court case but still came out a winner. Pepsi's move had been blocked. (Ironically, Dr. Pepper and 7-Up themselves merged in 1988 to form the nation's third-largest soft drink company.)

Roberto's Rules of Risk Taking and Deal Making

When he became CEO, Goizueta created a manifesto for the future of Coca-Cola—a 900-word, little brown booklet describing the new chairman's vision. One of Goizueta's sayings from the Little Brown Booklet: "It is my desire that we take initiatives as opposed to being only reactive and that we *encourage intelligent individual risk-taking*" (his emphasis). He also proclaimed a willingness to sacrifice short-term gains for longer-term benefits.

"I think you cannot encourage an action-oriented corporate culture. But you surely can *discourage* it," Goizueta explains. "I think what you don't do is more important that what you do. . . . With regard to risk, what is important is to solicit ideas, and once the person believes in them, you assure yourself that person has done his or her homework, then back him up. If it's a mistake, well, if somebody bats .300, he's a good hitter in baseball. So if you have two or three good hits, it pays off for the number of times that you don't hit the ball.

"Risk taking is a day-to-day thing. It is not something you can dictate. You cannot tell somebody, 'Now you are going to be creative.' You have to provide an atmosphere in which creativity can flourish. In the advertising business, for example, if somebody has a contract and they say they want out, the last thing you want to say is, 'Well, goddamn it, I'm not going to let you out of your contract. You're going to be there creating new commercials for Coca-Cola!'

"You cannot tell somebody, 'You're going to be action-oriented. I want ten proposals from you every week.' Rather . . . you have to [encourage risk taking] with little things. If somebody makes a mistake, don't hit them over the head. Also, set goals for the person. Tell the person what you want, but don't tell the person how to achieve it."

Goizueta also devised his own set of risk-taking and deal-making rules. "Deal making brings to mind pictures of corporate barons in smoke-filled rooms, high-stakes poker games, daring entrepreneurs, white knights and the like. . . . But deal making has proven to be one of the fastest ways to increase shareholder value, and the market is rewarding companies that are breaking out of the mode of business-as-usual and showing a willingness to take risks in order to increase their returns," he says.

255

Here are the rules Goizueta recommends to other would-be corporate deal makers:

(1) **Know Where You Are Going:** The first step is to devise a simple, clear strategy. "Once the [action] starts it moves fast," he says. "You have to know where you're going and what you want. . . . If you don't know where you are going, the last thing you will want to do is get there in a hurry."

(2) **Do Your Calculations:** "Back in 1982 we surprised many—even shocked a few—with our acquisition of Columbia Pictures. You might say that was the formal announcement of the new spirit we adopted. . . . *We saw* an industry poised on the verge of tremendous opportunities for a company with the resources, skills and willingness to realize them . . . . *We saw* an industry which is not dependent on high technology or heavy capital investment for growth—two things we at Coca-Cola are not good at handling. . . . *We saw* an industry whose profits are largely U.S.-based, a quality we like in order to help balance the large percentage of our earnings which come from overseas. . . ."

(3) **Invest the Time and Resources to Do It Right:** In Goizueta's view, the pressures of risk taking require a special—usually separate—commitment of people and resources.

(4) **Think Long-Term; Think Strategically:** Coke accepted a short-term drain on earnings to acquire Columbia because, explains Goizueta, "We were buying for the long term: the hub of a wheel that would generate profitable growth for the company as a whole."

(5) **Recognize the Risks of Both Action and Inaction:** For every risky situation, there are both risks of moving ahead and risks of doing nothing. "Measure one set of risks against the other," advises Goizueta. "Both a decision to do nothing and a decision to take the most dramatic of actions should be based on the same deliberate study of the risks involved." That's what Goizueta did before granting the Coke name to his new diet cola in 1982. He saw bigger risk in doing nothing. Now, he boasts, his "risk" is the number one diet soft drink in the world, outselling its nearest competitor by a five-to-one margin.

(6) **Allow No Room for Personal or Corporate Egos:** To Goizueta, this means having the guts to admit a mistake if a risk doesn't work. Then get on with the next risk.

256

(7) Don't Let the Status Quo Slow You Down: Coke's mood shift was late in coming. "Our bias against debt made the leveraging of financial resources the hardest move of all. Once we overcame our reluctance, its value exceeded all our expectations."

(8) Risk Daily: "Make deal making an integral part of the daily operating life of your business. . . . It will have a rapid and dramatic effect on any organization." The compound annual return on Coca-Cola stock was about 1 percent during the 1970s. But Goizueta's aggressive "risk daily" manifesto brought it to more than 20 percent in the 1980s. When Goizueta took over, Wall Street priced Coke shares at less than two times book value. By mid-decade, those shares were selling at closer to four times book value as investors jumped aboard Coca-Cola's new Risk-Taking Express.

(9) Coax, Don't Bully, Others into Risking: Goizueta manages his inventive troops with a loose grip, letting them set some of their own goals. "If you can *negotiate* what you want it's a lot better," he says. "For example, say I ask you for something, and ask when you can have it for me. And you say, 'I can have it by December 14th.' If *I* had said December 14th, then you would be meeting *my* deadline. But if you say December 14th, then you are meeting *your* own deadline. You tend to work harder at achieving that because you've set that deadline for yourself."

FOLLOW-THROUGH

*"I don't know where speculation got a bad
name, since I know of no forward leap which
was not fathered by speculation."*

—JOHN STEINBECK

Golfers and tennis players, in particular, know that striking the
ball is a minor part of the swing. The *follow-through* is largely
what determines the stroke's accuracy. In enterprise, risk-taking
follow-through is equally crucial. No rest for riskers. Once a company takes a risk, bird-dogging it becomes even more critical than
the initial risk itself. Follow-through could mean backing off. It
could mean raising the risk ante. It could mean changing course
midstream.

Salomon's Rise and Stumble

To see the dangers of rapid expansion *without* proper follow-
through, companies like Shearson Lehman need only have looked
crosstown to Salomon Brothers Inc., an investment banker for

institutional clients. Salomon's meteoric rise, and subsequent stumble under the tutelage of its risk-taking leader John Gutfreund, was a classic demonstration of what happens when a company runs ahead of its risks and doesn't follow through.

Salomon's rise began roughly in 1981 when Gutfreund, chairman and CEO of Salomon Brothers, merged the firm into Phibro Corporation, a commodities trading house, to form Phibro-Salomon. That move shocked Salomon's old-school partners. But Gutfreund had a vision of Wall Street's future, and Salomon's role in it. That future would require a much higher admission price than Salomon could have afforded on its own. The deal gave Salomon access to Phibro's deeper pockets—money with which Gutfreund could take larger and larger risks.

Gutfreund began building Salomon into a financial superpower by seeing things in new ways, by taking risks that old-line firms wouldn't touch. It was Salomon that virtually invented the commercial market for mortgage-backed securities, and turned it into a multibillion-dollar business. The firm became a leader in other areas of "securitization"—transforming different types of debt into tradable securities. Gutfreund himself went to work for Salomon in the 1950s and rose swiftly through the ranks as a daring trader.

Once at the top, he didn't let up. Says Gutfreund, "Some managements ask, 'Why rock the boat?' But I think you *should* rock the boat, even if only as a discipline. My suspicion is that if you believe things are going along today just as they were yesterday, you're going to be dead very shortly. It's an illusion that things remain the same and that you can grind out the same old product or service year after year. . . . It's a great temptation to say, 'If it ain't broke, don't fix it.' But that could be a mistake. It may not be broken, but you have got to constantly try to improve it." Unfortunately for Salomon, what Gutfreund *said* and what he *did* weren't always the same.

By 1984, Gutfreund had regained full control of the firm after sharing power briefly with Phibro's chief. That's when his risk taking broke into a full gallop. Those were boom times for the financial industry, not just on Wall Street, but worldwide, where investment houses of many nations battled for shares of the new global market. From 1981 to 1987 total employment at Salomon tripled. In 1986 alone it grew 40 percent, to over 6,000.

"No longer can an investment bank get by on old-school ties and fancy china in the partners' dining room," observed *Business Week* during those years. "To compete today, a firm must be able to put huge sums of its own money at risk in complex and volatile markets from Singapore to London. . . . What sets Salomon apart is the sheer scale on which it operates in the markets, reflecting an appetite for risk unrivaled among financial middlemen." Salomon had become the largest participant by far in the worldwide market for U.S. government securities, literally gambling *billions* of dollars of the firm's money by purchasing those securities based on its predictions of what would happen to interest rates. Profits soared fivefold.

Gutfreund was dubbed "King of Wall Street." He had transformed Salomon from a firm with $200 million in capital to one with almost $3.5 billion. Salomon was bulging its britches, so Gutfreund committed himself to a gigantic real estate project with Mortimer Zuckerman that would include new corporate headquarters—a grandiose $1.5 billion cathedral of finance on New York's Columbus Circle. Salomon drew up plans to occupy 1.5 million of the project's estimated 2.3 million square feet of office space.

It was *Business Week* again that showered Gutfreund and Salomon with praise. "Not so long ago, Wall Street's elite was dismissing Salomon Brothers as a bunch of brutish bond traders," the magazine gushed in December 1985. "But timing, guts, and John H. Gutfreund's iron will—and willingness to take risks—have transformed Salomon from a stodgy partnership into the model of a modern investment bank. . . . With $68 billion in assets, it is twice Merrill Lynch's size and roughly on par with American Express Co. If Salomon were a commercial bank, it would be the nation's fifth largest. But no one, not even Citicorp, the largest U.S. bank, can match Salomon's momentum. It is on one hell of a roll."

Hot Streak Illusion

Being on "one hell of a roll," however, can be dangerous to risk takers. Hot streaks are an illusion. Athletes believe in them. But when researchers studied actual shooting statistics in professional basketball as well as baseball batting averages, for example, they found the hot streak to be a myth. Two dangers lurk: taking too big a risk because you feel "hot," and letting down your guard for the same reason.

Salomon seemed to be on just such a hot streak. The firm had become the most feared competitor among all the Wall Street investment houses. It was also the most profitable publicly owned securities house in America. "The firm is carrying about $38 billion in securities inventories—nearly four times as much as such leading rivals as First Boston and Merrill Lynch. A mere seven percent drop in the market value of those holdings would wipe out Salomon's entire net worth," commented *Business Week.*

Gutfreund committed huge parts of Salomon's resources in Tokyo, London, Zurich, Sydney and Frankfurt. The firm's expenses to foot that expansion soared, too. In Tokyo, a capital infusion of $300 million early in 1987 made Salomon Brothers Asia Limited Japan's fifth largest securities firm, trailing only the old-line Japanese firms.

In London, Salomon moved into majestic new quarters near Buckingham Palace. By this time, *everybody* in the securities business believed that global markets would be the next great fountain of profit opportunity. When those profits did not immediately materialize, Salomon, along with dozens of other global investment banks, found itself overextended and financially pinched.

Comfort Can Kill

A comfortable risk taker is a poor risk taker, one disinclined to follow through with more risks. Gutfreund got comfortable. Ironically, rapid growth had become Salomon's status quo. That's precisely what Gutfreund had warned against: *believing that things will be the same tomorrow as they were yesterday.* They were not.

In 1986, when Gutfreund took Salomon into the hot area of financing corporate takeovers with high-yield securities, he was asked about the wisdom of such a move. His answer revealed how much he'd lost sight of creative destruction, the willingness to change things when they're still working well. Follow-through change was gone. Said Gutfreund, "I'm *not* prepared to dismantle what got us where we are." If he *had* been prepared to do so, Salomon might not have stumbled so badly later. Salomon's CEO had become tentative about changing to meet his firm's future. No follow-through.

The risk Gutfreund needed to take earlier than he did was to break that status quo. The follow-through risk was in shifting course, slowing down, consolidating. Risk, he forgot, deals with *change—in any direction.* Gutfreund was not alone in failing to spot the changes, but his firm had one of the worst cases of ego.

By early 1987, signs of trouble had surfaced. Earnings fell badly as the costs of rapid expansion grew. "Central control at Salomon was lacking," Gutfreund confided to one reporter. As troubles mounted, the firm's stock price slipped. From a high of near $60 per share it would eventually sink into the low 20s. Salomon's CEO hadn't stayed fixed on the long-term "big picture." The resulting overexpansion would later cost nearly 1,000 people their jobs.

London's *Financial Times* speculated on why this all happened to Gutfreund. Salomon had started out primarily as a "trading" firm—the raucous business of buying and selling securities. The pace can make its participants black and blue, but the decisions are usually black and white. "The trading mentality still permeates all that Salomon does," commented the *Times* in 1987. "Generations of buy/sell, long/short, win/lose, have tended to reduce management thinking to a binary system." Salomon, in other words, was risking for the short term, not the long. And its leaders weren't thinking like risk takers—they weren't thinking *transmutatively.*

As Salomon's position weakened, corporate raider Ronald Perelman, who'd acquired Revlon, Inc. two years earlier, made a move to take over Salomon. Gutfreund was forced to seek help from his friend, the well-known investor Warren Buffett, chairman of Berkshire Hathaway Inc. Buffett bailed him out, but extracted a sweet deal from Salomon in the process.

Even before the stock market crash of 1987, Salomon was forced into major cutbacks and restructuring that cost $250 million to implement. Backing out of the Zuckerman real estate project alone cost the firm $50 million or more. Buffett was getting $63 million yearly in special dividends from Salomon as the price of rescuing the firm from Perelman's attack. The firm's shocking exit from the municipal bond business cost another $75 million.

Salomon had proven that jam-the-foot-on-the-accelerator-type risk taking without proper follow-up wasn't necessarily *intelligent* risk taking. The pitfall comes from believing that expansion is always best. But it's not. Salomon was daring, but not wise. Taking headlong expansionary risks does not constitute a complete risk-taking strategy. ARTful executives also need the ability to spot the point at which those risks cease being dynamic, constructive ones, and begin leading the company over the edge.

In good risk-taking form, however, Gutfreund proved to have other essential risk-taker qualities—resilience and confidence. The year of the restructuring, he eliminated his own $2 million bonus, taking "only" a $300,000 salary. And in a demonstration of confidence, he replaced the bonus with stock options that would be valuable only if Salomon's stock price improved—if *he* made them valuable by turning the firm around.

Ironically, that decision by Gutfreund steals a page from Henry Kaufman's book. Kaufman, longtime superstar chief economist at Salomon, clashed with Gutfreund and left to form his own consulting firm in 1988. Kaufman had opposed Salomon's expansion into junk bond financing, a phenomenon Kaufman believes poses great risk to corporations that rely on it too heavily. "Abuse of the debt creation process contributes to failures and debauches the essence of an economic democracy," he says. "Equity, in contrast, allows freedom of decision making [and risk taking] and often reflects confidence in society and its political and economic institutions."

Kaufman argues that when the consequences—positive or negative—of corporate risk taking fall to the firm's equity owners rather than its bond (debt) holders, corporate executives will be more willing and able to take creative and innovative risks. To emphasize the point, he has advocated total elimination of taxes on capital gains (the profits investors make when those equity values rise), and a doubling of taxes on dividends (cash payouts to investors that could otherwise be risked on financing future

263

growth)—quite the opposite of what the huge tax rewrite of 1986 accomplished.

And to put more spice into the risk-taking soup, Kaufman further suggests that top corporate managers be paid in relation to the fortunes of their companies. Gutfreund took that advice.

BOOK
VI
REVOLUTIONARY RISK

"Risk? Risk is our business. That's what this starship is all about. That's why we're aboard her!"

—JAMES T. KIRK,
captain, Starship *Enterprise*

MAKING MENTAL
MEASUREMENTS

*"Entrepreneurship is 'risky' mainly because so
few of the so-called entrepreneurs know what
they are doing."*

—Peter Drucker

Mention the words "risk" and "business" in the same breath
today and, more often than not, the word "entrepreneur" comes
sailing back. Academics who study financial and business risk
taking invariably equate it with entrepreneurship. So do most
other people.

America's self-indulgent love affair with entrepreneurship in
the 1980s, however, blurred the meaning of the concept. Suddenly every company wanted to become "more entrepreneurial,"
without understanding what that really meant. Entrepreneurship
became dangerously synonymous with success. In reality, it often
suggests failure. Perhaps worst of all, the idea became *romantic*.
Ugh. Entrepreneurial risk became thoroughly pasteurized and
homogenized through the filters of pop culture.

What, then, is an entrepreneur . . . really? And what is entrepre-

267

neurship's link to active risk taking—ART? Webster's says it's "a person who organizes and manages a business undertaking, assuming the risk for the sake of the profit." Joseph Schumpeter's definition is virtuously brief as well: "The function of entrepreneurs," he says, " . . . consists in getting things done."

But true entrepreneurs are rarely *outlandish* risk takers. They say so themselves, and so do many experts who've studied the genre. Arthur Lipper III, chairman and CEO of *Venture* magazine, and a veteran of the venture capital field, claims that "typically, entrepreneurs are not gamblers and do not think of themselves as risk takers." *Some* entrepreneurs take major risks. But most classify themselves as only moderate, cautious or "calculated" risk takers. Many entrepreneurs like to define and minimize risks. They are ARTists, but their ART is more subtle, more muted. They are not people trying to play chicken with an economic locomotive.

Measuring Risk's Distance

Psychologists who have studied entrepreneurial behavior tend to agree that the entrepreneurial tree blossoms best under conditions of *moderate* risk and uncertainty. Too much risk makes entrepreneurs feel they are not in control. Ratcheting down that risk a few notches to the point where the entrepreneur feels his or her actions can *influence* the outcome will produce a more active and willing risk taker.

One of America's leading experts on the psychology of executive decision making, David C. McClelland, a Harvard University psychologist, once used a child's game to demonstrate this process:

Two groups of five- and six-year-olds were asked to play a game of ring toss. Each child was allowed to choose where to stand—up close, far back, or anywhere in between. Children in the first group—selected because they were considered *low* achievers—demonstrated no marked preference for where they stood. Many stood up close, many others stood very far back.

The children in Group B—identified as *high* achievers—did show a marked preference for where they stood. Most of them chose a moderate distance—*far enough to make getting the ring on the peg a strong challenge, but close enough so they had a fighting chance of actually making it.*

McClelland concluded from this experiment that today's entrepreneurs are probably those high-achieving Group B children, now grown up. They take risks, but calculated risks that they feel they have an ability to influence. Says McClelland, "[The children] are behaving like the businessman who acts neither traditionally nor like a gambler, but who chooses to operate in a way in which he is most likely to get achievement satisfaction. . . . " In other words, *results.*

David Liederman, the cookie entrepreneur of the David's Cookies chain, draws the distinction between casino gambling and entrepreneurial risk taking. "I hate casino gambling for the simple reason that, let's say I put a dollar on red, it comes up red. Well, if I win, how come I didn't put a million dollars on red? And if I lose, why am I a schmuck for losing the money on red? I can't win. If I lose, I've lost, and if I win, I didn't win enough. So in business I gamble, but they're *calculated* gambles."

John Welsh, head of the Caruth Institute of Owner-Managed Business at Southern Methodist University, Dallas, and an entrepreneur himself, agrees that entrepreneurs are not necessarily the highest risk takers. They are not bench sitters either. Welsh describes them as *challenge takers:* "Entrepreneurs are neither high risk nor low risk takers. They prefer situations in which they can apply their wits and their brawn to influence the outcome. They are highly motivated by a challenge in which they perceive the odds to be interesting, but not overwhelming."

Entrepreneurs take risks not because they like danger in their lives, but because they know that only through risk will they find value. Entrepreneurs create enterprise, jobs, innovation where there otherwise would be none, just as other risk takers create action out of inaction.

THE HOUSE THAT HARRY BUILT

*"We do what is necessary. We're guerrillas. We're
street fighters. We're not planners. We don't think.
We practice hunchmanship. And the nature of risk
taking is hunchmanship. You play your hunch
when you take a risk."*

—HARRY V. QUADRACCI,
founder and president,
Quad/Graphics, Inc.

Harry V. Quadracci is a risk taker who doesn't fit any convenient
molds. In 1971 he bought a small abandoned factory for $150,000.
He paid for it with a rubber $10,000 check as the deposit, a second
mortgage on his home, and a fervent hope he could arrange more
financing by the time the deal closed.

He needed the building to house a new $1 million printing
press he hoped to buy from a British manufacturer, although he
had little idea how he'd finance that either. The new press, in
turn, would become the centerpiece of a printing company he
hadn't yet formed. And although Quadracci didn't realize it at the
time, two more roadblocks loomed. The market niche he intended
to enter wouldn't catch hold for another ten years, and the press
he wanted to buy was the wrong type for the job anyway. Harry's
problems appeared terminal before he ever opened shop.

Nearly two decades later, however, Harry's firm, Quad/Graph-
ics, Inc., had long since become the fastest-growing and one of
the largest printing concerns in the United States, with nearly
$500 million in sales and over 4,000 employees. It claimed to be
the world's largest printer of newsweeklies. Since 1978, Quad/
Graphics has grown at an average annual rate of 40 percent—an
outrageous pace in a manufacturing industry where 10 percent
growth was considered exceptional. Such explosive gains make
Quad look more like a computer or biotechnology company than
the more mundane enterprise of applying ink to paper.

But numbers aren't the real story at Quad. Active risk taking
(ART), or as Harry calls it, "hunchmanship," has made Quad/

270

Graphics one of the most dynamic members of a new corporate breed emerging in American business. Quadracci is the Houdini of hunchmanship.

Once Quad was rolling, its founder would face the full complement of financial risks and roadblocks associated with empire building. But what Harry Quadracci intended to fashion was a complete new set of risks *on top of the "standard" economic ones.* He aimed to build a radically new type of corporation in American heavy industry. It would be run by different rules that Quadracci would devise along the way. He would risk millions over the years on rapid expansion, on developing new printing industry technologies, on turning a small local printing operation into a national force in the industry while keeping the work force focused on a risk-taking, "think small" approach. But those financial development risks would often be secondary to the risky new *style* and *structure* Quadracci would create for his company and his ever-growing numbers of employees.

Shaking Things Up

Quad/Graphics has shaken up the printing industry with its offbeat methods. It instituted the 36-hour three-day workweek, creates and markets its own new technologies, makes its own inks, publishes its own magazine, makes every worker a "partner" with unheard-of responsibilities over quality control and multimillion-dollar equipment. To its competitors, Quad/Graphics is totally outrageous.

Quad is owned partly by its workers through an Employee Stock Ownership Plan (ESOP) once ranked the best in the country. Workers with high school educations or less are rapidly advanced to managers and encouraged to take risks immediately after they are indoctrinated in Quad's way of doing things. Quad is continuously changing and experimenting with new ways to improve quality, performance and profitability. This upstart, privately held company has become not only one of America's premier printing companies, but a front-running developer and supplier of leading-edge printing and graphics industry technology. And it has done it all on Quadracci's addiction to ART.

Harry Quadracci is single-handedly changing the American

271

printing industry's image. Until now, printing had always been a heavily unionized, capital- and labor-intensive, dirty, noisy back-breaking line of manufacturing. In short, it's about the *last* business most high-tech entrepreneurial jockeys of the 1970s and 80s would ever have considered starting. But not Harry. This Ivy League–educated product of the middle American work ethic has a socially experimental conscience wrapped inside a master business tactician's mind, coated with the individuality of a lawyer's training and the "let's do it" drive and inventiveness of ART. Harry is a walking endorsement of the exclamation point. He eats risk for breakfast, and preaches the doctrines of "Think Small," "Take Risks" and "Don't Think About It, Do It."

Quad/Graphics is mainly a printing company, but to say it is *just* a printing company is like saying Larry Bird is *just* a basketball player, or Laurence Olivier *just* an actor. They are masters of their craft, and they bring innovation to it in a way that nobody else has.

The first five years of Quad's existence were a survival battle for Quadracci and his tiny band of employees. "For five years we had to find *some* way for the press to print," says Quadracci. "The press doesn't know what it prints, was our philosophy. We printed anything to survive, to get the money in the door and out the door. We just went after it.

"We do what is necessary. We're guerrillas. We're street fighters. We're not planners. We are doers. *We don't think. We practice hunchmanship.* And the nature of risk taking is hunch-manship," adds Quadracci. "You play your hunch when you take a risk. Entrepreneurs don't take huge risks, they take intermediate risks, *lots of little, informed risks.* It's like a doctor's diagnosis is nothing more than a hunch, based upon the facts. In terms of entrepreneurial risk taking, that's a hunch based upon the overt facts as you, the risk taker, see them, not as they appear in somebody else's eyes."

Harry sets many of the latest beliefs about entrepreneurship and business "excellence" on their ear. Entrepreneurs are supposed to be most successful by finding a niche, and doing that one thing well. But as Quad/Graphics blossoms, its head hunch-man becomes *less* certain about what business he's really in. "There is one common thing that unites Quad/Graphics," says Harry with a touch of irony: "We don't know what business we're

272

in. We're in marketing, magazines, chemistry, printing, trucking, computers—all these different divisions. I can only define the business by what we're *not* into. We're *not* in the business of manufacturing plastic sink toys!" According to Quad/Graphics' founder, "We're in the business of being the best at whatever business we're in."

FREEDOM: CONCOMITANT
OF CONTROL

*"Indeed, risk and faith do produce much more
waste and inefficiency than any well-trained
planner could tolerate or defend. But such
waste and irrationality is the secret of
economic growth."*

—GEORGE GILDER,
economist

In managing enterprise, there are two forms of control. One is
venture capitalist Fred Adler's type—inhaling information, then
standing eyeball-to-eyeball with whatever needs doing and making sure it gets done the way *you* want it. Call it control Type A.
The other type is Harry Quadracci's. His control is more subtle.
It is control with mirrors. This is control Type B. Once his dominance is established he sees how far he can back *away* from control—shifting it to other people. Type A control is a means of
confronting risk. Control Type B is a risk itself; it is variable
speed, loose, changeable control. It is control hooked to freedom.
It relies heavily on *trust*.

Most of America's business managers grew up on the wholly rational idea that to "manage" was to exert steady-handed control, maintain order, exercise authority in directing others. Managing was a supervisory and an administrative task. Its creative, ARTistic sides were suppressed or ignored. Administrator-type managers were, and are, judges and observers in the business courtroom, more often than participants.

After a decade of wrenching economic change, however, with more in store, corporate America is realizing that the job of management isn't at all what it was thought to be. Managers are now becoming experimenters, role models for risk. For managers like Quadracci, management is about how much control they recognize they do *not* have and are willing to *give up* through the process of risking. Management is *not* about order for them, but has more to do with perceiving and extracting value and opportunity from purposeful chaos. As Quadracci points out, it's *not* the exercise of authority at all that takes managers to the top. It is the exercise of risk and responsibility, often in the *absence* of authority.

Management expert Peter Drucker has described it similarly: "The main goal of management science must be to enable business to take the right risk. Indeed, it must be to enable business to take *greater* risks—by providing knowledge and understanding of alternative risks and alternative expectations. . . . "

Thus, top managers need to understand risk through experience in order to lead their companies in that direction. Two major studies in the 1970s and 80s involving thousands of business managers reached the same conclusion: Managers who rise to the top have made it there because they take more risks. Some psychologists, in fact, believe that a willingness to take risks is an early sign of future success.

Management risk takers also tend to perpetuate their own species—they hire other risk takers. While risk-averse managers put great stock in past experience, risk takers will first sniff out an applicant's willingness to take risks. Risk-taking managers are the ones who continually stretch the bounds of their authority. They also believe most strongly that responsibility and authority are not granted . . . they are *assumed*.

All too often, managers want risk taking to be more like dieting, where results are immediately clear and easily quantifiable on the bathroom scale. Risk works differently. The links between risk and success aren't always clear or immediate.

Experimenters at the University of British Columbia, Vancouver, have conducted one of the most extensive inquiries ever undertaken into risk taking by business managers—a twelve-year study involving more than 509 senior-level Canadian and American executives. The study's authors, Kenneth MacCrimmon and Donald Wehrung, both professors at the university, concluded that successful managers *do* take the most risks—that those at the senior vice president level and above had attained those positions in part, at least, from being greater risk takers.

This study, which began in 1972, was initially funded by the Canadian government's Department of Industry, Trade and Commerce in hopes of finding out why Canadian executives seemed less willing to take risks than their American counterparts. Although it went beyond that, the study ultimately concluded that nationality had nothing to do with it, even though Canadian managers believe *themselves* to be more risk-averse than Americans.

Academic studies of risk in business, however, tend to come up dry in the end. They poke at the surface characteristics of risk takers, hoping to find common links but turning up very little of concrete use. While the Canadian study concluded that "more successful managers took more risks than less successful managers," it failed to answer the more pressing question: Did their risk taking contribute to that success, or was it simply a by-product? As other such inquiries have found, risk in enterprise does not lend itself easily to laboratory scrutiny. Posing hypothetical situations, which may represent risks only to the researchers who select them, and testing individuals without anything *really* at risk, produces few tangible results. One conclusion of the Canadian study, for example, was that "managers with more wealth took more risks for some measures of risk. However, they took less risk when other measures were used." Not much to go on there.

This study did point out that while common wisdom suggests that people have a fixed propensity to take or avoid risks, this isn't necessarily so. Managers who seemed willing to take risks in one case, became risk averters in another. A key reason is that risk is so highly relative. The individual's perception of what is a risk, and what isn't, can change under different circumstances. On the flip side of that, however, risk *averters* appear far more consistent in avoiding risks, according to this study. "This intriguing result," the authors say, "leads us to conclude that risk takers may not be as set in their ways as risk averters." What's more, the risks people take in their personal lives are poor indicators of how they will react to risky business situations.

And the Canadian study also confirmed one other general observation about risk: Most managers rate themselves as greater risk takers than they actually are. When it was obvious which choice would make them *appear* to be bold risk takers, study participants made that choice. But while more than half of the managers in the study called themselves risk takers, only about 26 percent demonstrated actual risk behavior in their actions, as determined in the study's hypothetical situations and a review of the participants' personal financial profiles. Conclusion: "The managers were more risk-taking in their attitudes than in their behavior."

That last phenomenon gives headaches to companies trying to hire risk takers. Just asking somebody whether he or she is willing to take risks won't identify a risk taker. Farley, the Wisconsin psychologist, calls such a person a pseudo Type T—somebody who lives a vicarious risk-taking existence, but remains a couch potato at heart. When faced with risky decisions in enterprise, this self-avowed risker may suddenly turn conservative.

Risk taking by groups is another paradox. Common belief holds that groups are more cautious in their decisions than individuals —they are less creatively daring. Most people believe that the process of compromise that characterizes group decisions inhibits risky choices, waters down decisive actions, and dampens daring. But many individuals become *bolder* when they are in a group. In the relative safety of a group they do not have to stand alone, and the consequences of a wrong choice will be shared. Individuals can *appear* to be big risk takers without putting much at stake. As a result, group decisions actually tend to display *greater* risk.

And because group leaders tend to be greater risk takers, that also pushes group decisions in riskier directions. Academics call this phenomenon (first identified in a study by James Stoner in 1961) the "risky shift." It really shook people up when it was

277

identified. If groups took bigger risks, would the military, which functions on group decisions at the top, be more adventurous than we'd like because of group decision making? And what were the implications for juries? Testing the "risky shift" hypothesis became a favorite academic topic of the 1960s and early 70s. Follow-up studies, however, found that the phenomenon wasn't quite as general as first thought. Some psychologists now suggest it is more of a polarizing effect—the group will *tend* to be more extreme in the direction of the predominant individual sentiment. If most individuals favor a risk, the group will favor a risk, and then some.

Walkaway Management

While many CEOs have adopted the "management by walking around" approach popularized some years ago, Harry Quadracci seems to do it more by *walking away*. He uses freedom and trust as companions to control. Harry manages by letting people manage themselves, and through that responsibility, achieve things they never thought themselves capable of achieving. Quad's form of employee participation goes far beyond the simple weekly beer bashes that are legend around Silicon Valley companies. Harry V. Quadracci has refined the concept of employee participation into an art form from which even the Japanese could learn, and in fact have.

And like the creative process of art, Harry's brand of ART can't be reduced to formulas or dictums. It just happens and it is constantly changing. "Let me define management for you," Quadracci commands. "At Quad/Graphics, management is defined as this: All of management is an experiment." For Harry, being a manager is a question of *coordinating*, far more than *controlling*, what goes on inside the company. His unique brand of risk is in giving up control to an outrageous extent.

He pleads with his own managers to experiment and develop their own styles. Quad's management "is not just one person, or a select committee of individuals, or a collection of interconnected committees," he explains. "At Quad/Graphics, management is a rather mysterious process because it just seems to happen. We don't have any committees or committee meetings. We don't have

278

private or executive meetings or conferences. We don't have *any* formal way of getting things done. But in fact we do get things done." And that's not an accident. It's Quadracci's grand design, very specific in its own chaotic way.

Such a decentralized, unstructured way of running a fast-growing $500 million company in a traditional line of manufacturing is highly unusual. It would seem more appropriate for a high-tech, research-based firm where behind-the-scenes work by scientists and engineers is often more important than the divisions that actually turn out the product. But a printing company must please its demanding clients anew with every issue of the magazine they print, be it monthly or weekly. Each issue is an entirely new product created from scratch.

Following in his father's footsteps, young Harry formed his first company, Quad/Photo, at age fourteen, aimed at exploiting the photo market for eighth graders going through their first confirmation. In 1952, at age sixteen, he started printing church bulletins, calling cards and tickets with another company he called Quad Litho. From Marquette High School in Milwaukee, Quadracci made a crucial choice that would influence him greatly in coming years—he decided to attend Columbia University in New York City. He earned an undergraduate degree in philosophy and worked at Krueger Printing in Wisconsin during the summers; then he earned a law degree from Columbia Law School. In 1961 he returned to Milwaukee to practice law, but ended up joining Krueger Printing, where his father, Harry R., was now executive vice president.

"I got so involved with the work that after four or five years' time I knew more about the company than anybody else did," he recalls. He soon became vice president and general manager of the company that his father had formed behind his grandfather's store.

During the late 1960s, Krueger prospered. Then two events rapidly engineered Harry V.'s departure. When the president of the company retired, Harry was passed over for the position. It went instead to a friend of his, Bob Mathews, who had been sales vice president. Harry, they said, was just too young to take the reins of so large a company. So Quadracci decided to quit. But the outgoing president asked him to stay on, for a while anyway. The firm's contract with the powerful printers' union was coming due soon, and they needed somebody to handle the negotiations. If Harry would do them a favor and stay for another six months to handle those negotiations, they'd pay him for a full year.

So Harry stayed, but regretted it. Negotiations with the union broke down, and the workers went out on strike. "The strike was terrible," Harry remembers. During the fourteen-week struggle, Quadracci developed a distaste for the hard-line, anti-labor stance the company's management was taking. When the strike eventually ended, Harry was gone, and the underpinning of later risks he would take in structuring a new approach to employee relations was set.

Harry and his wife, Betty (they were married in 1967) left their two babies with the grandparents and headed to California for a two-week vacation. "Then I came back, started looking for a job, and frankly I couldn't find one. It was a terrible, terrible time in the job environment. I was now a manufacturing person. In the time between graduating from law school and this period in the early 1970s I became a lapsed lawyer."

He first looked for a job in Milwaukee. That's where his roots were and that's where he wanted to stay. "But I couldn't get a job in Milwaukee," he says. "So I started looking through the entire country. Well, I couldn't get a job *anywhere* at the level I had reached. I've said before that I started my own company because nobody would hire me. Well, that's absolutely true. I was either overqualified or overarrogant, one of the two. Too arrogant to accept a lesser job, or overqualified for the jobs that were presented to me. I suspect it was more overarrogant than overqualified."

Quadracci took a job briefly at a printing company in Detroit, traveling back and forth between Michigan and his family in Wisconsin. It was in Detroit that Quadracci made a crucial discovery. He heard about a new-generation printing press that was being made by a British manufacturer. It could print high-quality color faster than old presses, and more efficiently. The first such press to be installed in North America was at a printing company in Canada, so Harry went to have a look. Seeing the new machines in action triggered the "Eureka Factor" for Quadracci. "This is it," he said to himself. "This is the press that I can use to start my own company, and to sell investors on. This is different."

On his trips back to Milwaukee, Quadracci started putting together an operational plan, a marketing plan and a finance plan to launch a new printing company. He worked up a presentation about where he saw the printing market and the new technology going, and pitched it to anybody who would listen. His idea was to tap a printing market he felt certain was about to explode—high-quality, four-color newspaper inserts. "My idea was that people were becoming more color-conscious," explains Quadracci. "And that they would soon be demanding more high-quality color printing on newsprint. It would be fantastic. With the new press I planned to buy I could produce better-quality four-color, at lower prices than anybody else in the whole country." As he'd learn later, Quadracci was right about demand for color, but he was years *too early*—a classic risk-taking trap. Right idea, wrong time.

But running one printing company in Detroit while drumming up support to start another in Wisconsin didn't work. So Quadracci quit to devote full time to launching his own company. As he puffed on the feeble spark of an idea, the printing industry in general was depressed, and poised to enter a decade of wrenching change.

Most of the best commercial printing work was still being done on sheet-fed presses (one sheet at a time) but was beginning to move toward the new web-press technology (printing multiple pages on rolls of paper) as its quality improved. Big magazines were printed on rotary letterpress—the dinosaurs of the industry —and were just beginning to move to web press. In 1970 about 80 percent of all magazines were produced on rotary letterpresses, says Quadracci. By the mid-1980s there were none. Change was gripping the printing industry, and Quadracci was one of the people who saw it coming. Over the next ten years, more than 35,000 printing industry jobs would be rendered obsolete by those changes.

Harry's plan was to raise $500,000 by selling $25,000 units to investors. But he knew nothing about starting a business, and found advice hard to come by. "This was in 1971," says Quadracci, "and that was a period of time when it was difficult to find anybody who had ever started their own business. I didn't know of anybody to talk to about how to go about it." That left Harry to figure things out for himself. "The question was, how do you start a printing company whose major asset is a million-dollar piece of equipment, if you have no money? And, how do you keep any control over it? I went around and around and around and got absolutely nowhere."

He knew what printing press he wanted. He knew it would cost almost $1 million to buy it. And he knew what type of printing he wanted to do (color newspaper inserts). It also occurred to Harry that he'd need a building for his company, and that it must have a railroad siding for hauling in tons of paper and equipment. So Harry started shopping for a building to house the company he hadn't yet formed that would run the press he didn't have the money to buy.

A friend told him of a building just west of Milwaukee in the little town of Pewaukee, Wisconsin. "It was absolutely perfect," says Harry. "A vacant old millworking company—20,000 square feet on seven acres on a railroad siding." The owner wanted $225,000, which seemed reasonable to Harry. So he called the real estate broker. "Look," Quadracci told him, "what I want to do is not really buy this property, I just want to get an option on it. So if I get this company going, and get this press, I'll have a place to put it." But the broker had another suggestion. "Why don't you do this, Harry," he responded, "why don't you just put in an offer on the property, and start the negotiations, and talk about the option later?"

"Well, how much do you think?" Harry replied.

"Well, he's asking 225," said the broker, "and he's already turned down an offer of 190, so you can probably buy it for 210. Why don't you put in an offer to buy at 175, and maybe by the time you dicker a little you can decide whether or not you can get your deal together."

Harry thought about it and said, "I really don't want to start at 175. Why don't we do it this way. Why don't we start at 150, with an offer of 10 percent down, the balance to be carried on a land contract [like a mortgage] at 8½ percent interest, with no payment of principal for the first five years." To seal the offer called for $10,000 in "earnest money" so the buyer would know Harry was serious about purchasing, and not just playing games. Harry recounts what happened next:

"So I signed the offer to purchase. And I wrote out a rubber check for $10,000 because I didn't have $10,000. Four hours later the owner *accepted* the deal. Now I have no choice. I have a $10,000 check up in the air—and that could be called illegal. This is sixteen months after leaving Krueger Printing, and we had exhausted all of our funds. I went home and talked to Betty and told her about the check, and we decided there was only one thing we could do. All we had was our home, and I said the only thing we can do is mortgage the house. So I went to the bank and I borrowed $35,000, and the $35,000 is what we used as the money to buy the building that would house Quad/Graphics."

"But what happens if it doesn't work?" asked Betty.

"If the company doesn't go we'll have to sell the house and move into the plant," replied Harry, "and our kids can brag about having the largest playroom of any of their friends."

Taking the risks proved to have a liberating effect on Quadracci's thinking more than anything else. "I was feeling mainly relief," he recalls, "because all this time I hadn't been getting anywhere, and this took away all of my options. I mean, this was now a commitment. I thought, 'This is it, kid. There is no way I can consider going to work for another company now.' How would I get rid of this property? The previous owner had it on the market for three or four years and hadn't been able to sell it until I came along, and thank God there was a defective title so I could put off the closing for several months."

With one minor miracle under his belt, Quadracci now needed a way to acquire a $1 million press with little or no money. His first move was to approach the British manufacturer. Quadracci asked the company to guarantee part of a bank loan he hoped to get to pay for the press. The manufacturer, figuring Harry hadn't a chance to get the loan anyway, agreed. Meanwhile, Quadracci had already been to the bank. He asked *them* if they'd be willing to make the loan if the manufacturer would guarantee part of it. The bank—figuring the press manufacturer would never do such a thing—had agreed, too.

Suddenly a deal to buy the press was close. Harry's plan was to have a limited partnership of investors be the entity that would actually buy the press, and then lease it to the newly formed

283

operating company. The lease would be assigned as security to the bank for the underlying loan, and all payments on the lease would go to the bank. Says Quadracci, "Then I, as an individual, personally guarantee that transaction between Quad/Graphics, the leasing company, the bank and the press manufacturer. And we go out and buy $1 million of insurance on my life."

Quadracci recognized that it wasn't the personal guarantee that meant so much itself, but the demonstration of a personal commitment to the new company. "Banks want to see a commitment," he says. "They don't want the entrepreneur to be able to walk away scot-free if the venture goes bust."

When the press deal went before the bank's loan committee, however, it was turned down as too risky. Harry wasn't about to accept that decision. He argued that the bank's officer had made a commitment, and that the bank couldn't back out now. The committee reconsidered and approved the press loan the next day. "So there we go," says Harry. "I buy the building and spend some money on improvements. I get the loan for the press, we have $120,000 in the till, and we're set to go."

Not quite that easy. Trouble struck again one October evening in 1971 as Harry sat at home watching television, secure in knowing his newly acquired printing press was being shipped from Great Britain to Pewaukee and would be arriving soon. That night a grim-faced Richard Nixon appeared on national television to announce special economic measures aimed at stemming a serious drain on the nation's gold reserves. When Nixon declared an emergency duty surcharge on all imported goods, Quadracci grimaced. The surcharge came to $60,000 on Harry's new press— wiping out half of his new company's working capital in seconds. Quadracci paid the duty under protest.

It was 1972 when Quad/Graphics began operations with its eleven employees and single Baker Perkins press, in the midst of a recession and an acute paper shortage that was causing havoc for printers and publishers. "We opened the doors to start printing, and absolutely nothing happened," recalls Quadracci, who soon realized his blunder. He had developed a workable business plan and structured the entire venture—even choosing his million-dollar press—based on his belief in greater demand for color on newsprint.

"The only problem was, nobody was interested in it. This was ten years before *USA Today*, and nobody was talking about color newspapers. My business plan was well thought out and based on reasonable assumptions. *But it didn't work.* We were in the wrong market with the wrong press at the wrong time, and we quickly found out that we *had* to start taking more risks—try any new idea we could think of in order to survive."

Quadracci hired a sales force. He had a few good industry contacts and was able to get "overflow" work—mostly small printing jobs that busier companies would pass along. "Quad would print anything, except pornography, that would be sold on general newsstands," says its relentlessly upbeat founder. "We would grant credit when other people were not granting credit. We lost money only one year."

Between 1971 and 1975, Harry had just enough cash coming in to keep his firm alive, and a dangerous cycle developed. Just when more money arrived, the press would break down and drain it away. In 1973, Quad's outlook was grim. "The press wouldn't print, the market we envisioned wasn't there, and the sales department wasn't selling worth a damn," remembers Harry. He stepped back, reassessed his risks, and took action. That summer he fired his last salesman, packed his bag, and went to New York City—the mecca of magazine publishing—to try to sell his company's services himself.

That was Quad's turning point. Although he was a midwestern product, Quadracci had been educated in New York and wasn't intimidated by Gotham. If major magazine printing contracts were to be had, New York was the place to find them. For the next six years Harry personally handled sales for the company.

According to Quadracci, it is self-confidence that makes one person more willing to take risks than another person. "The best thing that ever happened to Quad/Graphics is not that I went to law school," he says, "but that I went to law school in *New York City*. I lived from age eighteen to twenty-six in Manhattan at 110th Street and Amsterdam. New York became *my* city. When I came here in 1973 and had to start selling because my salesmen weren't doing it, and I didn't know anything about selling, at least it was my city. I can't sell a milk can to a dairy farmer because I don't understand those people. But I understand New York. I really am a shy guy, but I have self-confidence in New York, and

285

90 percent of our business comes from New York. At one time it was 100 percent of our business. That's the nature of risk taking. I didn't choose Boston. I didn't choose San Francisco. I got involved with New York, the city I *understood*."

Theory Q

Quadracci's unorthodox risk-taking style is known around Quad as "Theory Q"—a loose collection of thoughts and ideals that demonstrate "Harry's way" of doing things. Two key tenets of Theory Q are: (1) being informed, and (2) *not* bothering to make plans. "Over the last fifteen years Quad/Graphics has grown at the rate of 40 percent per year," he says. "And I think those fifteen years are long enough to statistically validate my premise that Quad/Graphics has *not* had any more opportunities presented to it than any other company. We just made more of the opportunities that we had. We've done that by, number one, being informed, hands on; having the heart, the feeling, the pulse of the market, or whatever it is.

"And secondly, not being blinded by plans. I go by a philosophy my wife's father thought of—MPYPIDK: 'My Plan, Your Plan, I Don't Know.' Let's just see what happens. That's basically the way that Quad/Graphics has been run. We have used one opportunity to beget another opportunity, to beget another opportunity, but always moving. When one area is conquered, we go to the next one so that we always have an *intensity of focus*."

Quadracci used Theory Q as an ART blueprint while he laid the bricks of his company's unique new foundation. One financial example was budgets. Quad/Graphics has none, its president states: "Each of our ten operating companies has a profit-and-loss statement, *not* measured against a budget. No budgets. Rather, we measure a division against its own previous performance."

Quadracci surely isn't the only executive to operate a fast-growing business without a budget. But he is one of a precious few to risk doing so by specific design. Said Theory Q's creator: "A budget is a substitute for being able to get some other meaningful standard of measurement. Isn't actual performance a better guide, a better budget than a budget? Now that P&L information is available momentarily, who needs a budget? A budget is based on a certain level of sales, and as soon as the sales aren't there the budget is out the window anyhow.

"So why sit there in November or October and try to develop a budget for the following year based upon something that happened the first six months of *this* year? That's what a budget is. It is so far removed from the reality of the market that the decisions aren't being made immediately. Those decisions are being made in a vacuum, they're not being made in a live environment. Because of computers, we no longer need to budget. We've taken all of the effort that goes into budgeting and are using the computer to massage the facts and come up with daily production records for decision-making."

Daring to Think Differently

Quadracci dared to think differently about how a company should confront growth. Besides, Harry and his company simply move too fast for things like budgets to take root. According to Quadracci, each of his departments looks 30 percent different every six months. "Those changes include production speeds, waste, quality levels, everything. The whole company is changing that rapidly," he says. "How could we possibly operate with a budget under those circumstances? If I were to project my operations forward, based upon what I was doing six months ago, I'd be a minimum of 30 percent off in every area."

Quadracci puts little stock in the standard business balance sheet, believing that most assets are inaccurately stated anyway. "The only thing that's valid about a balance sheet is the liabilities," he says. Even his annual report—though strictly a voluntary exercise, since Quad is a private company—argues that numbers seldom reveal the really decisive factors in a company's success. "Thus," he says, "our managers are taught early to have a healthy skepticism when approaching numbers for the valuation of worth, or as an index of performance." By doing that, Quad/Graphics avoids a statistical trap that stifles so much corporate risk taking— the overreliance on number crunching in the mistaken belief that these data can somehow help eliminate risk.

Quadracci savors his well-crafted image as a risk-taking nonconformist, perhaps even flaunts it. In one of his annual reports,

Quadracci even described the company as a circus—an analogy few chief executives would attempt. "Experienced Quad/Graphics observers would not find the use of circus imagery in such a traditionally staid document as an annual report to be inappropriate, as they would confirm my own proud judgment that Quad/Graphics *is* a circus," said Harry in the President's Letter. "Rather than a single show on center stage, Quad is a continuous performance in many rings of highly creative and individualistic troupes. . . . Clowns are a perfect symbol of the Quad/Graphics philosophy of management, because, unlike so many others, they are not wedded to conventional wisdom. They retain their childlike ability to be surprised and the flexibility to adapt to, or even thrive on, change. . . . The more we analyze, agonize and think, the less we get done. So we have to stop thinking and just do, and in doing the thinking will evolve. . . . This is the kind of wisdom the clown instinctively understands, but which is too seldom recognized in modern industry.

"Our creativity, our willingness to thumb our noses at convention and our outrageous style have become the hallmarks of Quad/Graphics' success. It is, of course, more difficult to stick your neck out, to be different, to take risks others might feel unthinkable," said Harry, who made his entrance to the company Christmas party that year riding an elephant.

Recent American business history is filled with the remains of new companies that grew too fast. People Express Airlines had phenomenal early success, but its founder, Donald Burr, ran out of ways to feed the growing giant and was forced to sell. Adam Osborne saw his Osborne Computer Corporation grow into a $100 million company, and then go bankrupt, all within the span of twenty-six months. Fred Adler was called in to rescue Bethesda Research Laboratories when it grew too far too fast. Even Apple Computer found itself in trouble in 1985's computer industry slump, only to pull itself up again.

When it comes to the risks of rapid growth and spending on capital equipment, Harry Quadracci is fearless. Even one of the printing industry's own trade journals called Quad's growth rate "rare and probably unmatched among major American printing firms." For most small printing companies seeking to expand, the multimillion-dollar price tag on a new press presents a catch-22.

288

To justify buying it they first need the print orders. But in order to get the orders they need the press to print them on. Such things are never a problem for Harry Quadracci. He took the maximum risks and bought equipment any way he could, whether he needed it immediately or not. He still operates that way.

In 1976, at age five, Quad/Graphics had a hundred employees and plant and equipment worth $3.7 million. By 1980, Quad had $21 million in plant and equipment and 390 employees. Two years later there were eight presses and 620 employees. A new plant in Sussex, Wisconsin, opened in 1983—the same year that Harry Quadracci placed what his company says was the largest single equipment order in magazine printing history—a $50 million contract to buy thirteen presses and six bindery lines over a three-year period. Even before that equipment was all delivered, however, Harry was out shopping for more. Not once, but several times.

Although Quadracci stretches his assets to the maximum to feed expansion, he likes to pay off his debts early. According to Harry, a debt term should not exceed more than one-half the useful life of the asset being purchased with that debt. Harry avoids highly leveraged, long-term financing that leaves little cushion if the economy turns sour.

So far, that hasn't been a problem. Another new plant, this one in Saratoga Springs, New York, was christened in January 1985. By mid-1985, Quad had ballooned to four plants with twenty presses, worth $154 million, and over 1,800 employees. That year Quad's operations consumed *268 million pounds of paper* and 6 million pounds of ink.

A year later Quad had two dozen presses rolling and sales topped $265 million, up $120 million in a single year. And a year after that a fifth plant was in the works, the company was operating about thirty printing presses, and sales jumped yet another 40 to 50 percent. And so it goes.

Within months of opening, Quad's new plants were already expanding. Construction is a constant at Quad. The company started with 20,000 square feet of plant space in 1971, but had over 1.8 million square feet under roof by 1987. It now has its own construction division.

With its link to publishers via orbiting earth satellites, Quad has become part of a complex communications network every bit as current as television or radio. Quad's nonstop growth gives the firm a competitive edge by assuring it will always have the latest equipment. At any given time, 90 percent of Quad's printing capacity is represented by equipment less than five years old. Presses roll 24 hours and print more than 7,000 *miles* of paper each day.

At last count, Quad's sales were growing at 50 percent per year, profits at 100 percent, and contributions to employee profit sharing at 100 percent as well. The company was creating more than three new jobs every day of the year, bringing in a hundred new clients in a year's time, while losing not a single old one. Quad ships 1.5 million pounds of magazines and catalogues from its plants *every day*. Quadracci was now planning to spend upwards of $100 million per year on new plants and equipment.

If you read magazines or shop from catalogues, chances are you're reading from something Harry Quadracci has printed. In addition to major magazines such as *Time, Newsweek, U.S. News & World Report, The Atlantic, INC., Playboy, People* and *Sports Illustrated,* Quad/Graphics has printed slick new-car catalogues for Chrysler, Ford and General Motors. Even rock music listeners have sampled Harry's handiwork. When Bruce Springsteen released his *Live 1975–1985* album, Quad printed millions of the thirty-two-page insert containing photos and lyrics.

When it appeared that Congress would change the tax laws in 1986 to eliminate some tax benefits of investing in capital equipment, Harry bought more new printing presses, to nab those tax credits before they expired. By rapidly pushing the new presses into service, even if they weren't really needed, Quad gained an $8 million investment credit to carry forward. "For the other guys, the rest of the competition that didn't buy, it will be more costly and more difficult to catch up to us now," said Quadracci.

"You've got to move quickly. Stop thinking. Just if it feels good, do it. Then we worry about whether it's right or not. To make the wrong decision is better than to make no decision at all. At least you've explored the alternatives. With the new presses that was it. We bought them, and we built plant space to put them in. There are still presses on order that we don't know what we will do with when they come in."

* * *

Since the company's founding, Quadracci has emphasized that corporate growth "makes absolutely no sense unless it provides opportunity for growth of the individual as well." After one expansion binge, Harry climbed the podium at dedication ceremonies to commend his troops. "It takes a special kind of courage to take the plunge," he said, "to work harder and longer, to try new and different ways to achieve seemingly unattainable goals. There are no charts to follow or set formulas to guarantee success. But we learned a long time ago that careful planning and taking the comfortable, safe road was not for us. . . . We're moving ahead to meet even more challenges and take more risks, because that's the way we're made. We just can't be satisfied with the way things are.

"What makes us special? Are we superhuman? I think not. What we have is the opportunity to stretch ourselves to the limit, to find out how good we can be. Let the planners and the thinkers stand aside."

One thing Quadracci insists on doing is constantly taking the temperature of his markets, by getting out and talking to his customers. "You've got to be hands-on," he says. "You've got to be out in the marketplace. You can't be up there in your office. Even the size company we are today, I pride myself on the fact that I still practice the trade that I started in 1973—90 percent of my job is to hit the bricks. I'm out on the street. You gotta know what's going on. That's hands-on, bottom-up management."

He also takes on site selection for new printing plants as a personal responsibility. When he decided to add a plant in 1984–85, Harry narrowed the field to eight possibilities in the Northeast. Why the Northeast? Because Quadracci is a contrarian . . . a risk taker. Most other printing companies had been moving south to serve the growing Sunbelt areas and to escape the greater influence that labor unions hold in the North. "I thought it would be great to have a plant where everybody else isn't," explains Harry, who built *his* next new plant in Saratoga Springs, New York.

"Based on my speculation, my feeling alone, without any commitment from publishers that they would use us, we risked $25 million on a plant, on the belief that one of the newsweeklies [the plums of the printing trade] would have no alternative but to print there because we'd be the best [nearby] source," he says. "When

291

you buy presses, they are all on speculation. But those are risks based on my judgment that there is a demand for our goods. It's hunchmanship . . . no statistics."

When the new Quad plant opened in 1985, recalls Harry, "it didn't have one stitch of work scheduled" for its thirty-three employees. Less than three years later the plant was printing *Time* and *People* magazines (part of their total distribution), and employed four hundred. His gamble had worked. Again.

Quad workers seem to love their unorthodox ARTistic leader. At the close of each year, Harry gathers them together for a "State of the Company" address, where he reveals financial details seldom released by privately owned companies. In one such address, Quadracci brought 3,000 employees and guests to their feet when he announced that Quad would add a fifth plant and seven new presses the following year. A sixth plant was later planned for the Midwest, and another for California.

No business doublespeak here. Harry lays it on the line. In one company speech, after listing large gains in plant, equipment and value of product produced, Harry added, "Our earnings, however, decreased slightly as a result of the additional interest burden of borrowing to buy new presses. But not to worry," he boomed. "From the standpoint of cash generated from operations—the amount of money that sticks to our hands after the accountants are done playing with depreciation and other games—our cash flow went from $13.2 million to $14 million. And in true Quad/Graphics style, we then took that $14 million, went out and borrowed $56 million, and bought $70 million of new plant equipment. That, in turn, created 700 new jobs."

Alert to Opportunity

Quadracci's "Act Now, Think Later" mentality keeps him alert to opportunity with little advance planning. He makes certain he's armed ahead of time to take risks when those opportunities arise. In 1985, for example, he arranged a $30 million line of credit with a major New York bank, Manufacturers Hanover. That, according to Harry, was "money we could play with."

Later that year Quadracci learned that John Blair marketing, a firm that published color advertising coupon inserts for newspapers, might be for sale. Blair Marketing, a division of John Blair & Company, a radio, television and entertainment company, was once considered the Rolls-Royce of the freestanding insert business. (Freestanding inserts are those aggravating coupon booklets that plump up your Sunday newspaper and litter your floor.) Although it was generating $150 million in revenues, the firm fell on hard times and had lost $17 million the previous year.

Still, it was a line of business that Harry had eyed since launching Quad in 1971, and he knew of Blair's prior reputation and subsequent troubles. As Harry tells it, he went to see the president of the company at four-thirty in the afternoon on a Wednesday and said, "I understand you want to sell your company." Blair's president replied, "Yes, we'd rather sell it to our employees, but that didn't seem to come together." Harry had briefly studied Blair's financial condition. "Well, why don't you let me buy it, and we will keep your employees," he countered. "How much do you want for it?" The price was between $9 million and $11 million. "Sold," said Harry. "I'll buy it." He'd let his financial experts work out the final terms. While he headed down to Washington, D.C., on other business, he recalls, "My financial guys got together with their financial guys, put together a contract, and I came back the following day and signed. And that was it."

Within weeks Blair had become another of Quad's many operating divisions, Quad/Marketing. That his newest division was based in New York tickled Quadracci to no end. Ten months into his ownership of the newspaper insert company, Quadracci was standing behind the desk in his corner office in the center of Manhattan, shimmering with enthusiasm and a cinematic smile. "One year ago, owning this company was the farthest thing from my mind. I had no idea we were going to do this. And here I am, sitting in the geographic center of all my dreams—Rockefeller Center, across the street from the Time-Life Building. And it was *not* in my plans. In fact, anything I planned never seemed to happen."

What was he doing with a $150 million company if it wasn't in his plans? It's Theory Q risk taking at work: "I walked in, the opportunity was there, and I moved faster than anybody else did. And that was it," says Harry.

From start to finish, the Blair acquisition had consumed weeks, not months or years. Emergency surgery to stem the losses took

293

even less time. According to Harry, he brought in four women and eight men, took over the key operations, and within nine days had eliminated the operating deficit. Blair, he discovered, had been buying products and services from a sister company, and was being grossly overcharged. He also knew that by printing the huge volume of inserts at Quad, the firm could save equally huge amounts of money. At thirty-two pages, each color insert is like a complete magazine, except there is no editorial material. A circulation of 48 million, delivered to nearly five hundred newspapers, produced advertising revenues of nearly $9 million per issue.

That kind of printing volume is enough to keep eight presses active twenty-four hours a day, all year long, enough to fill four hundred truckloads every two weeks. Using his newly installed press capacity, Quadracci was able to cut costs by nearly a third, from $7.25 per 1,000 printed inserts to less than $5 per 1,000. At Blair, complex page layouts were still being done manually, via the old scissors-and-paste method. Quad brought in a specially designed computerized system, for an annual savings of another $4 million to $5 million.

Wasn't Quadracci fearful of harming the rest of the company by taking on a money-losing new business? "Oh sure," he says. "But I had infinite confidence in the ability of our people to turn the thing around." To him, that confidence in his and his staff's abilities meant he had *control of the risk*, and that, in turn, made it a minimal risk to Quadracci, not a long shot.

Until now, Quad had grown mainly from within, albeit at high speed. The Blair acquisition added another quick layer to growth —and this time in a field outside printing. Quad was beginning to *look* like a large company. Wouldn't bigness threaten Quad's unique culture? Not according to Harry. "We made a conscious decision not to lose sight of what made us big so fast," he says, "and that was being small. As long as we retain that feeling of smallness, the culture we've created will perpetuate itself, no matter how big we get."

R&D That Pays Off

At Quad/Graphics, research and development is second nature. The in-house nomenclature makes Quad sound more as if it should be in San Francisco's Silicon Valley or Boston's high-tech Route 128 than in Pewaukee, Wisconsin, printing magazines. One innovation breeds another until the whole place is a simmering vat of change. By 1983, Quad had figured out numerous ways to run its presses faster (speed improvements are constant; press crews compete in a kind of perpetual press speed Olympics), but soon discovered that the inks it was using wouldn't stand up to such high-velocity application. The company went to its commercial ink manufacturer, but they were slow in responding. So Quad did what Quad does best—started making its *own* customized inks. Quad's Chemical Research and Technology (CR/T) division, formed in February 1983, now supplies all of the ink for the company—and beyond. CR/T has become a leader in the high-test ink business, turning out tons of the stuff yearly.

Cutting costs for clients is also a major obsession at Quad. And one client's special need has often led Quad to develop new technology that benefits many others. *Family Computing Magazine* is one such case. When *Family Computing* was looking for a printer, the magazine wanted a company that could offer an economical way of printing, binding and mailing several different versions of the same magazine. Apple owners would get the Apple version, IBM owners the IBM version, and so on. Since magazines can save huge sums in postage costs by sorting their issues by zip code before they enter the post office, a new method of channeling the separately printed *Family Computing* issues into a single mail stream (thus saving money) would be necessary for the idea to work economically.

So in hopes of landing the new account, Quad/Tech—one of Quad's most successful semiautonomous divisions—set out to develop the new equipment that would be needed. Quad/Graphics became *Family Computing*'s printer, and even though the magazine's publisher abandoned the idea of multi-versions of the magazine, Quad/Tech's engineers continued to build a new machine called a Multi-Mailer, based on the concept of saving postage costs by sorting many magazines all at once. If one large magazine could use the concept to save money on mailing multiple versions, they reasoned, why couldn't several smaller magazines also save money by channeling their publications into a combined mail stream?

The finished product, a computer-controlled electro-mechanical system that channels multiple magazine titles into a common mail stream, made it possible—for the first time—for smaller magazines to enter the mail prepared by zip code or carrier route. It altered the way magazines are distributed, and brought down mailing costs—one of the largest single expenses of magazine publishing. The magazines involved in the system share the resulting postage savings, based on their volume. Among the first five magazines that were collectively saving nearly $2 million in yearly mailing costs because of Quad's innovation were *The Atlantic* and *Harper's*.

Monitoring press "registration" during the color printing process has historically been one of the industry's most vexing problems. Since each color of ink is applied separately, one at a time at high speed to form a full-color image on paper, each color-to-color layer must be aligned precisely on top of the other to avoid blurring. This alignment is called press registration, and in the past it was done largely by human hands. Quad/Tech developed its own microcomputer-driven Register Guidance System—a kind of Seeing Eye robot—to check press registration, automatically bring the press into register, and keep quality high and waste low. The device was developed by two Quad electricians whom Harry sequestered at his winter vacation home with instructions to develop such a system. It has since gone through numerous revisions and won international awards for technical development.

Early in his firm's growth, Quadracci recognized that while electronics had long ago been introduced to the printing industry, those developments dealt almost exclusively with the "pre-press" area. That's the process of preparing a publication for print, including color separations, typesetting, and making the films used in the photo offset printing process. The technological advances, however, seemed to halt at the door to the pressroom's heavy equipment. In that sweaty realm, change was slow in coming. With multimillion-dollar price tags, printing presses are big-ticket items. In any given year there may be only a hundred companies worldwide in the market for a press. With so few being made, advancements were slow.

This situation was tailored to Harry's ART—Quad/Graphics simply taught itself how to manufacture its own advancements. Quad/Tech began life as a small research and development division within the company. Today it's a world leader in developing new printing industry technology, a major supplier of microcomputer control systems to the printing industry in the United States. Those control systems help printers cut waste while increasing running speeds and maintaining quality. But Quad/Tech has a special edge over its competitors in press technology—an entire company to serve as its experimental laboratory. Quad/Tech can sell equipment *for* printers that has been developed *by* printers.

At first, Quadracci tried to sell his company's inventions to the large press manufacturers, but those firms weren't much interested if they hadn't invented it themselves. So Harry began selling Quad's technological innovations *to his own competitors* in the printing business, a sideline that now provides as much as 10 percent of Quad's revenues. According to Harry, one regional printing company outside Quad's area sends blank purchase orders with standing instructions to Quad/Tech: Send whatever you develop as soon as possible. Quad/Tech has 150 employees and accounts for $20 million in yearly sales. And, according to Harry, it is "wildly profitable."

The numerous technological innovations have helped Quad, as well as other printing companies, improve average press running speeds from about 480,000 pages per hour in 1976 to 1.6 million pages per hour a decade later, with the same five-man press crew, and with a vast increase in quality.

SEEING THE BIG PICTURE

*"Existing means of production can yield
greater economic performance only through
greater uncertainty; through taking greater
risks."*

—BOEHM-BAWERK'S LAW,
a basic economic theory

Risk is something that can be practiced, which, as we've seen, makes it an active affair, not a passive state. One does not "accept" risk so much as seek it out. Risk *making* is not simply asking, "What risks will my company be forced to cope with?" It is action *initiated*. Positive risking is intentional. It requires proper attention and "feeding" (adding resources) to keep the enterprise in good health for the future. This is another way of saying that risk taking is an *investment* in the future. Businesses that ignore this economic fundamental face great peril.

Enterprise is often victimized by the myth that its future will mirror its past. Wall Street, for example, has great fondness for lists showing the "Best Performing" or "Worst Performing" mutual funds. Individual investors rush to bet their money on last

298

year's top funds—and by association, the managers running them. The illogical assumption behind the myth goes like this:

> Yes, there is uncertainty in the market, but the uncertainties that cause failure can be figured out, and these people [the managers of the "best" performers] have somehow figured out what causes the errors and have made the necessary adjustments.

But, in fact, uncertainty and change are not static, and by definition cannot be thought out rationally. They are laden with surprise, with novelty, with risk. In this technological, information-driven age, business tends to be smug—sure of its ability to avoid risks profitably. But the inevitable unpredictability of enterprise means that the natural state of men and women who function within it must be one of ignorance and peril, *not* knowledge and security.

Since change is unending, uncertainty infinite, risk taking must be a *continuous process*. It is not something corporate management can study once, develop an opinion about and devise some tactics for, world everlasting, amen. Taking risks is what change and uncertainty require enterprise to do, but the method is itself subject to change and uncertainty.

There's no ultimate risk—one big gamble that will solve everything. Instead, enterprising risk makers, especially ones like Harry Quadracci, *tend toward a continuous series of smaller risks*. The reason is more pragmatic than profound: Opportunities to take "The Big Risk" are simply more rare. And for most people there's greater danger of messing it up out of sheer fear. Nonetheless, in the latest rush to reinvent the corporation, some businesses have succumbed to the fantasy that the greater the risk, the better the idea. The most successful risk-inspiring situations, however, as with the most effective innovations, start small. Holding out for The Big One assigns too lofty a position to risk, when it should be viewed more as a frequent, sometimes messy, always uneven necessity of daily enterprise.

Thinking in terms of continuous small risks, as Quadracci, Bob Swanson and Fred Adler do, helps the risk taker see the entire picture more clearly. For example, in Quadracci's risk-taking scheme, selling his company's newest technological discoveries to the competition is not a conflict. In his view, it is not other printers that are his competition, but other media—television,

299

radio, newspapers that compete with his bread-and-butter clients in the magazine trade. The way Harry sees it, anything he can do to lower the cost of publishing magazines is good for him. Lower costs means more advertisers will buy space, and that will return more business to Quad. *Quadracci is able to see beyond his own concerns*, to the bigger picture.

Quad's Risk-Taking Culture

The employee-management architecture Quadracci created at his company was crafted to squeeze out the best risk-taking abilities of each employee. How does Harry encourage others to take risks? "First and foremost," he says, "you have to *raise their sights*. You have to make them believe that they are capable of becoming something better than they ever hoped to be.

"You take a look at our company and you see we are very much technology and printing, but our average employee is at best a high school graduate. We don't have 3,500 engineers out there like some of the high-tech companies in Silicon Valley. And yet we are operating as if we *do* have 3,500 engineers out there. Our kids have all the equipment, but maybe they didn't go on to college.

"First you get them fired up to the fact that they can become something more than they ever hoped to be; that they're as good as anybody else; that nobody is any better than they are. That's raising their sights. That's first and foremost." Then there's "mentoring"—the system at Quad where employees learn from each other. It establishes a controlled environment, explains Harry, which lets each person know he is free to make all the mistakes in the world, but protects him from doing anything that would be disastrous personally or for the company. "You don't make him drive a car before he can walk," says Harry. "You expose him to risk taking, but you control the risks."

According to Harry, Quad's emphasis on experimentation produces more risk takers. "When I get a new manager in, they come and they sit there just as you're sitting there now," he tells an interviewer. "And I say, 'Look, you're now in management. Congratulations. But let me tell you this, you're not a pressman one day and a manager the next. There is a difference. I can teach you

300

how to run a press, but I *can't* teach you how to manage. You can only find out how to manage [by] yourself, by trial and error. You try something and if it works, it works. You can't act like Harry Quadracci. Don't ever copy anybody. Develop your own style because you are you. You'd sound silly sounding like me, just like I'd sound silly sounding like you.' "

Among Quad's newer divisions is Quad/Rail, created in 1987. It seems Harry bought an old railroad sleeper car called the Silver Chalet which he planned to restore and use as an overnight guest quarters at one of Quad's plants. When a Milwaukee company hired to do the restoration fell behind on the job, Quadracci did what he had done so many times before—created a new division and did it himself. Now Quad/Rail is a permanent division that repairs and restores railcars for other companies.

Duplainville Transport, another of Quad's many divisions, was born one day when the shipping department asked Harry about generating revenue by hauling loads on return trips rather than coming back empty. Before they knew it they were in business, with simple instructions from Quadracci: Figure out for yourself what to haul. Harry doesn't get involved in telling Quad's divisions what they should be doing, or even setting goals. "That's your responsibility," he tells his bumper crop of managers. He watches from a distance, offering guidance when other managers have trouble adapting to the Quad way of risk taking.

Toasting a Perfect Zero

Taking risks is cause enough for celebration at Quad—whether or not they succeed. When Quad/Tech spent three years and $1 million developing a new folder that didn't work, Harry threw a champagne party and awarded a medal to the project leader. "You've got to have a perfect zero every once in a while as well as a perfect success if you've explored alternatives," explains Harry. Quadracci can't imagine reprimanding employees, let alone firing them, for taking risks that fail. "You have to find a way for it to work."

At Quad/Graphics, the traditional nomenclature of work roles, such as "boss" and "worker," doesn't exist. As a result of Quadracci's legal training, employees at Quad/Graphics are all known as "partners." Bosses have been replaced by sponsors and mentors; and the rank and file are students, who are all the time learning to become managers or mentors themselves. A few other things you won't find at Quad: organizational charts, procedural manuals, time clocks and, of course, budgets.

"We encourage all of our pressmen, for example, to run the press the way they want to," say Harry. "Back in 1973 when we started adding presses, I refused to put somebody in charge of the pressroom. Just as each lawyer is a partner and they run their own part of the business, I said each pressman is going to run their own press." Other managers objected. "You can't do that," said one. "Why not?" replied Harry. "Because you'll fragment management" was the answer. "I think that sounds like a good idea," said Quadracci. "Let's fragment management. I'd rather have fifty people out there all thinking independently—being in conflict with ideas without conflicting in personality—and working together independently to develop an operating policy which I can then validate, than for me to sit up here from the top down and say this is the way we're going to do it."

In Quad's egalitarian culture, the only difference in the uniforms (supplied clean daily) worn by supervisors and other workers is that the supervisors have their last name on the pocket, others their first name. Harry's uniform is different, often favoring bow tie and suspenders, though his office is unassuming and highly accessible. He uses one end of a conference table as his desk, and if Harry isn't around other employees will readily occupy his office for their own needs.

Pressmen are called press *managers* at Quad. "If you are responsible for a $6 million press I have news for you," says Harry. "You're as much responsible for profits as I am." Employees who make manager are promptly given a ticket to New York, where they stay with their spouse in one of the three apartments Quad owns in midtown Manhattan. "It's part of their encouragement, their training to get out in the world," explains Harry.

Quad is even unconventional when it comes to work hours. Harry was one of the first to introduce the three-day, thirty-six-hour workweek, and make it successful. Employees love it, and it has been a boon to the company. Since the printing plants are in production twenty-four hours a day, having only one shift change made scheduling easier. After Quad went to the three-day week, productivity increased by 20 percent. If the purpose of organization in enterprise is to permit common people to do uncommon things, as one management expert has said, then Quad/Graphics has come up with the right formula to pull it off.

Earning Accolades

Quadracci's experiment with risk has earned the company increasing recognition. In 1985, the liberal magazine *Mother Jones* named Quad/Graphics one of the ten best businesses in America, based on workplace conditions, degree of employee ownership and participation, social value of product produced, and concern for the environment and community service, among other factors. Quad's Employee Stock Ownership Plan (ESOP) has also won praise. When *Psychology Today* magazine explored the effects of employee ownership on company performance in 1986, it singled out Quad's program as "The Ultimate ESOP." Said the magazine, "For Quad/Graphics employee-partners, working at the company is its own reward, both financially and personally." Although employee ownership of companies was little more than a curiosity when Quad was formed, it has grown in popularity, due in part to favorable tax incentives for company contributions to an ESOP. Under these programs, companies can deduct the value of stock contributed to employee ownership plans.

A recently completed four-year study by the National Center for Employee Ownership (Arlington, Virginia), the basis for the *Psychology Today* article, said, "An employee stock ownership plan is at the heart of [Quad's] philosophy and culture. A large part of the impetus behind the start-up of Quad/Graphics by Quadracci and his co-founders was the desire to diminish any class division among workers. . . . The workers act as though Quad's presses belong to them, because they do. They act as though every order is their personal responsibility, because it is." At Quad, the employees as a group own about 20 percent of the company; original employee founders about 60 percent (48 percent of that is Harry's); and outside investors about 20 percent.

Harry Quadracci is the kind of innovative businessman who practices a brand of risk taking that terrorizes other managers.

Many executives pay lip service to the freedom of risk taking and making mistakes, hoping they will never have to take big chances. Perhaps nowhere else in American manufacturing today is a work force so free to pursue its own initiative, and make those mistakes without fear of retribution, as at Quad/Graphics. What's more, if they succeed, they will share the rewards. Where some firms talk of initiative, Quadracci puts the ball into play daily. If there is initiative to be unchained, the printing house that Harry built can do it.

One particularly curious experiment in management risk taking occurs each May at Quad/Graphics. That's the date of the annual "Spring Fling"—the day management plays hooky, leaving the "rank and file" in charge of the company. It's a tradition that started in 1974. Harry had planned to close the plant for a day while the senior executives met for strategy sessions and some socializing. When some unexpected printing work came in, Harry decided to keep the plant open and let the workers handle whatever needed to be done.

As one business magazine observed, this practice of leaving employees unsupervised for a day can be a high-stakes business gamble. But not to Harry. Although a small slipup—an incorrect color tint, a misplaced page—could cost the company six figures on a print run of millions, Quad's brand of "management by walking away" has proven to be a major morale booster for the employees, and problems have been few. After all, Theory Q maintains that responsibility belongs to everybody; that workers don't always need somebody telling them what to do. Harry is willing to take the risks that will help train his employees to act like the owners of the company they are.

At the core of Quadracci's vision for the future is a belief that his firm's competitive edge depends on educating its employees. *An informed, confident employee is one more willing to take the risks that lead to innovation,* he says. To ensure that edge, Quad has developed an extensive, in-house education system. Quad/Ed teaches courses ranging from remedial reading to computer programming and press operation. Attendance is strictly voluntary and there's no pay for attending classes. But in one recent fall semester, more than half of all Quad employees were attending Quad/Ed courses each week. The setting couldn't be more appropriate—an old country schoolhouse Harry bought in 1984,

304

painted red and surrounded by farmers' fields, across Duplain-ville Road from the Pewaukee, Wisconsin, plant.

Instructors come from within Quad's own work force. The company frees its skilled workers so they can learn how to share their knowledge with others. The company describes Quad/Ed this way: "Passing one's knowledge on to those that come after is an integral part of Quad/Graphics. This precept flies in the face of printing industry tradition—and most journeymen trades, for that matter—that says knowledge is a thing to be guarded. Quad/Graphics doesn't believe that by sharing knowledge, it puts its own position in peril." It's one more way that Quadracci has risked being unconventional.

The company also bucks tradition by operating a school for customers, set at Camp Quad's forty-acre nature preserve in a nearby county. Harry felt that many print buyers really knew very little about the technology of the printing process, and had been "bluffing" their way through for years. Nobody had ever taken the time to show them in detail what goes on behind the scenes. Now Quad holds the customer sessions about eight times yearly.

While shared responsibility is a Quad cornerstone, employees must prove they are worthy of that responsibility and of participating in decisions. Nobody confuses Harry's brand of loose management with low standards. Quadracci is a tough taskmaster—a risk *leader*. He challenges his people; he doesn't coddle them. Nobody sloughs off and survives around Quad. Employees have pride of craftsmanship drilled into them if it's not there naturally; they are brought along by their mentors, who constantly reinforce the Quad way of doing things.

Those who become managers are given a heavy load. They can get help if they need it, but there's little time at Quad for extensive hand-holding. The emphasis is on professionalism. "Instead of thinking of themselves as printers, we get them to think of themselves as trained technicians who run the computers that run the presses," explains Quadracci. New recruits go through a lengthy training process. According to Harry, they are told something like this:

> Welcome to boot camp. You're eighteen years old. You're coming to work for Quad/Graphics. Yours is not to reason why. For the next three years you're going to learn *our* way—and it's your

305

responsibility to learn. We're going to give you the proper equipment and it's your responsibility to educate yourself to use it.

Those uncomfortable with such responsibility—the ones who
prefer to be told what to do—don't make it. The rest learn Theory
Q's emphasis on customer satisfaction. Says Harry, "You need to
listen to the client, but you need to hear him, too. Clients buy
satisfaction, not products and services. It therefore follows that
we are in the business of satisfying customer needs rather than
simply supplying printing. And to satisfy needs you must know
and understand the customer. We are all in the customer satisfaction business, not just the sales department. 'Keep your eye on
the customer, not the competition,' is the motto here. Keep your
eye on the customer, and to hell with the competition." Among
his other ARTist's traits, Quadracci is a good listener.

Although the printing industry is heavily unionized, there are
no unions at Quad/Graphics and no seniority system. Few would
want a union. Harry's progressive management style places Quad/
Graphics above standard union or anti-union sentiments prevailing elsewhere. One printing trade journal credits Harry's legal
training with sharpening his appreciation of the delicate balances
that must be struck between the needs of the employees and those
of the company.

Quad's thousands of employees feel they have little in common
with their counterparts elsewhere in the printing trades. At Quad,
the field is open—workers are free to pursue and learn as many
new jobs as they can handle; Harry *trusts* people—a risk many
managers don't take. That's just the opposite of the highly structured shops where each person does one thing only. Elsewhere,
it might take an individual eight to ten years to become a first-
pressman—the person in charge of the press and the five-member
crew it takes to run it. Even then, he'd still be an hourly wage
earner. Quad has compressed that time period to three to five
years. Its first-pressmen have been as young as twenty-two years
old. They become salaried managers with a say in all areas that
affect their press, from scheduling to hiring and training their own
crews. A salaried manager is in charge of each major piece of
equipment, and each manager's compensation includes an annual
base salary plus a cash bonus awarded for both individual and
company performance.

Extended Family

The Quad culture reinforces the idea that all employees are tied together as an extended family, with similar goals. Since each department is responsible for doing its own hiring, the family concept can be quite literal. Employees like it so much they recommend their relatives for new jobs. Before Quad expanded to other states, more than one-third of its entire work force was related in some fashion—husband/wife teams, brothers and brothers-in-law, cousins, fathers, mothers and sons.

One Quad plant has its own full-time fitness director, and a $3 million sports facility. The day care center has hundreds of kids enrolled at peak periods. Nonsalary benefits at Quad (the hidden paycheck) total 40 percent of direct compensation per employee —among the top 2 percent of all employers in the United States. Quad provides five types of insurance: medical, hospital, dental, eye and life. It also pays its workers not to smoke. In one recent year, the company paid out nearly $80,000 to employees in no-smoking awards.

Employees are invited frequently to the company lodge on a Wisconsin lake. And when Quad parties—which it does often and hard—the local food vendors rejoice. At one of three annual summertime bashes, the Quad family gorged itself on 5,000 Italian sausages (the wurst of choice due to Harry's Italian roots), 1,200 hot dogs, 29 half-barrels of beer, 450 gallons of sodas and wine coolers, 150 pounds of green peppers, and nearly a quarter-ton of Jerry Kreuzer's famous baked beans.

And since Harry likes popcorn, the plant has old-style popcorn vending carts that dispense a new supply each afternoon. This is called Quad/Pop, of course, and the daily dose of popcorn has a message behind it as well. Harry wants it to be a constant reminder that employees should generate a flow of new ideas, like kernels of corn in a popcorn popper.

The enthusiasm at Quad spills over to the firm's clients. Norm Richey, production director for the *Journal of the American Medical Association,* was a typical Quadracci convert. The first time he went there he became lost trying to find Quad's plant amidst the lush southeastern Wisconsin countryside. Once he was safely inside the plant, Quad sold itself. As Quad employees tell the story, Richey soon became so caught up in the enthusiasm that reverberates throughout Quad that when other executives from the *Journal* came to visit, Richey was seen leading the tours himself.

The American Medical Association was hooked on Quad's commitment to employee health, too. And the AMA liked the idea of printing the nation's largest medical journal, a weekly, at a company that pays its employees to quit smoking, offers regular CPR training, and has exercise centers open to all.

Harry is an art enthusiast as well, collecting pieces that please him at every opportunity, and displaying them throughout the plant—including the employee locker rooms. His buying became so intense, his collection so large at 250 to 300 pieces, that Harry had no idea what he owned. So he hired away Barbara Nocon from the Milwaukee Museum of Art to become Quad's first in-house art curator. Quadracci has long maintained that the printing industry, despite its modern technologies, is still merely an evolution of art. "First came the concept, then the tool, then craftsmanship, then the machine that could reproduce multiple images," he once said in a speech at the Milwaukee Art Museum. "Finally, with infinite accuracy, we can print 6 million impressions an hour to tolerances of millionths of an inch. Still, art and technology are both man-centered. It's just a matter of how you use the tool and the machine."

For Harry Quadracci, building and improving the business has involved constant risk. Had Quadracci not been made of stern risk-taking material, there would be no Quad/Graphics Inc. He risked money; he risked unorthodox thinking; he risked losing it all countless times by refusing to back off from his "Think Small" rejoinder even as the corporation became much larger. He dared to build an enterprise from scratch in a way nobody else had quite done it before.

"It's hard to think small," says Harry. "But in taking risks, you have to break them down into *attainable* risks." Other entrepreneurs delude themselves by saying they'll become more innovative once they have some money to work with. But to Harry it's not a matter of money. "It's just a matter of thinking small, of starting in some small way, of doing *something*."

When the company finished yet another year of explosive

growth, Quadracci exhorted his troops not to get trapped in look-ing at Quad as a giant: "Don't say that, 'We're getting to be a big company, so let's get organized.' No. As a company, we've got to think small. We're getting to be a big company, so let's *not* get organized. Let's get disorganized. Think small. Think small." To help reinforce that, the company hosts regular "Think Small" din-ners where employees can discuss how to work better as a team.

Quadracci does have one terrific advantage that some other businesses don't, and it helps him take risks and be patient: Quad/Graphics is *privately* owned. He doesn't have public stockholders or Wall Street analysts to satisfy. Does that really make risk taking easier? "Oh, absolutely," says Harry. "I always tell the employ-ees, the greatest thing that ever happened to Quad/Graphics is that I can't be fired. Not being able to be fired is one fantastic, wonderful insurance policy. I can go out and take risks, and if they don't work I can say, 'Okay everyone, so big deal. So I made a mistake. So we didn't make the bucks this year. We'll make them next year.' That's one of the things that you lose when you're not in control as the entrepreneur. That's why I think some founding entrepreneurs are so successful—it's because they are allowed to continue to take risks and *be* successful. The next guy who comes along can't do things the same way."

For now at least, Harry Quadracci has no plans to try to cash in his success by taking his company public, as so many others have done. If he needs cash he finds other ways. In 1985, for example, the General Electric Pension Fund invested $20 million in Quad convertible subordinated debentures, giving Quad more growth money while allowing it to stay private. "I don't understand why so many entrepreneurs are in such a big rush to go public. I think there's a certain syndrome with wanting to cash out and own a $2.5 million house, with looking to build a fortune. I think it depends on the company. I think at the high-tech companies and the software companies, where you have a short shelf life for the product, the entrepreneurs tend to look at keeping score by how much money they can accumulate. But that's because it's a very fleeting thing."

Harry Quadracci keeps score other ways. "Let me put it this way," he says. "I remember clearly when I had sixty-five employ-ees working for me. But I don't remember reaching the point when I was employing 2,500. It doesn't take a genius to under-

309

stand that I would be quite happy with the income off of one web press, let alone thirty. So why am I doing what I'm doing? For the joy of the sailing. Like sailing, it's more important to compete than to win. And people say, 'What are you talking about, Harry?' And I say, well, how would you like to win the Super Bowl by having the other team not show up? I think the joy of competition, of winning, seeing people grow—all of that is fun."

America can no longer afford to believe that the tools of business end with profit-and-loss statements, quarterly earnings reports, economic projections and market research studies. These are no more the stuff of enterprise than are bags of coins a banker's tools.

Risk, and a willingness to embrace it, are what differentiates an economic system that merely "provides" from one that has the potential to build, innovate and make something where nothing existed before. That is the essence of dynamic risk, the essence of enterprise.

Progress and profit in enterprise *do* require its participants to roll the dice of risk. But unlike gambling, the art of taking calculated risks—of being *both* daring and wise—is a positive force of economic creation. By understanding what risk really is and is not, its uncertainties and its powers, risk takers can load those dice and turn up more winners, more often.

ACKNOWLEDGMENTS

Novelists, in a sense, have it easy. They make up their own "facts." But nobody writes a work of nonfiction without help. Information from hundreds of books, articles, studies, speeches, observations, and interviews all gets tossed into a brew that eventually emerges as a finished book.

I owe a debt to the scores of people who gave their time to be interviewed. Many of them are named throughout the book where their comments appear. And although the direct thoughts of others did not survive the editing process, I am indebted to them as well for helping shape the thinking behind the book. Many others sent written materials or quotations on risk taking which proved helpful.

To avoid excessively cluttering the text with footnotes and numbers, all notes are contained in a Notes on Sources section in the back of the book, identified by page numbers and the key phrases to which they refer.

Special thanks go to Hugh J. O'Neill, executive editor at Times Books, who steadfastly provided a clear vision of how to transform the raw ideas here into the most practical, useful book it could be, offering sound advice on what it needed and what it did not.

My thanks go to Vaud Massarsky, who helped with some early research, and the Bobst Library at New York University for providing resources and a quiet haven in the midst of New York.

Heartfelt thanks to my incredibly loving wife and best buddy, Kaye, who encouraged me countless times to stay at (or get back to) the keyboard of my trusty AT&T 6300 personal computer, and

311

whose own outstanding professional acting talents and insights into human behavior often help me understand why people do what they do.

And a final expression of gratitude to my parents: my father, Paul Kehrer, whose special wit and business acumen first shifted my career toward financial journalism, and my mother, Margaret Kehrer, who aside from my editor and agent was the only one to read and comment on an early version of the manuscript.

NOTES ON SOURCES

A primary source of quoted remarks as well as many other facts
and observations in this book is dozens of interviews, many of
them tape-recorded, conducted by the author between 1985 and
1988 with the principals involved. In addition to the books, the
magazine, newspaper and journal articles, the wire service reports, the speeches, studies, letters, essays, papers, published interviews, research reports and corporate documents specifically
cited here, scores of others helped bring the concept of risk in
enterprise into greater focus. Company financial information is
generally from annual and quarterly reports, press releases and
SEC documents.

BOOK I: The Heart of Business Risk

4   WALTER WRISTON . . . OFFERS AN: Walter Wriston, *Risk and
Other Four-Letter Words* (New York: Harper & Row, 1986), p.
228. This remark was previously made in a speech by Wriston
before The Economic Club of Chicago, October 25, 1979, later
reprinted in his book.

4   "A SPECIFIC SKILL": Dictionaries offer many definitions of art.
This one comes from *The American Heritage Dictionary of the
English Language*, 1971 edition.

4   EARLIER IN THIS CENTURY: Joseph A. Schumpeter, who was a
professor of economics at Harvard University, described
"creative destruction" in his classic economic text *Capitalism,
Socialism, and Democracy* (New York: Harper & Brothers,
1942), pp. 81–86.

5   THAT MAKES WEATHER: The weather analogy is suggested by
        James Gleick in his delightful book on the science of chaos,
        Chaos: Making a New Science (New York: Viking, 1987).

6   "THE SYSTEMATIC SLOUGHING OFF": Peter F. Drucker,
        Innovation and Entrepreneurship (New York: Harper & Row,
        1985).

7   RICHARD FOSTER: Foster's arguments on innovation are
        presented in *Innovation: The Attacker's Advantage* (New York:
        Summit Books, 1986).

9   AS FAR BACK AS: The Kansas newspaper editor was William
        Allen White of *The Emporia Gazette*, who made the comment
        for *Life* magazine on his seventieth birthday in 1938. The story
        is recounted in the July 12, 1985, edition of *The New York
        Times*.

9   A MARKETING EXPERT AT HARVARD: This was Mark S. Albion, a
        marketing professor quoted in *The Washington Post*, July 22,
        1985.

12   NEW YORK EXECUTIVE SEARCH MAVEN: Roche described the
        incident in a *New York Times Magazine* "Business World"
        supplement, December 7, 1986, p. 9.

14   AND IN HIS RUSH: Goizueta's comment about not market-testing
        Diet Coke was made in "Putting the Daring Back in Coke,"
        The New York Times, March 4, 1984.

17   IN ONE MAJOR STUDY: The study referred to was a twelve-year
        effort conducted by Kenneth MacCrimmon, professor of
        management, and Donald Wehrung, associate professor of
        policy analysis and management sciences, both of the
        University of British Columbia. Results were published in
        Taking Risks: The Management of Uncertainty (New York:
        Free Press, 1986).

19   ACCORDING TO J.B.: J.B. Fuqua, "What's Wrong with Today's
        CEO?" *Chief Executive*, Spring 1987.

20   ONE OF THE FIRST: Readers can find a detailed account of Coca-
        Cola's testing process in Thomas Oliver, *The Real Coke: The
        Real Story* (New York: Random House, 1986).

24   FUQUA CITES: From J.B. Fuqua, "What's Wrong with Today's
        CEO?" *Chief Executive*, Spring 1987.

35   THEN IT GOT EVEN WORSE: Excerpts from angry letters were
        reported in *The New York Times*, July 12, 1985.

35   COKE-BASHING BECAME: The Sugar Association's comments ran over the PR Newswire on April 30, 1985.

37   ALL THE TIME: Keough, as quoted in "Coca-Cola's Big Misjudgment," *The New York Times*, July 12, 1985.

40   "CEOs OFTEN VIEW COMPROMISE:" From J.B. Fuqua, "What's Wrong with Today's CEO?" *Chief Executive*, Spring 1987.

42   AT THE CORPORATION'S ANNUAL MEETING: As reported in "Keeping New Coke Alive," *The New York Times*, July 20, 1986.

44   THE COMPANY'S EXECUTIVES: "Coca-Cola Faces Tough Task in Marketing Old and New Coke," *The Wall Street Journal*, July 12, 1985.

45   THE YEAR AFTER THE FORMULA CHANGE: *Advertising Age*, December 29, 1986.

45   AS ONE NEWSPAPER REPORTED: *The Washington Post*, July 22, 1985.

47   ACCORDING TO A *WALL STREET JOURNAL* STUDY: A series titled "Struggle Against the Odds: Blacks in Business." This item was published May 17, 1988.

48   "INDEED," OBSERVED *THE NEW YORK TIMES:* "Kodak Pays the Price for Change," March 6, 1988.

48   PRODUCT ACCELERATION: The reference to the Japanese word *wai-gaya* comes from "Manufacturers Strive to Slice Time Needed to Develop Products," *The Wall Street Journal*, February 23, 1988.

49   "AT ANY OTHER COMPANY": "Keeping New Coke Alive," *The New York Times*, July 20, 1986.

BOOK II: Paying the Price

56   GENERAL FOODS FOUND: "The Numbers Racket: How Polls and Statistics Lie," *U.S. News & World Report*, July 11, 1988, pp. 44–47.

59   ON A NOVEMBER DAY: Richard Darman made his comments in a speech before the Japan Society in New York on November 7, 1986. *The New York Times* carried reactions of business leaders November 11. Darman followed up with an article, "In Search

of Pioneer Spirit," *The Wall Street Journal*, March 20, 1987, p. 36–D.

62   As TOM PETERS NOTES: Tom Peters, *Thriving on Chaos* (New York: Knopf, 1987), p. 392.

63   "IN THE UNITED STATES": Sadlow made these comments in a presentation titled "Cultivating Innovation within the Corporate Environment," published in a collection of papers called *Managing Product Innovation* by the British–North American Committee, October 1984, pp. 19–26.

63   IN THEIR BOOK: Walter Adams and James Brock, *The Bigness Complex: Industry, Labor, and Government in the American Economy* (New York: Pantheon Books, 1986).

66   NEUHARTH CONSIDERS THE LAUNCHING: Neuharth expressed his thoughts about this early risk taking in remarks made January 22, 1986, on accepting an award for entrepreneurship from the Wharton Entrepreneurial Center, Philadelphia.

67   JACK GERMOND, THE POLITICAL COLUMNIST: Germond's comment has been widely repeated, including in a *Washington Journalism Review* profile on Neuharth, August 1986, p. 23, and in Peter Prichard, *The Making of McPaper: The Inside Story of USA Today* (Kansas City, Mo.: Andrews, McMeel & Parker, 1987), p. 79.

67   HE ONCE ATTRIBUTED: "Neuharth's Urge to Merge Enlarges Gannett's Operations," *The Wall Street Journal*, September 11, 1985.

74   OF *THE WASHINGTON POST'S* VENTURE: Peter Prichard, *The Making of McPaper*, p. 93.

79   AS PSYCHOLOGISTS HAVE POINTED OUT: An excellent article, "Successful Executives Rely on Own Kind of Intelligence," appeared in the Science section of *The New York Times*, July 31, 1984.

80   ACCORDING TO A REPORT: *Psychology Today*, October 1981, p. 24.

80   YOU AND I WILL FLIP: Two articles that provide a fascinating and in-depth analysis of the psychology of risk-taking decisions are: Kevin McKean, "Decisions, Decisions," *Discover*, June 1985, pp. 22–31; and William F. Allman, "Staying Alive in the 20th Century," *Science 85*, October 1985, pp. 31–37. Both rely heavily on the outstanding research in this area by Professors

Amos Tversky of Stanford University and Daniel Kahneman of the University of British Columbia, Vancouver.

86 THE KEY TO UNDERSTANDING: James Gleick, in *Chaos: Making a New Science* (New York: Viking, 1987), pp. 92–93.

93 CONSIDER VCRs: The best in-depth account of how the VCR market developed is James Lardner's *Fast Forward: Hollywood, the Japanese and the VCR Wars* (New York: Norton, 1987).

95 JAMES LARDNER: From *Fast Forward*, p. 74.

95 AVOIDING RISKS: Lester Thurow, *The Zero-Sum Solution* (New York: Simon & Schuster, 1985), pp. 137–38.

96 THE CHINESE HAVE LONG: James Lipton, "Here Be Dragons," *Newsweek*, December 6, 1976, p. 17.

96 WILLIAM C. CLARK: From Clark's paper "Witches, Floods, and Wonder Drugs: Historical Perspectives on Risk Management," published in *Societal Risk Assessment*, a General Motors Research Labs symposium, 1980.

98 "AN ESSENTIAL PART OF": William F. Allman, "Staying Alive in the 20th Century," *Science 85*, October 1985, p. 33.

101 ACCORDING TO ONE REPORT: Neuharth as quoted in Prichard, *The Making of McPaper*, p. 286.

102 AND SHORTLY AFTER: *Value Line*, December 17, 1982, p. 1811.

102 ON ITS THIRD BIRTHDAY: *USA Today*, September 13, 1985.

103 IT WAS DURING: Neuharth's conversation with Warren Phillips was recounted in "Gannett Expands at Faster Pace," *The Washington Post*, September 8, 1985.

106 "GANNETT IS DEPENDABLE": *Value Line*, March 14, 1986, p. 1813.

107 FRED SMITH: From text of *INC.* magazine interview with Smith, October 1986, pp. 35–50.

108 "IN DAILY NEWSPAPERS": *Forbes*, December 2, 1985.

110 THE IRONY OF: "TV Version of USA Today May Be Financial—If Not Critical—Success," *The Wall Street Journal*, February 4, 1988.

BOOK III: Seeing Through the Risk Mind

116　In one of his rare interviews: "A Chat with Michael Milken," *Forbes*, July 13, 1987, pp. 248–56.

119　Only a distinct minority: Most of Dr. Farley's comments are from an interview. This particular observation is from his article "The Big T in Personality," *Psychology Today*, May 1986, pp. 44–52.

120　A study of investment preferences: Stuart H. Blum, "Investment Preferences and the Desire for Security: A Comparison of Men and Women," *The Journal of Psychology*, 1976, Vol. 94, pp. 87–91.

122　As one woman entrepreneur: Robert D. Hisrich and Marie O'Brien, "The Woman Entrepreneur from a Business and Sociological Perspective," proceedings of the Babson College Conference on Entrepreneurship, June 1981, p. 25.

131　By 1988, he ruefully: "The Genentech Mystique," *Barron's*, January 11, 1988.

133　At Genentech, science and business: Alison B. Bass, "Managing for Success: The Genentech Story," *Technology Review*, May/June 1985, pp. 28–29.

135　Lee Iacocca: From his commencement address at Duke University, May 4, 1986, Durham, N.C.

136　"What this means": "Companies Turn to Incentives," *The New York Times*, July 19, 1985.

137　Sparking the risk spirit: This is a point forcefully made by economist George Gilder in the prologue to his book *The Spirit of Enterprise* (New York: Simon & Schuster, 1984), pp. 15–19.

138　Even business managers: Kenneth MacCrimmon and Donald Wehrung, *Taking Risks: The Management of Uncertainty* (New York: Free Press, 1986).

140　As risk expert Peter Moore: Peter G. Moore, *The Business of Risk* (Cambridge, England: Cambridge University Press, 1983).

147　They became entrepreneurs: "Biotech's First Superstar," *Business Week*, April 14, 1986.

149　"Here I saw my whole career": Swanson made this comment in a profile of him by Randall Rothenberg appearing in *Esquire*, December 1984, p. 372.

159 A WALL STREET ANALYST: The analyst was Linda I. Miller of
PaineWebber, Inc., quoted in "Biotech's First Superstar,"
Business Week, April 14, 1986.

161 SWANSON ALSO HAD PLANS: Swanson made his comments about
marketing Activase at the Health Care Conference sponsored
by Hambrecht & Quist in San Francisco, January 12, 1987.

163 SAID *FORTUNE*: Gene Bylinsky, "Genentech Has a Golden
Goose," *Fortune*, May 9, 1988, p. 53.

163 A 1988 *BUSINESS WEEK* SURVEY: "Who Made the Most—and
Why," *Business Week*, May 2, 1988, cover story.

BOOK IV: Grasping Risk's Geometry

168 IN 1987, WHEN: "The Changing Role of the CEO," *Business
Week*, October 23, 1987.

168 DON KELLY ... ADDED: Quoted in *Business Week*, ibid.

168 IN THE SCIENCE OF: The "butterfly effect" concept was
described by James Gleick in *Chaos: Making a New Science*
(New York: Viking, 1987).

170 FRED SMITH: From *INC*. interview, October 1986, pp. 35–50

172 MICHAEL MILKEN: *Forbes* interview, July 13, 1987, pp. 248–56.

179 SOME INSIDERS BLASTED ADLER: Daniel Burstein, "High-Tech
Angel," *New York* magazine, June 25, 1984, p. 36.

189 "AMERICAN BUSINESS": J.B. Fuqua, "What's Wrong with Today's
CEO?" *Chief Executive*, Spring 1987.

189 OR, AS ROSABETH KANTER: Quoted in "The Changing Role of
the CEO," *Business Week*, October 23, 1987.

190 CONSIDER THE INTRIGUING STORY: A highly interesting account
of the Stanley Steamer comes from Charles C. McLaughlin,
"The Stanley Steamer: A Study in Unsuccessful Innovation," in
Explorations in Entrepreneurial History, Hugh Aitken, ed.
(Cambridge, Mass.: Harvard University Research Center in
Entrepreneurial History, 1954), pp. 37–47.

201 THAT BLINDING MIST: "Tycoon's Travails: Pittsburgh Billionaire
Finds Venture Capital a Rough Game to Play," *The Wall Street
Journal*, September 17, 1986, p. 1.

208 OSBORNE: Steve Fishman, "Facing Up to Failure," *SUCCESS!*,
November 1984, pp. 48–53.

209 ALLEN MICHELS: From "Profile in Failure: One Man's Painful Crash," *The Wall Street Journal*, December 15, 1986, © Dow Jones & Company, Inc., 1986. Reprinted by permission. All rights reserved.

212 SIMILARLY, MANAGEMENT EXPERT PETER DRUCKER: Drucker discussed the "near-failure" in his classic text *Management: Tasks, Responsibilities, Practices* (New York: Harper Colophon, 1985), p. 796.

215 BY EARLY 1984, ONE BUSINESS MAGAZINE: Joe Flower, "Those Visionary Entrepreneurs," *Venture*, March 1984.

BOOK V: Risk-Taking Tactics

221 THE U.S. AIR FORCE: The fighter pilot analogy was made by Thomas M. Hout and Mark F. Blaxill of the Boston Consulting Group in "Make Decisions Like a Fighter Pilot," *The New York Times*, November 15, 1987.

223 LONG BEFORE: Akers made the comments in a speech to the European Management Forum, Davos, Switzerland, February 4, 1985.

225 CROW STARTED OUT: *The Wall Street Journal* published two major page-one features describing Crow's operations, March 24 and March 27, 1986.

228 GRAY DECIDED TO INVEST: "How Pratt & Whitney Lost Jet-Engine Lead to GE After 30 Years," *The Wall Street Journal*, January 27, 1988.

228 AN EXPOSÉ: *The New York Times Magazine*, September 20, 1987.

228 *BUSINESS WEEK* CAME UP WITH: "Jack Welch: How Good a Manager?," *Business Week*, December 14, 1987, p. 103.

231 IN THE WORDS OF: "Cable's All-Stars," *Channels Magazine*, March 1986.

240 "GANNETT IS THE FREEST SPENDING": "Does Gannett Pay Too Much?," *Fortune*, September 15, 1986, p. 59.

240 "NEUHARTH FORESAW THAT": "Gannett Chairman Expands Empire, Advancing into the 'Major Leagues,'" *Los Angeles Times*, July 6, 1986, Part IV, p. 1.

243   COHEN CLAIMS THAT MANAGING: Cohen made these observations
       in remarks to the New York Financial Writers Association,
       August 12, 1987.

245   As COHEN DESCRIBED IT: "Can Cohen the Consolidator Make
       Shearson-Hutton Work?" *Business Week*, December 21, 1987,
       p. 96.

247   AT HUTTON'S BUILDING: From a chronology of the acquisition,
       "A Done Deal: How Shearson Lehman Bought E. F. Hutton,"
       Dateline (publication for employees of American Express Co.),
       January 1988.

253   MEDIA INDUSTRY SUPERANALYST: Kagan as quoted in "Coca-
       Cola's Movie Mystery," *The New York Times*, September 24,
       1987, p. D–2.

255   GOIZUETA ALSO DEVISED HIS OWN SET: Coke's chairman spelled
       out these "rules" in remarks to the "Biggest Best Deals of
       1985" awards luncheon sponsored by Ernst & Whinney and the
       Atlanta Business Chronicle, February 7, 1986.

259   "SOME MANAGEMENTS ASK": From observations by Gutfreund in
       Sense, published by Lippincott & Margulies Inc., New York,
       issue 88, undated.

260   "No LONGER CAN": "The King of Wall Street," *Business Week*,
       December 9, 1985, p. 98.

262   "I'M *NOT* PREPARED": Gutfreund as quoted in "Can Salomon
       Brothers Learn to Love Junk Bonds?," *The New York Times*,
       November 16, 1986.

263   "ABUSE OF THE DEBT CREATION": Henry Kaufman made these
       remarks in his talk, "Promoting Economic Growth and
       Corporate Financial Risk Taking," before the Chief Executive
       Officers' dinner, Federal Hall, New York City, September 10,
       1985.

BOOK VI: Revolutionary Risk

268   JOSEPH SCHUMPETER'S DEFINITION: Joseph A. Schumpeter,
       Capitalism, Socialism, and Democracy (New York: Harper &
       Brothers, 1942), p. 132.

268   ARTHUR LIPPER III: Arthur Lipper III, with George Ryan, *Guide to Investing in Private Companies* (Homewood, Ill.: Dow Jones-Irwin, 1984).

268   ONE OF AMERICA'S LEADING EXPERTS: David C. McClelland of Harvard University described the risk-taking experiment with children in his book *The Achieving Society* (New York: Van Nostrand, 1961), pp. 211–12.

269   DAVID LIEDERMAN: Liederman's comments were included in John Mack Carter and Joan Feeney, *Starting at the Top* (New York: Morrow, 1985), p. 142.

271   QUAD IS OWNED PARTLY: A glowing account of Quad's Employee Stock Ownership Plan appeared in Corey Rosen, Katherine J. Klein and Karen M. Young, "When Employees Share the Profits," *Psychology Today*, January 1986. The article refers to Quad's as "The Ultimate ESOP."

275   MANAGEMENT EXPERT PETER DRUCKER: Drucker in *Management: Tasks, Responsibilities, Practices* (New York: Harper Colophon, 1985), p. 512.

276   EXPERIMENTERS AT: Kenneth MacCrimmon and Donald Wehrung, *Taking Risks: The Management of Uncertainty* (New York: Free Press, 1986).

288   EVEN ONE OF THE: "Power to the Printer's People," *Printing Impressions*, September 1984.

303   WHEN *PSYCHOLOGY TODAY:* "When Employees Share the Profits," *Psychology Today*, January 1986.

310   THESE ARE NO MORE: The "coins" metaphor was inspired by James Gleick, who used it in *Chaos: Making a New Science* (New York: Viking, 1987).

BIBLIOGRAPHY OF ADDITIONAL REFERENCES AND SUGGESTED READINGS

Allen, Robert G., *Creating Wealth* (New York: Simon & Schuster, 1983).

Avis, Warren, *Take a Chance to Be First* (New York: Macmillan, 1986).

Bennis, Warren, and Nanus, Burt, *Leaders* (New York: Harper & Row, 1985).

Boesky, Ivan, *Merger Mania* (New York: Holt, Rinehart, 1985).

Clifford, D. K., and Cavanagh, R. E., *The Winning Performance* (New York: Bantam, 1985).

Cook, James R., *The Startup Entrepreneur* (New York: Dutton, 1986).

Cox, Allan, *The Making of the Achiever* (New York: Dodd, Mead, 1985).

Diebold, John, *Making the Future Work* (New York: Simon & Schuster, 1984).

Drucker, Peter, *Managing in Turbulent Times* (New York: Harper & Row, 1980).

Fischhoff, B., Lichtenstein, S., et al. *Acceptable Risk* (New York: Cambridge University Press, 1981).

Garfield, Charles, *Peak Performers* (New York: Morrow, 1986).

Halberstam, David, *The Reckoning* (New York: Morrow, 1986).

Heller, Robert, *The Naked Manager* (New York: Dutton, 1985).

323

Henderson, Carter, *Winners* (New York: Holt, Rinehart, 1985).

Hornstein, Harvey A., *Managerial Courage* (New York: Wiley, 1986).

Keyes, Ralph, *Chancing It* (Boston: Little, Brown, 1985).

Levering, R., Moskowitz, M., and Katz, M., *The 100 Best Companies to Work For in America* (New York: New American Library, 1985).

Loden, Marilyn, *Feminine Leadership* (New York: Times Books, 1985).

McClintick, David, *Indecent Exposure* (New York: Morrow, 1982).

Peters, T., and Austin, N., *A Passion for Excellence* (New York: Random House, 1985).

Peters, T., and Waterman, R., *In Search of Excellence* (New York: Warner, 1982).

Pinchot, Gifford III, *Intrapreneuring* (New York: Harper & Row, 1985).

Rodgers, Buck, *The IBM Way* (New York: Harper & Row, 1986).

Rowan, Roy, *The Intuitive Manager* (Boston: Little, Brown, 1986).

Viscott, David, *Risking* (New York: Simon & Schuster, 1977).

von Oech, Roger, *A Kick in the Seat of the Pants* (New York: Harper & Row, 1986).

Wilson, John W., *The New Venturers* (Reading, Mass.: Addison-Wesley, 1985).

INDEX

Activase, *see* tissue plasminogen
  activator
Active Risk Taking (ART), 4–5,
  56–57, 60, 92–93, 118, 130,
  134, 141, 150, 157, 160, 167,
  169, 187, 225, 241–42, 263
  building blocks of, 62
  change championed in, 46
  in early automobile business,
    190, 192
  entrepreneurship linked to, 268
  exercise of control and, 275
  flexibility in, 39–40
  goals in, 80
  motivations in, 119–22
  opportunity as focus in, 78–79
  promotion of, 61–62
  of Quadracci, 270–72, 278, 286,
    292, 297, 306
  responsibilities generated by,
    85
  of VCs, 171–72, 182, 184, 196,
    199
  women in, 120–21
Adams, Walter, 63
Adler, Fred, 167, 173–86, 192–
  202, 212, 274, 299

background of, 181–82, 193–94
Biotechnology General
  investment of, 198
BRL opportunity turned down
  by, 174–75
BRL salvaged by, 175–80, 196,
  288
Daisy Systems investment of,
  196–97
entrepreneurs encouraged by,
  199–200
friends bankrolled by, 197–98
greenmailers criticized by,
  184–85
information gathering by, 182–
  83, 194, 200, 274
investment opportunities
  passed up by, 174–75, 201
on LBOs, 185–86
MicroPro investment of, 197
on money, 177–78, 195
OPB for, 192–93
pro-active investing of, 180–84
reputation of, 173–74, 176–77,
  198
on risk taking, 182–84, 188,
  192–94, 199–202

Adler, Fred (*cont'd*)
  seed capital put up by, 182
  on throwing good money after
    bad, 200–201
  Ztel investment of, 194–97
Adler & Company, 173, 176, 181
Advertising Age, 45, 229
Airbus Industrie of North
    America, 213, 215
Air Force, U. S., 221
Akers, John F., 203
  IBM revitalization and, 223–24
Allen, Herbert, Sr., 249
Allen, Herbert Anthony, Jr., 188
  Columbia Pictures acquisition
    and, 249–51
Allen & Company, 188, 249–50
Allman, William F., 98
Amdahl, 172
American Demographics, Inc., 6
American Express Company,
    244–46, 260
American High Speed Rail
    Corporation, 213–17
  financing of, 216–17
  formation of, 215
  legislative approval of, 215–16
American Medical Association
    (AMA), 308
America Today, 109
Ampex Corporation, 93–94
Amtrak, 213–15
Apocalypse Now, 206
Apollo Computer, 172
Apple Computer, 47, 172, 223,
    288, 295
ART, *see* Active Risk Taking
Atari, 171
Atlanta Constitution, 35
Atlantic, 67, 290, 296
Austin, J. Paul, 29, 42
automation, 64
automobile business, steam
    technology in, 190–92
Avco, 95

Barnes, Ben, 205
Barron's, 131
Baseball, Operation, 246
Beatrice International, 47

Vivian Beaumont Theater, 32
Beecham Pharmaceuticals, 162
Begelman, David, 249
Bell & Howell, 95
Benetton, 48
Berg, Paul, 150
Berkshire Hathaway Inc., 262
Bethesda Research Laboratories
    (BRL), 174–80
  Adler's salvaging of, 175–80,
    196, 288
  profitability of, 179–80
Betty Crocker Treehouses, 212
bet-your-company decisions, 43,
    87–88
*Bigness and Complex: Industry,
    Labor, and Government in
    the American Economy, The*
    (Adams and Brock), 63
Bingham, Robert Worth, 238–39
biotechnology:
  commercial potential of, 144–
    47
  Genentech's leadership in,
    150–51, 153–54, 156, 162–63
  patent issue in, 156–57, 163
  research in, 144–54
  VC investment in, 174–80,
    182–84, 198
Biotechnology General, 181, 183,
    198
Bird, Larry, 272
Black, Cathleen, 103
black entrepreneurs, 47
John Blair & Company, 293
Blair Marketing, 292–94
Blaxill, Mark, 221–22
Boehm, Suzy, 122–23
Boehm-Bawerk's Law, 298
Boesky, Ivan, 87, 193
bond financing, 116
Boorstin, Daniel, 15
Boston Consulting Group, 222
Bowman, Kathryn, 131
Boyd, Alan S., 213–17
  background of, 213–14
  high-speed rail service failure
    and, 214–17
Boyer, Herbert, 143
  financial success of, 155

research on gene splicing of, 144–49
Swanson's partnership with, 147
Braniff, 209
Braunwald, Eugene, 159
breaking patterns, 56
Brief History of Time, A (Hawking), 18
Brimmer, Andrew, 89
British Columbia, University of, 81, 138, 276
Brock, James, 63
Brooke, Peter, 172
Buffett, Warren, 262–63
Bureau of Labor Statistics, 121
Burr, Donald, 288
Bushnell, Nolan, 171
business:
  applying scientific analogies to, 57
  in buyer's market, 58–59
  failures, 203–12, 213–17
  reliance on statistics of, 55–56
  science blended with, 133, 142
Business Roundtable, 60
Business Week, 147, 163, 168, 189, 228–29, 260–61
butterfly effect, 168–69

Cable News Network, 75
cable television, 229–34
  sports programming of, 231–32
calculated risks, 81–82, 194, 199, 221–22, 235
  casino gambling vs., 139–40, 310
  Diebold on, 222
  in entrepreneurship, 268–69
  Goizueta on, 251–52
  of internals, 170
  Swanson on, 140–41, 151
California Institute of Technology, 149
capital gains, taxes on, 263–64
capitalism, 3–4, 9, 17, 32
Carter, Jimmy, 19
Cartridge Television, Inc., 94–95
cash flow, 198–99
Castro, Fidel, 12

CBS, 67, 93–95, 109–11, 237
Cervantes, Miguel de, 39
Cetus Corporation, 144, 148, 172
Champion International Corporation, 60
change, 3
  acceptance vs. creation of, 7
  championing of, 46–51
  Coca-Cola's avoidance of, 10
  Fuqua on, 24–25
  Goizueta on, 12
  predictability of, 57, 299
  risk as, 96, 262
  sensitivity to, 222
  spontaneous, 17
  unanticipated, 93
  unforeseen reactions provoked by, 48–49
Chaos (Gleick), 5, 86
Chapman, Alvah H., Jr., 238
Charles, Prince, 229
Cherry Coke, 14, 45
Chicago Tribune, 69
Chief Executive, 189
Chrysler Corporation, 60, 135, 209, 244, 290
Citibank, 4, 127, 181
Citicorp, 47, 260
Citicorp Venture Capital, Ltd., 142
City of Hope National Medical Center, 149
Clark, Peter, 237
Clark, William C., 96
Coca-Cola Classic, 14, 41–42, 45
  announcement of, 44
  delay in arrival of, 43–44
  New Coke vs., 49
Coca-Cola Company, 7–14, 15–16, 58, 93, 167, 248–57
  attempt to acquire Dr. Pepper by, 253–54
  Columbia Pictures acquired by, 29, 188, 248–53, 256
  criticisms of, 35–37
  debt assumed by, 29–30
  defense-oriented conservatism of, 7–8, 22, 28
  diet soft drinks introduced by, 12–14, 256

Coca-Cola Company (*cont'd*)
Fanta orange formula of, 18
flexibility demonstrated by, 40–41
global soft drink domination of, 29, 50
Goizueta's manifesto for, 255–57
marketing research division of, 20
mergers and acquisitions department of, 19
New Coke introduced by, 32–35, 37
new formulas tested by, 20–22, 26, 188
Pepsi's competition with, 10–11, 20–23, 27–28, 45, 254
reactions of financial community to, 36–37
reputation of, 9, 23
shareholders of, 42–43
traditional Coke formula resurrected by, 38, 43–45
traditional Coke formula scrapped by, 8–10, 20–22, 26–28, 30–38, 41, 43, 48–51, 159, 188
two Coke strategy adopted by, 41–42, 44–45, 49
under Woodruff, 28–29
yearly sales and profits of, 9–11, 20, 22–23, 25, 37–38, 45, 49
Cohen, Peter:
Hutton acquisition and, 241–42, 244–48
on risk taking, 242–43
Cohen, Stanley, 144–45
Columbia Pictures, 94
Coca-Cola's acquisition of, 29, 188, 248–53, 256
embezzlement scandal of, 249–50
film library of, 251–52
syndication rights owned by, 252–53
Columbia University, 279
Columbus, Christopher, 171
Combined Communications Corporation, 70

Commercial Credit, 244
Communications Satellite Corporation, 230
Compaq Computer, 172, 223
compromise:
Fuqua on, 40–41
as high-flex component, 40
computer-aided engineering, VC investment in, 196–97
Confessions of a P. R. Man (Wood), 221
confidence, self-reliance vs., 193
Congress, U. S., 214, 290
Connally, John, bankruptcy of, 205–6
Connally, Nellie, 206
Connecticut, University of, 169
constructive risks, 170
Continental Illinois, 209
contrarian, contrarians, 91–94, 241, 291
impediments to, 98
investments by, 97–98
Neuharth as, 98–111
surprises anticipated by, 92
in television technology, 94
control, 167–71, 184, 186
erosion of, 168
freedom and, 274–97
by illusion, 169–70
from information, 183
perception of, 168–69
Control Automation, 181
Convergent Technologies, Inc., 209–11
Cooke, Jack Kent, 237, 239
Cooley, Denton, 173
Coppola, Francis Ford, 206
corpocracy, 59–60
corporate takeovers, 57, 117, 184–85, 261
corporations:
as arenas for risk, 61–64, 255
cash flows of, 198–99
defense-oriented attitudes of, 7–8
employees loyal to, 136–37
fast-response, 222, 223, 227, 241, 243, 247
intrapreneurship and, 224–29

motivations of, 62–64
restructuring of, 61
costs of risk avoidance, 56
Cotting, James, 168
Create-a-Print, 47–48
creative destruction, 4, 6–7, 228
  at Coca-Cola, 10, 23, 32, 49
  in early automobile business, 192
  at Fuqua Industries, 23–24
  losing sight of, 261
creativity, 119, 235
Crow, Trammell, 190, 225
Trammell Crow Company (TCC), 225–26
Curley, John, 111

Daisy Systems Corporation, 181, 196–97
Dana Computer, Inc., 211
Darman, Richard G., 59–60
Data General Corporation, 181, 199, 202
David's Cookies, 269
deal making, Goizueta on, 255–57
Dean Wittter, 244
decision making:
  Adler on, 183–84
  on all company levels, 223–26
  bet-your-company, 43, 87–88
  erosion of control and, 168
  essential information for, 183
  of groups, 277–78
  perception of risk in, 80–81
  psychology of, 268
  in publication of USA Today, 88–90
  Quadracci on, 286–87, 290
  statistics in, 55–56
Democracy in America (Tocqueville), 241
Democratic party, 40
Des Moines Register, 236
destructive risks, 170
Detroit Evening News, 236–37
Detroit Free Press, 237
Detroit News, 237
de Windt, Del, 213

Dexter Chemical Corporation, 179
Diamond v. Chakrabarty, 157
Diana, Princess, 229
Diebold, John, 63–64, 224
  on calculating risk, 222
  on failure, 204, 207–8
Diebold Group, Inc., 63
Diet Coke, 12–14, 21, 256
Digital Equipment, 181, 223
Digler, Andrew, 60
Dior, Christian, 124–25
Christian Dior America, 124–26, 167
discontinuity, 86
Discover, 81
dividends, taxes on, 263–64
Doble steam cars, 191–92
Dow Chemical, 50
Dow Jones & Company, 6, 73–74, 103, 236
Drexel Burnham Lambert, 47, 116–17, 172, 238
Dr. Pepper Company, 253–54
Drucker, Peter, 6, 267
  on failure, 212
  on risk, 53, 56, 212, 275
Druskin, Robert, 246
Duke University, 135
  Fuqua School of Business of, 19
Duplainville Transport, 301

Eaton Corporation, 213
Eberstadt & Company, 174–76, 178
economics:
  growth, 60
  mathematics applied to, 86
  population growth and, 6
  of post-World War II period, 58–59
  statistics in, 56
  weather compared to, 5, 169
Economist, 46
Edison, Thomas, 226
Education Department, U. S., 121
Eller, Karl, 70
Embassy Communications, 253
Emerson, Ralph Waldo, 46
eminase, 162

Emory University, 28, 30
Emory University Hospital, 28
Employee Stock Ownership
   Plans (ESOPs), 271, 303
Enrico, Roger, 33
   New Coke criticized by, 34–35,
   45
entrepreneurship, 170
   blacks and, 47
   characteristics common in,
   141
   definitions of, 267–69
   encouragement in, 199–200,
   207
   fragmentation caused by, 137
   freedom to fail in, 208
   management and, 224
   restart rate in, 204
   risk in, 267–69, 272
   in securities industry, 243
   Swanson's interest in, 142–
   43
entropy, 17–18
Equitable Life Assurance, 244
escalation dilemma, 200–201
E-II Holdings, 168
Evening News Association
   (ENA), 236–37, 239
externals, 169

failure, 203–12
   acceptance of, 206–8, 224
   of Convergent Technologies,
   209–11
   definitions of, 205
   discoveries made from, 203,
   205, 207
   entrepreneurship and, 267
   fear of, 204–5, 208
   minimizing or eliminating of,
   207
   near-success vs., 212
   Quadracci's approach to, 301
   rebounding from, 205–6, 208,
   211–12
   risk linked to, 205
   stigma attached to, 207–8
   of U.S. high-speed trains, 213–
   17
Fairchild, 95

Family Computing Magazine,
   295
Fanta, 18
Farace, Andrea, 246–47
Farley, Frank, 118–20, 170, 277
Farley, William, 137
Farley Industries, 137
Fast Forward (Lardner), 95
Federal Express, 107
Federal Reserve, U. S., 89, 170,
   172
Federal Trade Commission
   (FTC), 254
Ferguson, Charles, 137
Financial Corporation of
   America, 209
Financial Times, 262
Financial World, 107
Finegold, Aryeh, 196–97
First Boston Corporation, 215,
   217, 261
Flagler, Mary Lily Kenan, 238
flexibility, 6
   in risk taking, 39–43, 59, 184,
   186, 188
   following through, 258
   Salomon Brothers' expansion
   and, 259–64
Food and Drug Administration
   (FDA), 130, 154, 156, 159,
   161–62
Forbes, 64
Forbes, Malcolm S., Sr., 66,
   108–9
Ford, 23, 116, 290
Fortune, 47, 106, 128, 141, 160,
   163, 240
Forum Group Inc., 206
Foster, Richard, 7
Fox Television, 233
Francese, Peter, 6
freedom, control and, 274–97
Freud, Sigmund, 79, 115
Friendly, Fred, 110
Fuqua, J. B., 18–19
   on compromise, 40–41
   on risk sharing, 188–89, 192
   on risk taking, 24–25, 188–90
Fuqua Industries, 18–19, 188–89
   creative destruction at, 23–24

gain:
    avoiding risk in pursuit of, 81,
        119
    perception of, 81, 88
    as result of risk, 82, 84, 187
Galbraith, John Kenneth, 208
gambling:
    entrepreneurship and, 268–69
    risk taking vs., 138–40, 310
Gannett Company Inc., 64, 65–
        77, 82–84, 159, 167
    acquisitions of, 69–70, 76, 109–
        11, 235–40, 248
    as contrarian, 99–111
    critics of, 83–84
    in decision to launch USA
        Today, 88–90
    financial success of, 67–69, 77,
        84
    losses assumed on USA Today
        by, 100–102, 105–6
    national base of, 69–70
    Neuharth's advancement in,
        68–69
    Neuharth's reassurances to, 87–
        88
    professional praise for, 107–9
    USA Today prototype produced
        by, 83, 88–89
    USA Today research of, 70–74,
        77
    Wall Street analysts on, 104–6
gasoline engines, steam engines
    vs., 190–92
gender, willingness to take risks
    and, 120–27
Genentech, Inc., 117, 127–34,
        141–44, 147–63, 172, 201,
        204
    basic research of, 147–50
    business risks confronted by,
        156
    cloning successes of, 149–51,
        153–54, 159–63
    employee-equity plan of, 130–
        32, 154, 162
    financing of, 157–59, 162–63,
        175
    formation of, 147
    launching of, 128–29

marketing department of, 151–52
    patent issue and, 156–57, 163
    public stock offerings of, 155–
        56
    risk-taking atmosphere of, 132–
        34
    rivals of, 144, 160–62
    Swanson's goals for, 127, 129–
        30, 132–33, 141, 150–51
    TPA developed by, 129, 151,
        159–63
Genentech Clinical Partners, Ltd.
    (GCP), 158–59
General Electric Corporation
    (GE), 50, 93, 194–95
    employee cuts at, 226–27
    individual initiative
        encouraged at, 226–29
General Electric Pension Fund,
    309
General Foods, Great Shakes
    product of, 56
General Mills, 212
General Motors (GM), 23, 50, 93,
    116, 290
gene-splicing, 129–30, 134
    commercial potential of, 144–
        47
    research in, 144–54
Germond, Jack, 67
Gesell, Gerhard, 254
GIBCO Corporation, 179
Gilder, George, 274
Gilson, Lawrence, 215–26
Glavin, William, 59–60
Gleick, James, 5, 86
goals of perfectionists, 205
Goeddel, David, 131
Goizueta, Roberto C., 8–14, 15–
        18, 167, 248–57
    attempt to acquire Dr. Pepper
        by, 253–54
    background of, 8, 12
    on bottling franchise owners,
        30–31
    on bringing out Coca-Cola
        Classic, 43–44
    on change, 50–51
    Coke's fading market share and,
        10–11, 22–23, 31

Goizueta, Roberto C. (*cont'd*)
  Columbia Pictures acquisition
    and, 29, 248–53, 256
  deal-making rules of, 255–57
  diet soft drink introduced by,
    12–14
  Fanta orange formula and, 18
  flexibility demonstrated by, 40–
    43
  manifesto of, 255–57
  on market studies, 251–52
  New Coke introduced by, 32–
    35
  optimism of, 42
  public criticism of, 35, 37–38
  reactions of financial
    community to, 36–37
  on risk, 11, 15–17, 25–26, 42–
    43, 251–52, 255–57
  traditional Coke formula
    resurrected by, 38, 43, 45
  traditional Coke formula
    scrapped by, 8–10, 20–22,
    26–28, 30–36, 38, 41, 48–51,
    159, 188
  two-Coke strategy considered
    by, 27–28, 41, 45, 49
  Woodruff and, 29–30
Golden Nugget Inc., 117
Good Morning America, 100
government, bureaucracy of, 59
Graftek Technology Corporation,
    181
Graham, Donald, 74
Gray, Harry, 227–28
Great Shakes, 56
Greeley, Horace, 73
greenmailers, 184–85
Greenwald, Gerald, 60
Greylock Management
    Corporation, 172
Merv Griffin Enterprises, 253
groups, risk taking by, 277–
    78
GTG Entertainment, 109–10
Gutfreund, John H.:
  risk-taker qualities of, 263–
    64
  Salomon Brothers' rapid
    expansion and, 259–64

Hammer, Armand, 219
Handler, Philip, 150
Harper's, 296
Harralson, James, 33
Louis Harris & Associates, 109
Harvard Business School, 9–10,
    89, 189
Harvard Lampoon, 107
Harvard Medical School, 159
Harvard University, 59, 137, 142,
    181, 191–92, 268
Hawking, Stephen, 18
Hay Group, 136
health-care products, 152–63
  Swanson's focus on, 152–54
Hearst Corporation, 239
Hefner, Christie, 225
Heidrick and Struggles, 12
Heller, Robert, 219
Heraclitus, 46
high-definition (HD) television,
    95
high-flex, 59
  compromise and, 40
  see also flexibility
Highman de Limut hypothesis,
    223
high-speed trains, 213–17
  U. S. government opposition to,
    214–15
Hillman, Henry, 201
Hillman family, 195
Hoechst A. G., 161
Hoechst-Roussel
    Pharmaceuticals, 161
Hollywood General Studios,
    206
Home Box Office (HBO), 230
Home Health Care, 172, 201
Hout, Thomas, 221–22
human growth hormone, cloning
    of, 154
Humulin, 154
Hutton, Edward Francis, 244,
    247
E. F. Hutton Group Inc.:
  legal and financial problems of,
    244, 247–48
  Shearson Lehman's acquisition
    of, 241–48

Iacocca, Lee, 115
  on risk taking, 135–36
Inc., 107, 170, 290
Indecent Exposure: A True Story of Hollywood and Wall Street (McClintick), 249–50
Industry, Trade and Commerce Department, Canadian, 276
information:
  on Coke's formula change, 20–21
  gathering of, 16–17, 182–83, 194, 200, 251, 274
  learning limits of, 18
  risk defined by, 25–26, 167, 182
  too much, 18–19, 93
innovation, 6, 138
  link between risk and, 132
instinct, definition of, 194
insulin, cloning of, 153–54
insurance, gambling vs., 140
intelligent risk taking, Goizueta's definition of, 15–16
interferon, 154, 159
internals, 169–70
International Business Machines (IBM), 50, 93, 163, 203, 295
  fast-response focus of, 223
  intrapreneurship at, 224, 226
International Harvester, 168, 209
International Herald Tribune, 71–72
International Institute for Applied Systems Analysis, 96
Intersil, 181
intrapreneurship, 224–29
  setting tone for, 225–29
investing:
  on basis of past performance, 298–99
  men vs. women in, 120
  pro-active, 180–84
  risk in, 85–87, 97–98, 105, 298–99
  in time and resources, 256
  in *USA Today*, 105
  see also venture capitalists
Ivester, Douglas, 252

Janeway, William, 174–76, 179
Japan, 60, 136, 213, 242, 253, 278
  flexibility in, 59
  product development in, 46, 48
  Salomon Brothers in, 261
  U. S. high-speed trains and, 213–15
  VCR market dominated by, 93–95, 222
Japan National Railroad (JNR), 214
Jobs, Steven, 60
Johnson, Lyndon, 40
joint operating agreements (JOAs), 236–38
joint ventures, 188
Journals of Psychology, 120
Journal of the American Medical Association, 307–8
Journal Publishing Company, 99
Joyce, James, 203, 205
junior stock, 131
junk bonds, 116–18, 263
Justice Department, U. S., 238

Kagan, Paul, 253
Paul Kagan Associates, 253
Kahneman, Daniel, 81
Kanter, Rosabeth, 189
Kaufman, Henry, 263–64
Keller, Helen, 113
Kelly, Don, 168
Kelly, Grace, 100
Kennedy, John F., 68, 205
Kennedy, Robert, 53
Kentucky Fried Chicken, 49
Keough, Donald, 21, 30, 37, 44
Kerkorian, Kirk, 249
Keynes, John Maynard, 135
Kidder, Peabody & Company, 106, 228
Kilgore, Bernard, 73
King, Larry, 161
Kipling, Rudyard, 1
Kleiner & Perkins, 142, 144, 147, 155–56, 195, 199
Kleiner Perkins Caulfield & Byers, 172
Knight-Ridder, 237–38

Kodak, 95
Create-a-Print product of, 47–48
Koplovitz, Kay, 229–34
background of, 230–31
financial risks taken by, 232–33
major league sports deals of, 231–32
programming risks taken by, 233
on risk taking, 230–31, 233–34
Koplovitz Communications, 230
Krueger Printing, 279–80, 283
Kuhn, Bowie, 231

Lane, Jeffrey, 245
Lano Corporation, 24
Lardner, James, 95
leadership:
ARTful, 130
in biotechnology, 150–51, 153–54, 156, 162–63
military concept of, 134
Lear, Norman, 229, 236–37
Lehman Brothers Kuhn Loeb, 244–45
Lehrer, James, 109
leveraged buyouts (LBOs), 185–86
Lewis, Drew, 215
Lewis, Reginald, 47
Liederman, David, 269
Life Technologies, 179–80
Eli Lilly, 153–54
Lincoln Center, 32–33
Lindbergh, Charles, 33
Lipper, Arthur, III, 268
Lipton, James, 96
Live 1975–1985, 290
Lockheed, 209
London Business School, 140
Los Angeles Olympics, 217
Los Angeles Times, 69, 105, 216, 240
loss:
choosing risk to avoid, 81
risk taking associated with, 138
see also failure
Lotus Development, 172

Louisville Courier-Journal, 236, 239
Louisville Times, 239
loyalty, risk taking rated above, 136–37
L. P. Media Inc., 236–37
Lubrizol Corporation, 155–56
Lynch Jones & Ryan, 238

MacArthur, Douglas, 65
MacArthur Foundation, 81
McCall Pattern Company, 47
McClelland, David C., 268–69
McClintick, David, 249–50
MacCrimmon, Kenneth, 276
McDonald's, 49, 72
McKinsey & Company, 7
McLaughlin, Charles C., 191–92
MacNeil, Robert, 109
MacNeil/Lehrer NewsHour, 109
Madison Square Garden (MSG) Network, 229–31
Magnavox, 95
management, 6
atmosphere for risk taking and, 61
control exercised by, 275–76
decentralization of, 189, 192–93
entrepreneurship encouraged by, 224
failure feared by, 204–5
information gathering by, 17
no-risk, 65
Quadracci and, 278–79, 287–88, 300–306
as risk motivator, 62, 64, 81, 275
risks modified by, 188
risk taking by, 275–77, 299
risk taking negatively viewed by, 138
in securities industry, 243
by walking around, 278
by walking away, 278–79, 304
Mandelbrot, Benoit, 87
Mannillo, Paula, 121–22
Manufacturers Hanover, 292
markets, 57
buyer's, 58–59

Coca-Cola's share of, 10–11,
20–23, 27, 31, 45, 50, 254
for color on newsprint, 71–72,
77, 83, 284–85
fragmentation of, 6
Quadracci's attitude towards,
291–92
seller's, 58
market studies, 310
by Coca-Cola, 20–22, 26, 188,
251–52
on *USA Today*, 70–74, 77, 89
Massachusetts Institute of
Technology (MIT), 128–29,
133, 137, 141–42
Alfred P. Sloan School of
Management of, 95, 142
mastery, relationship between
risk taking and, 122–23
Mathews, Bob, 279
Matsushita, 95
Maxwell, Robert, 109
MCA Inc., 95, 232
MCI, 117
Medical 21, 181
Meese, Edwin, 238
men, 120–23
mentoring, 300, 302
Merchandise 7X, 9
Merchandise 7X-100, 9
mergers and acquisitions, 63
see also *specific mergers and
acquisitions*
Merrill, Dina, 247
Merrill Lynch, 181, 242, 244,
260–61
Miami Herald, 69
Michels, Allen, 209–12
on failure, 209–11
Michigan State University, 230
MicroPro International, 181,
197
Milken, Michael, 116–18, 172
Miller, Paul, 68
Milwaukee Museum of Art, 308
Montgomery Ward, 93
Moore, Peter, 140
Mother Jones, 303
Motion Picture Association of
America, 95

motivation, 62–64, 79, 81, 275
of ARTists vs. risk averters,
119–22
of Nicholas, 126–27
Motorola, 95
Murdoch, Rupert, 67, 74, 233

National Academy of Sciences,
150
National Basketball Association
(NBA), 231
National Cash Register
Corporation (NCR), 24, 194–
95
National Center for Employee
Ownership, 303
National Hockey League (NHL),
232
National Institutes of Health, 159
National Observer, 73–74
National Press Foundation, 107
National Soft Drink Association,
13
Navistar International, 168
NBC, 109, 227, 229
near-success, 212
need satisfaction levels, 80
Nestlé, 47
Neuharth, Allen H., 65–77, 82–
84, 159, 167
acquisition risks taken by, 235–
40
advancement in Gannett of,
68–69
background of, 65–66
as contrarian, 98–111
criticisms of, 84, 87, 108, 239–
40
ego of, 110
Gannett criticized by, 67–68
interviews given by, 102–3
lessons learned in risk taking
by, 66–67
newspaper owners criticized
by, 74–75
potential rewards of risk
considered by, 82
professional praise for, 106–9,
240
public need identified by, 92

Neuharth, Allen H. *(cont'd)*
  responsibility for risk accepted, 87–90
  on risk taking, 74–76, 97, 105, 239
  Today project of, 68
  USA Today considered investment by, 105
  USA Today losses and, 101–2
  USA Today price hike and, 103–4
  USA Today research and, 70–74, 77
New Coke, 14, 21, 28, 45
  Coca-Cola Classic vs., 49
  considered replacement of, 41–42
  criticisms of, 34–35
  introduction of, 32–35, 37
Newsweek, 74, 137, 290
New York Daily News, 102
New York Times, 11, 14, 29, 48–49, 69, 74, 87, 136, 162
New York Times Company, 74, 239
New York Times Magazine, 228
New York Tribune, 73
New York Yankees, 231
Nicholas, Colombe, 123–27, 167
  background of, 124
  image strategy devised by, 124–25
  risk-taking motivations of, 126–27
Nippon Life Insurance Company, 244–45
Nixon, Richard, 284
Nocon, Barbara, 308

Occidental Petroleum, 219
O'Connell, Jack, 35–36
Old Coca-Cola Drinkers of America, 35
Olds, Ransom, 191
Olivier, Laurence, 272
OODA loop, 221
opportunity, 96, 116, 207
  in investing, 97
  link between risk and, 78–79, 85, 92–93

placing risk after, 84
Quadracci's alertness to, 292–93
responsibility and, 85
Osborne, Adam, 208, 288
Osborne Computer Corporation, 208, 288
Other People's Brains (OPB), 189, 192–193, 205
Other People's Money (OPM), 189

Packard, Dave, 152
Paine, Thomas, 85
Paine Webber, 244
Paramount Pictures Corporation, 232
patents, 156–57, 163
pattern recognition, instinct as, 194
PBS, 109
People, 290, 292
People Express Airlines, 208–9, 288
Pepsi-Cola U. S. A.:
  attempt to acquire 7-Up by, 254
  Coca-Cola's competition with, 10–11, 20–23, 27–28, 45, 254
  Coke's formula change and, 20–21, 27, 31, 33–34
  two-Coke strategy and, 41
Perelman, Ronald, 262–63
Perenchio, A. Jerrold, 236–37
perfectionists, 205
Perkins, Tom, 131
Perot, H. Ross, 60, 91
personalities:
  of risk takers, 118–20
  Type T, 119–20, 170, 277
Peters, Tom, 62, 203
Phibro Corporation, 259
Philip Morris, 249, 254
Phillips, Warren, 103
Pink Panther, 16
Playboy, 290
Playboy Enterprises, Inc., 225
Polaroid, 95
Pratt & Whitney, 227–28
prices, changes in, 86–87
Prime Computer, 172

printing industry, 270–73, 278–
    97, 299–310
  innovations in, 280–81, 295–
    97, 299–300
  Quadracci's background in,
    279–80
  Quadracci's misjudgment of,
    284–85
  spending on capital equipment
    in, 288–89
pro-active investing, 180–84
probabilities, 98, 140
Procter & Gamble, 50
productivity, 60
products:
  consumer perception of, 26
  development time for, 46–48
  health-care, 152–63
  life spans of, 23–25, 46–47,
    222, 252, 309
  sequential development of, 48
Protropin, 154, 159
Prudential-Bache, 181
Psychology Today, 80, 303
Purification Engineering, 181

Quad/Ed, 304–5
Quad/Graphics, Inc., 270–73,
    278–79, 283–97, 299–310
  budgets abandoned by, 286–87
  Chemical Research and
    Technology (CR/T) division
    of, 295
  circus compared to, 288
  diversification of, 272–73
  egalitarian culture of, 301–2
  ESOP of, 271, 303
  extended family concept of,
    307–8
  growth of, 270, 286–92, 296,
    309
  off-beat methods of, 271
  printing contracts acquired by,
    285, 290
  private ownership of, 309
  research and development at,
    295–97, 299–300
  risk-taking culture of, 300–301
  three-day week of, 271, 302–3
Quad/Litho, 279

Quad/Marketing, 293
Quad/Photo, 279
Quad/Pop, 307
Quadracci, Betty, 280, 283
Quadracci, Harry R., 279
Quadracci, Harry V., 270–73,
    278–97, 299–310
  approach to employee relations
    of, 280, 292, 300–307, 309
  art collected by, 308
  background of, 279–81, 285
  capital equipment purchased
    by, 283–84, 288–90, 292
  companies acquired by, 293–94
  exercising control and, 274–75
  fearlessness of, 288–89
  hunchmanship of, 270–72,
    291–92
  management style of, 278–79,
    287–88, 300–306
  new printing company started
    by, 280–85
  new technologies sold by, 297,
    299–300
  nonconformity of, 287–88, 305
  on risk taking, 270, 272, 275,
    285–86
  self-confidence of, 285–86, 294
  State of the Company addresses
    of, 292
  Theory Q of, 286, 293, 304, 306
Quad/Rail, 301
Quad/Tech, 295, 297, 301
quality control, 72
Quinn, John, 107

RCA, 93–95, 227–28
Reagan, Ronald, 59, 214–15
real estate, intrapreneurship in,
    225–26
Reavis & McGrath, 181
Reich, Robert, 137
responsibilities:
  avoidance of, 85–86
  in risk taking, 85–90, 198
restriction enzymes, 174
Revlon, Inc., 262
Richey, Norm, 307–8
Risk, J. Fred, 206–7
risk arbitrage, 87, 193

risk management, 61
risk/reward ratio, 55
    Neuharth's consideration of, 66,
        76–77, 102, 105
risks, risk taking:
    acceptance of, 57
    of action vs. inaction, 256
    active varieties of, 57, 298
    adjusting of, 168
    avoidance of, 6, 55–61, 63–64,
        79, 85–86, 93, 95–96, 115–
        16, 118–19, 136, 140, 167,
        187, 189–90, 192, 207, 224,
        275–77, 299
    cautious, 188, 194
    comfort in, 261–62
    confrontation in, 274
    as continuous process, 299, 308
    control of, 294
    creation of, 62, 298
    delays in, 17
    descriptions of, 4, 53, 57, 96,
        138, 200
    dispassionate, 173
    elimination of, 55, 57, 96, 193,
        207
    encouragement of, 79, 208, 255,
        257
    as essential, 79
    fear of, 190
    ignoring of, 93
    increasing abilities in, 97
    legal boundaries of, 117
    looking dumb in, 27
    magnitudes of, 169–70, 200
    making choices about, 55
    measuring costs and benefits of,
        56–57, 63
    minimization of, 57–58, 167,
        187–88, 294
    misreadings of, 7
    negative effects of, 58, 187–88
    passive varieties of, 57, 61
    perceptions of, 80–81, 115–16,
        171, 276–77
    positive potential of, 187
    prevention of, 204
    recognition of, 93
    relative nature of, 26, 276
    research on, 138, 183
    from strength, 235–38, 241
    of tampering with success, 26
    as unavoidable, 79
    uncertainty in, 48–49, 57
    weapons against, 55
risky shift, 277–78
Roche, Gerard, 12
Rogers, Will, 3
ROLM, 172
Roosevelt, Theodore, 165
Rotter, Julian, 169
Royal Crown Cola Company, 33
rubber band risk taking, 39–40

Sadlow, Chester A., 63
Salomon Brothers Asia Limited,
    261
Salomon Brothers Inc., 37, 246
    assets of, 260
    cutbacks and restructuring of,
        262–64
    profitability of, 261
    rapid expansion of, 258–64
San Francisco, University of
    California (UCSF), 143, 147,
    149
Santa Clara University, 85
Sarnoff, David, 94
satellite transmission technology,
    71–73, 77, 108
Saturday Review, 107
Schumpeter, Joseph, 4, 184, 268
science:
    business blended with, 133,
        142
    business vs., 57
Seagate Technology, 201
Sears Roebuck, 94, 181, 244
Securities and Exchange
    Commission (SEC), 117, 193,
    249
securities industry, 241–48
    entrepreneurship in, 243
    impact of 1987 crash on, 241–
        42, 244
security, control vs., 168
seed ventures, 172, 174, 182
self-reliance, confidence vs., 193
Sellers, Peter, 16
semiconductor industry, 137

sequential product development, 48
7-Up, 254
Sevin-Rosen Management, 172
Shaykin, Leonard, 185
Shearson Lehman Brothers Holdings Inc.:
  acquisitions of, 241–48
  ownership of, 244–45
Shearson Lehman Hutton Inc., 47, 60, 180, 245, 247, 258–59
Shugart, Alan, 201
Simon, William E., 47, 137, 140
six packs, 29
Smith, Adam, 17
Smith, Fred, 107–8, 170
SmithKline Beckman Corporation, 160
SoDak Sports, 65–66
somatostatin, cloning of, 148–50, 153
Sony Corporation, 46, 94–95, 190, 222
South Dakota, University of, 65
Southern Methodist University, Caruth Institute of Owner-Managed Business at, 269
Soviet Union, fear of failure in, 208
Speidel Newspapers, 69
Sports Illustrated, 290
Springsteen, Bruce, 290
Standard & Poor's, 244
Standard & Poor's 500 stock index, 43, 227
Stanford University, 81, 142, 150
Stanley, Freelan and Francis, 190–92
Stanley Motor Carriage Company, 190, 192
statistics:
  in decision making, 55–56
  risk taking stifled by, 287
Statman, Meir, 85–86
steam-powered autos, 190–92
Steinbeck, John, 258
Steinbrenner, George, 231
stock market crash (1987), 87, 241–42, 244, 262
Stone, Oliver, 248

streptokinase, 160–62
success:
  links between risk and, 276
  see also failure
Success!, 208
Sugar Association, 35
Sun Microsystems, 47
Supermanagers, The (Heller), 219
superoxide dismutase (SOD), 183
Supreme Court, U. S., 95, 157
Swanson, Robert A., 117–18, 127–34, 140–63, 299
  background of, 141–48
  commercial potential of gene-splicing and, 144–47
  description of, 127–28
  equity-participation plan of, 130–32, 154
  on failure, 204
  financial maneuvering of, 157–58, 175
  financial success of, 155–56
  Genentech's goals established by, 127, 129–30, 132–33, 141, 150–51
  Genentech's risk-taking atmosphere created by, 132–34
  health-care products focused on by, 152–53
  launching Genentech and, 128–29, 147
  patent issue and, 156–57
  research on gene-splicing and, 144–50
  on risk taking, 140–41, 143
  TPA development and, 159–61

TA Associates, 172
Tab, 13
Tagamet, 160
Tandem Computers, 172, 199
Tandem Productions, 253
taxes, 290
  on capital gains and dividends, 263–64
Technology Review, 133–34
telephone switching technology, VC investments in, 194–96
Texas Air, 209

Theory Q, 286, 293, 304, 306
Thriving on Chaos (Peters), 62, 203
Thurow, Lester, 95–96
Time, 87, 93, 290, 292
Time Inc., 76, 111, 209, 232, 249
Tinker, Grant, 109, 229
tissue plasminogen activator (TPA), 158–63
  Adler's familiarity with, 182–83
  cloning of, 129, 151
  FDA approval of, 161–62
  sales of, 162
TLC Group, 47
Tocqueville, Alexis de, 241
Today, 68, 99
Townsend, Robert, 235
Transamerica Corporation, 244
transformational thought, 118, 262
Transportation Department, U. S., 215
Treasury Department, U. S., 59, 205
Treybig, James, 199
Triangle Industries, 117
Tribune Company of Chicago, 239
Tri-Star Pictures, Inc., 253
Trust Company of Georgia Bank, 9, 30
tumor necrosis factor (TNF), 158–59
Turner, Stephen, 174–75, 178–79
Turner, Ted, 67, 75, 111, 229, 252
TV Cable Week, 209
Tversky, Amos, 81
Type T personalities, 119–20, 170, 277

UA-Columbia Cablevision, Inc., 230
UA-Columbia Satellite Services, Inc., 230
Ueberroth, Peter, 217, 246–47
uncertainty, 96
  in investing, 98, 299
  profiting from, 94
  Type T personalities and, 119–20

United Technologies, 227
Universal Pictures, 95
USA Network, 229, 232–33
USA Today, 65–77, 82–84, 92, 236, 285
  accepting responsibility for success or failure of, 88
  birth of, 99
  as contrarian move, 98–111
  criticisms of, 100
  decision to proceed with, 88–90
  distribution problems of, 101
  field-testing for, 83
  high-quality color printing in, 71–72, 77, 83
  innovations of, 83–84
  Neuharth's interview on, 102–3
  professional praise for, 107–8
  projects leading up to, 68
  raising price of, 103–4
  research on, 70–74, 77, 89
  risks in launching of, 66–67, 88, 159
  start-up costs of, 65–66, 82, 88, 100–102, 105–6, 111
  televised version of, 110
  television as competitor of, 71–73, 77, 107–8
USA Weekend, 109
U. S. News & World Report, 67, 111, 290

Value Line, 101–2
VCRs, 71, 92–95, 190, 251–52
  Japanese domination of market for, 93–95, 222
vending machines, 29
Venrock Associates, 172
Venture, 268
Venture Associates, Inc., 216
venture capitalists (VCs), 171–86, 192–202, 212, 268
  activities of, 171–72
  in biotechnology, 174–80, 182–84, 198
  in computer-aided engineering, 196–97
  earnings of, 173
  escalation dilemma of, 200–201

examples of, 172
increasing risks accepted by, 201–2
LBOs and, 185–86
OPB technique adopted by, 192–93
risks shared by, 188
sophistication of, 172–73
in telephone switching technology, 194–96
VisiCorp, 172
von Oech, Roger, 187

Whack on the Side of the Head, A (von Oech), 187
Wall Street Journal, 44, 47, 67–68, 126, 155, 201, 225, 227, 242, 249–50
Michels interviewed by, 209–11
USA Today and, 71, 73, 83, 102–5
Wall Street Transcript, 107
Walsh, Michaela, 121, 123
Washington Journalism Review, 107
Washington Post, 69, 74, 175
Washington Post Company, 73–74, 239
Washington Post Weekly Edition, 74
Washington Redskins, 237
Washington Star, 76
Watson, Thomas, 163
WDVM-TV, 237
wealth creation, 137–40
casino fallacy of, 138–40
weather, economics compared to, 5, 169
Del E. Webb Corporation, 226
Wegbreit, Ben, 209–10
Wehrung, Donald, 276

Welch, Jack, 50
GE employee cuts made by, 226–27
individual initiative encouraged by, 226–29
Welsh, John, 269
Wendt, Henry, 160
Wesray group, 47, 137
Westinghouse Electric Corporation, 63
Wharton School of Business, 107
Wilder, Thornton, 91
Williams, James B., 9
Wilson, Ian, 29
Wisconsin, University of (UW), 118–19, 170, 277
women, 120–27
Women's Economic Development Corporation, 121
Women's World Banking, 121
Wood, Robert J., 221
Woodruff, Robert Winship:
background of, 28–29
Goizueta and, 29–30
WordStar, 197
Workslate computers, 210
Wriston, Walter, 4, 84, 127
WUSA, 237
Wynn, Stephen, 117

Xerox, 47, 60

Yaeger, Chuck, 78
Yale University, 12

Zenith, 93, 95
Zoetrope Studios, 206
Ztel, 194–97
Zuckerman, Mortimer, 67, 111, 260, 262–63